The Science of the Singing Voice

The Science of the Singing Voice

Johan Sundberg

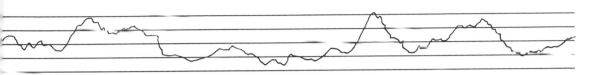

 NORTHERN ILLINOIS UNIVERSITY PRESS

DEKALB, ILLINOIS 1987

© 1987 by Northern Illinois University Press
Published by the Northern Illinois University Press,
DeKalb, Illinois 60115
Manufactured in the United States of America
All Rights Reserved
Designed by Jo Aerne

Library of Congress Cataloging-in-Publication Data

Sundberg, Johan, 1936–
    The science of the singing voice.

    Translation of: Röstlära.
    Bibliography: p.
    Includes index.
    1. Singing. 2. Voice. I. Title.
MT821.S913   1987   784.9   87-5499
ISBN 0-87580-120-X

ISBN 0-87580-542-6 (pbk.)
        4   5   6   7   8

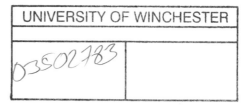

For Gunnar Fant

Contents

Preface

This is an attempt to present and discuss research on the human voice in singing as compared with speech. A book with this aim seemed needed: research reports in this area are scattered in various journals ranging in subject from astronautics to musicology; thus, locating them is sometimes difficult. As I have had the fortunate and probably unusual opportunity of doing research on the singing voice for almost twenty years, systematic searches and good luck have brought together a good many interesting articles.

This book does not treat the singing voice in the usual way. Actually, most of the several terms normally used for singing are not at all mentioned in this text, the reason being that different persons tend to mean different things with these terms. Instead, I use a terminology that has been borrowed from phonetics, acoustics, and medicine. I hope that this will eliminate many possibilities for misunderstanding.

The book addresses everyone who is curious about the functioning of the human voice. Reading it should require no special background in fields that may tend to appear exotic for some singers, such as mathematics or medicine. This is not to say that the book will not offer some challenges to its readers. Several sections on phonetics may cause readers to slow their reading pace.

The book is dedicated to Gunnar Fant. I have had the fortunate opportunity of working at his lab for twenty-five years and have profited greatly from both the daily contacts with his standards for doing research and the fundamental contributions to theory of voice production his works have yielded. Both the science of the singing voice and I owe much to this man.

This book was originally written in Swedish, and I have translated it to English myself. Toward this end, I received much friendly help from members of the patient staff of the NIUP. I have also profited greatly from a number of other people in writing this book. Two persons have been particularly important for building my musical background in terms of showing how the voice can be used as a musical instrument: my singing teacher, Dagmar Gustafson, and Anders Öhrwall, the leader of the Stockholm Bach Choir, in which I sang for a great number of years. Other persons of great importance have been the many members of the staff at the Department of Speech Communication and Music Acoustics at KTH: Jan Gauffin, Erik

Jansson, Anders Askenfelt, Sten Ternström, and many others. My friends in phoniatrics, Björn Fritzell, Peter Kitzing, Rolf Leanderson, and others have taught me important aspects of voice medicine. Thomas Rossing and Richard Miller read the English manuscript and offered many valuable suggestions. An indispensable requisite for my spending so many years in the esoteric area of singing voice research was a series of grants from the National Bank of Sweden Tercentennary Foundation.

The Science of the Singing Voice

What Is Voice?

The question that heads this chapter seems at first glance simple enough to answer. But it is worthwhile to consider some of the principal voice terms and to ask what they actually signify. What do we really mean by *voice, voice organ, speech, singing, voice sound?*

We would all agree that we use our voice when we speak or sing. To speak or to sing is to move one's lips, tongue, jaw, larynx, and so on, while an airstream from the lungs passes the vocal folds. In this way we generate sounds, which we call *voice sounds*. These voice sounds may be either speech sounds or sung notes, depending on the purpose of producing them. The voice also generates other types of sounds, for example, hawking, whispering, and laughing. Most of us probably would agree that such sounds can also be labeled voice sounds. This suggests the following definition: all sounds can be considered voice sounds if they originate from an airstream from the lungs that is processed by the vocal folds and then modified by the pharynx, the mouth, and perhaps also the nose cavities. This definition implies that the voice is associated with vibrating vocal folds and the vocal tract. The different structures that we mobilize when we use the voice can be called the *voice organ*. The voice organ, then, includes the breathing system, the vocal folds, and the vocal and nasal tracts. We may ordinarily regard the voice organ as a tool for making sound; a singer uses this tool as a musical instrument.

The voice organ allows us to generate a great variety of voice sounds. Some of this family of sounds are speech sounds; if such sounds are arranged in adequate sequences, *speech* is produced. In *singing* there are both speech sounds and other types of sounds. They can be called *singing sounds,* if we want, or more commonly *notes* or *tones,* and they can be regarded as more or less modified speech sounds.

Let us devote some thought to the voice sounds called *speech sounds*. Speech sounds are the constituents in an acoustic code for interhuman communication. This definition suggests that a given speech sound is always the same, no matter who pronounces it, but this is obviously far from true. The exact sound characteristics of a speech sound, for example, a vowel such as /i:/, reflect and thus also depend on many different factors. One such factor is the pronunciation, or *speech habits,* of the individual speaker. Speech habits tend to vary according to both geographical and sociological origin.

Apart from speech habits, other factors also contribute to the exact sound characteristics of a specific speech sound. One such factor is the personal characteristic of the voice organ, which is significant for *personal voice timbre.* As a consequence, the same vowel may sound very different depending on whether a man, a woman, or a child pronounces it. The reason is that the shape and size of the pharynx and mouth cavities impose their characteristics on the sound of a person's voice. Such differences exist not only between groups of people, such as men, women, and children, but also between individuals. Thus a great many of the voice timbre differences between individuals of the same age and the same sex are due to *morphological differences,* which are differences between the details of the individuals' voice organs. We will return to such matters in chapter 5. We conclude that the acoustic details of the same speech sounds differ because of voice differences between individuals.

It is not only the vocal tract dimensions that are significant for personal voice timbre. The mechanical characteristics of the vocal folds (length, thickness, viscosity) are also of decisive importance. Such differences partly explain why different persons speak with differing voice pitch. A low pitch range is a typical characteristic of the adult male voice, because, normally, only the vocal fold dimensions of an adult man can produce such a low voice pitch.

Still, nature set rather generous limits within which we can change our personal voice timbre; it can, for instance, be altered quite substantially by means of voice training. Impersonators, of course, exploit this ability to change voice characteristics. The sound of the voice depends on the individual shape of the vocal tract and of the vocal folds as well as on the habitual use of a particular speaker's voice organ. Basically, this fact is well known to all of us; educating and training a voice implies changes in the sound of the voice. Such changes would be impossible to achieve if all voice characteristics were innate.

This is not to say that voice characteristics are easy to modify. On the contrary, it may be very hard to improve an individual's voice habits so that the voice better endures the strains to which it is exposed. The point is to take optimal advantage of all possibilities that the individual characteristics of the person's vocal folds and vocal tract offer.

Initially we posed a question: What do we mean by voice? Has this question been answered above in a satisfactory way? Hardly; what has been said so far is possibly even confusing, from the point of view of finding an answer to the question. The term *voice* cannot be equated with *voice organ,* nor *speech sounds,* nor *singing sounds,* because voice is something personal. Furthermore, not all speech sounds are voice sounds; it would seem odd to judge a person's voice quality from an unvoiced sound sequence, such as a whisper. Indeed, it seems that we know exactly what we mean by the word *voice* as long as we don't try to define it!

Apparently, we have already run into a dilemma. Often the most efficient solution in such situations is to make a crude, arbitrary decision. Accepting this solution, we state that in the present book the term *voice* will be used for the sounds generated by the voice organ, including the vibrating vocal folds, or to be more precise, by means of an airstream from the lungs, modified first by the vibrating vocal folds, and then by the rest of the larynx, and the pharynx, the mouth, and sometimes also the nasal cavities. Thus, *voice* becomes a synonym of *voiced sound*. The voice timbre (the sound characteristics of the voice) is determined in part by the way in which the voice organ is being used and in part by the morphology of the voice organ. In this book we will see how the voice organ is constructed, how it functions, and what determines personal voice timbre.

Before abandoning the prevailing atmosphere of introduction, it may be appropriate to offer the reader a sketch of the content of this book. In the second chapter, "The Voice Organ," we will see how the voice organ is constructed (its anatomy) and how it works when we use it (its physiology). Here the explanation is presented for the fact that we are able to generate sounds with our voice organ. The chapter explains why the vocal folds start to vibrate, why they generate sound when they vibrate, why some vowels sound different from others, and how the timbral character of a vowel is controlled by the shape of the tongue, the lips, and the jaw openings.

The third chapter, "Breathing," presents a detailed picture of how our breathing system works and how we use it for the purpose of phonation. Different characteristics of the breathing system, for instance—lung volume, air flow, and air pressure—are presented, all of them possible to measure objectively. An account is given for the differences in these dimensions between speech and singing. The well-known fact that improvement of voice function often can be obtained by means of changing the breathing habits is discussed, and possible explanations are presented.

The fourth chapter, "The Voice Source," is a central chapter in the book. It deals with the sound generated by the vibrating vocal folds, which constitutes the raw material of the voice. This sound is generally called the *voice source*. The chapter presents and discusses results from recent scientific research concerning the vibrational mode of the vocal folds and the acoustic consequences of these vibrations significant for voice timbre. Here, accounts are given of the current view on the effect on the voice source of changes in vocal effort, pitch, and type of phonation. Also, research results are presented concerning voice source differences between varying types of voice, for instance, male and female voices, and falsetto and normal voice register (or *modal register*, as we will call it in this book). Careful reading of this chapter is recommended for those readers who are unfamiliar with phonetics and speech science.

The fifth chapter, "Articulation," is also important. It describes how the sounds of the voice are affected by the lip and jaw openings, the tongue shape, and the vertical larynx position, or the *articulators*, as they will be called in this book. An initial section describes the effects of the articulators on the vocal tract resonances, or the *formants*. These formants determine the vowel quality and also much of the personal timbre of the voice. In the three following sections, the text becomes somewhat more specialized. Accounts are given of the formant frequency differences that have been found between different voice types, such as male and female voices, tenor and bass singers, and so on. Several characteristics regarding the choice of formant frequencies in male and female operatic singing are described in separate sections. The male opera singers' so-called "singer's formant" (which actually is not a formant) and the female opera singers' pitch dependent choice of formant frequencies are considered in two such sections. The relationships between the formant frequencies and the dimensions of the vocal tract are also discussed.

Most people who use their voices for musical purposes are choir singers. Still, very little research has been devoted to choir singing, perhaps because it is generally regarded as a less heroic and spectacular form of voice use than solo singing. The sixth chapter, "Choral Voice," summarizes the few articles presently available on this topic.

The seventh chapter, "Speech, Song, and Emotions," describes how the emotional state of a person affects the way in which the voice is used. It is well established that emotions affect the voice. For instance, it is generally assumed that stress is the cause of several voice disorders. Moreover, we are often able to draw correct conclusions on the emotional state of a speaker just by listening to the voice. The ability to draw such conclusions necessarily plays an important role in the emotional experience we may enjoy when we listen to a good singer. The chapter reviews several articles dealing with the influence of emotions on voice behavior in speech and in singing.

The eighth chapter, "A Rhapsody on Perception," is devoted to a description of phenomena that are relevant when we listen to voice sounds, particularly those occurring in singing. The first section explains the fact that the speaker or singer and the listener perceive the voice quite differently. The distortion of the auditory picture that the singer or speaker receives of his or her own voice is described as is the sensation of body vibrations which are particularly felt by singers who use them to control their phonation. The remaining sections deal with the perception of certain aspects of voice sounds, occurring mostly in singing, such as vibrato, vowel color, identification of vowels in high-pitched singing, and singing in and out of tune.

The last chapter, "Voice Disorders," briefly summarizes part of a book of the Swedish phoniatrician Björn Fritzell (1973), head of the phoniatric department at the Huddinge Hospital, Sweden. The chapter also contains a review of articles that describe how the vocal fold vibrations and the voice source are affected by voice disorders. One aim of this chapter is to help readers avoid certain types of voice disorders arising from unwise use of the voice. With these words the author wishes his readers progress, pleasure, and good vocal health during as well as after reading!

This introductory chapter would be incomplete without one more word on terminology. Sometimes, the same term may mean opposite things to two voice experts, as is suggested by the results of an experiment in which the author participated (Sundberg and Askenfelt, 1983). A pair of synthe-sized sung, ascending scales with different timbral characteristics were re-peatedly presented to twenty-nine subjects, all of them voice experts. Their task was to characterize, in their own terminology, the differences in sing-ing technique underlying the two scales. In the long list of adjectives used by these experts there were several instances of similar terms with appar-ently opposite meanings. There is therefore a great risk of causing misun-derstandings if one uses the traditional terminology, including even such basic concepts as support, projection, and the like. Therefore most terms commonly used in singers' terminologies have been deliberately avoided in this book.

The Voice Organ

In this chapter we shall see how the voice organ is built. The first part of the chapter contains a description of the landscape, so to speak, and the latter describes the way in which the machinery behind the voiced sounds functions. Using medical terms, we call the first part the *anatomy* of the voice organ and the second part the *physiology* of the voice organ.

Anatomy

The voice organ is constituted of three different systems: the breathing apparatus, the vocal folds, and the vocal tract. A very condensed presentation of their construction will follow next, but it should be complemented by a close examination of figures 2.1 and 2.2. Readers eager to learn more are urged to examine the work of Zemlin (1968) and Shearer (1979). (The author must confess that all his attempts to gain a clear view of the construction of the larynx were in vain until he had the opportunity to see a dissection of excised human larynxes. Thus, the reader is recommended to arm himself with curiosity, patience, and energy.)

The *lungs* are spongy structures suspended in a sac within the rib cage. The small cavities in these spongy structures are connected to tubes called the *bronchi*. These join the trachea, which is terminated by the vocal folds.

The vocal *folds* are constituted by muscles shaped as folds and covered by a mucous membrane. They are also called the vocal cords; but since they are really folds rather than cords, we will use the term *folds* in this book. The vocal folds are approximately 3 mm long in the newborn infant and grow to about 9 to 13 mm and 15 to 20 mm in adult females and males, respectively. The importance of the vocal fold length to the voice has recently been scientifically analyzed by Sawashima et al. (1983), who showed that the longer the vocal folds, the lower the pitch range of the voice. They also showed that vocal fold length does not significantly depend on body length but rather that there is a significant correlation with the circumference of the neck.

The slit between the vocal folds is called the *glottis*. The vocal folds originate on the posterior surface of the *thyroid cartilage* near the thyroid angle. The folds run posteriorly, and each fold inserts in an *arytenoid cartilage*. The anterior angle of the thyroid cartilage can easily be seen in many adult

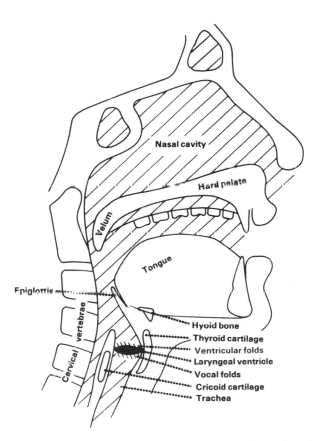

Figure 2.1. Schematic representation of a mid-sagittal profile of the voice organ.

males (particularly on skinny persons) and is referred to as the Adam's apple. Thus the Adam's apple marks the location of the vocal folds in the throat.

The arytenoid cartilages can be moved very quickly. They open and close the glottis by a rotating movement, which separates or pulls together the posterior ends of the vocal folds. The action of the arytenoid cartilages in bringing together the vocal folds is called *adduction;* and the opposite movement, that is the separation of the vocal folds, is called *abduction.* Unfortunately, these two terms sound very similar. However, if one recalls that the Latin word *ab* means *away from* (think of abstinence, for instance) and that the Latin word *ad* means *to* (think of addition), the meaning is easy to remember. Then one must only have distinct articulation, which presumably will cause persons interested in the sounds of the voice no trouble.

Adduction and abduction are movements that enable us to shift from unvoiced to voiced and from voiced to unvoiced sounds, respectively. In order to pronounce a voiced sound, the vocal folds must be adducted; and in order to pronounce an unvoiced sound, they must be abducted. When we pronounce a word such as "dissect," the vocal folds must be adducted until the /s/ sound is reached. Then, they must be abducted during the /s/, adducted again for the vowel sound, and then again abducted for the final

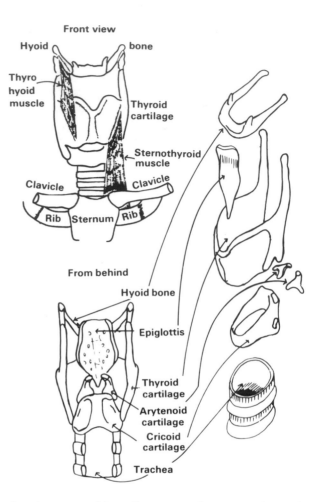

Front view

Hyoid   bone

Thyro
hyoid
muscle

Thyroid
cartilage

Sternothyroid
muscle

Clavicle   Clavicle

Rib   Sternum   Rib

From behind

Hyoid bone

Epiglottis

Thyroid
cartilage

Arytenoid
cartilage

Cricoid
cartilage

Trachea

Figure 2.2. The various cartilages of the larynx. Also shown are the hyoid bone and two tracheal cartilage rings. (After Shearer, 1979.)

/k/ and /t/ sounds. Clearly, the arytenoid cartilages must be very active and precise in their operation during speech production.

A few millimeters above the vocal folds there is a similar pair of folds, covered by mucous membrane. These are called the *ventricular folds* or the *false vocal folds.* We will avoid the latter, somewhat moralistic, name here. Between the vocal folds and the ventricular folds there is a small cavity, the *laryngeal ventricle* (also the *sinuses of Morgagni*). The glottis serves as the bottom of a small tube-shaped cavity, which is called the *larynx tube.* Posteriorly, this tube is limited by the arytenoid cartilages, anteriorly by the thyroid cartilage and the inferior part of the *epiglottis,* while the lateral parts of the larynx tube are constituted by the tissues that join these structures. The larynx tube is a rather narrow, short tube, about one or two centimeters long. This tube is inserted into the bottom part of a much wider and longer tube, namely the *pharynx.* Therefore, the pharynx partially surrounds the larynx tube,. On the right and left of the larynx tube, the bottom part of the pharynx forms pear-shaped cavities called the *piriform sinuses.*

At the bottom of the pharynx, in the posterior part of the sinus piriformes, just behind the arytenoids, there is an opening to the stomach system. It is through this opening, which is normally closed, that we pass food and beverage when we swallow. Food and drink are not welcome in the lungs. For this reason the larynx tube closes the entrance to the airways as soon as we swallow. In this closing operation, the epiglottis plays an important role. If we fail to close the larynx tube during swallowing, so that something meant for the stomach enters the airways, we start coughing violently, so that the wrongly delivered substance is thrown out.

The back wall of the pharynx is constituted by the cervical vertebrae, the side walls by *constrictor muscles.* The anterior wall is the larynx tube at the bottom, then the epiglottis, which is a cartilage shaped somewhat like a spoon, and higher up, the tongue. The tongue, which originates in the hyoid bone, is composed of a number of muscles. The root of the tongue goes well below the upper tip of the epiglottis, so that there is a cavity between the root of the tongue and the upper part of the epiglottis. The ceiling of the pharynx cavity is constituted by the *velum,* which serves as the gate to the nose cavities and which forms the most posterior part of the mouth.

The combination of the pharynx and the mouth is referred to as the *vocal tract.* The nasal cavity is split up into two halves in its anterior part, with the nostrils as their apertures. In the ceiling of the nasal cavity narrow channels lead up to other cavities, the *maxillary* and *frontal sinuses,* which are located in the bone structure of the skull. When these cavities are suppurated, one has *sinusitis.*

From the point of view of the student of the voice, the entire point of the apparatus just described is that it allows us to make a variety of sounds—not only a small variety—as do many animals, but a huge variety that can be successfully used for complicated acoustic communication systems such as speech and singing. In order for this to be possible, the variability of both the vocal folds and the vocal tract needs to be very great. This variability is made available to us by means of a large number of muscles. In the past section some of these have been presented. Instead of enumerating them all (and at the risk of boring some readers eager to learn more about the voice), we will instead present some remaining important muscles, as we discuss their functions and their contributions to voice timbre.

Physiology
Functioning

As mentioned above, the voice organ is composed of three units: the breathing apparatus, the vocal folds, and the vocal tract. Each of these serves a purpose of its own (see figure 2.3). The vocal purpose of the breathing sytem is to compress the air in the lungs, so that an airstream is generated past the glottis and the vocal tract.

It is necessary here to introduce and define two crucial terms. *Phonation* means sound generation by means of vocal fold vibrations. In phonation the

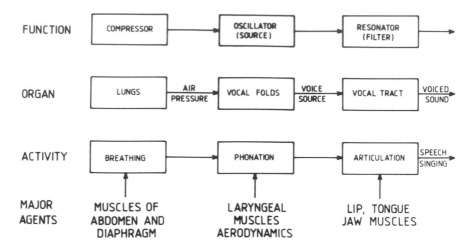

Figure 2.3. Block diagram illustrating the three functional constituents of the voice organ: the breathing apparatus acts as a compressor supplying an overpressure of air; the phonatory apparatus constituted by the vocal folds acting as an oscillator converting the transglottal airstream to a sequence of air pulses corresponding to the voice source; and the vocal tract resonator.

vocal folds generate a primary sound, as the airstream passes them. This sound is called the *voice source.*

The voice source passes through the vocal tract, and thereby it is shaped acoustically. The nature of this shaping depends on the vocal tract configuration, which is controlled by *articulation.* One who is used to the vocabulary of engineers might prefer to speak about the breathing system as a *compressor* and to regard the vocal folds and the vocal tract as an *oscillator* and a *resonator,* respectively. We will return to these terms a number of times in this and future chapters; the reader will certainly end up realizing that they do good service. So what do they mean in the first place?

A *compressor* is used to compress a gas like air by decreasing the volume containing it. An *oscillator* is a name for anything that generates a signal of some kind. When it is an acoustic oscillator, as in the case of the voice organ, it is an acoustic signal that is being generated. Such a signal is composed of small (indeed microscopic) and rapid variations of the air pressure. In voiced sounds, it is the vocal folds that give rise to such variations. When the airstream passes the vocal folds, they may start vibrating, so that they alternately open and close the passage for the airstream. In this way the airstream gets chopped into a series of small air pulses, and at regular intervals these raise the air pressure above the glottis. The pressure then falls and is raised anew, as soon as the vocal folds allow the next air pulse to pass. Thus, by alternately opening and closing the passage for the airstream, the vibrating vocal folds generate an acoustic signal composed of variations in the air pressure (see figure 2.4). As long as the vocal folds open and shut the glottis at identical time intervals, a tone is generated which possesses a certain *frequency.* This frequency is equal to the vibration

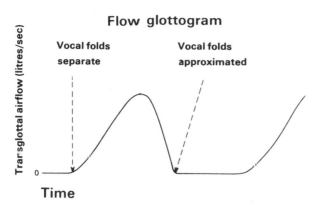

Flow glottogram

Vocal folds separate

Vocal folds approximated

Transglottal airflow (litres/sec)

0

Time

Figure 2.4. Schematic representation of the waveform of the voice source constituted by the air pulses generated by the vocal fold vibrations; when the vocal folds close the glottis, this air stream goes to zero, and when the vocal folds open, a momentary airstream results, which is terminated by the following closing of the glottis.

frequency of the vocal folds, as a moment's reflection will tell us. It is also equal to the frequency of the generated note. Thus, if a soprano sings the note A5* having the frequency of 880 Hertz (Hz), the vocal folds open and close 880 times per second.

The vocal folds are not the only oscillator in the voice organ enabling us to generate sounds. Other parts of the voice organ can also work as oscillators to create unvoiced sounds. If the airstream from the lungs is forced to pass a narrow slit with reasonably rigid walls, the airstream becomes turbulent. Thereby noise is generated, a signal lacking pitch. Noise also corresponds to air pressure variations, but in this case the variations are irregular, or aperiodic. If we pronounce an unvoiced sound, such as /f/, it is the slit between the lower lip and the front teeth that works as the oscillator. But noise-generating oscillators can be formed in other places as well. In whispering, the vocal folds are so tense that they are not set into vibration. At the same time they form a sufficiently narrow passage that the airstream may become turbulent and generate noise. A noise generator can also be formed between the tongue dorsum and the velum (as in the pronunciation of the German *ach*) or between the tongue tip and various places along the hard palate, as in the pronunciation of the initial sounds in the words *shaft, chief,* and *sip.*

Everything that possesses the properties of mass and compliance is a *resonator.* An air volume possesses both these properties. Even if air does not weigh much, it still weighs something and therefore possesses mass. Also, it is possible to compress air, which then strives to resume its original volume (otherwise, rubber tires would be a poor idea!); this implies that it possesses compliance. For this reason the air enclosed in the vocal tract acts as a resonator.

*Here we will use a system for labeling the pitch frequencies, which is charming because it is so logical. Each octave is given a number of its own, and each octave starts on the note of C and ends on the note of B. Octave number zero is the lowest one in which our hearing system can discern a pitch. The piano keyboard generally starts in this octave number zero. This system relieves us of the awkwardness of regarding some octaves as smaller than others, of regarding a certain C as the middle one (in what sense then?), and other labels which may be falsely thought-provoking. The system is easy enough to remember; the frequency for the pitch of A4 is equal to 440 Hz.

Sound within a resonator decays slowly. If one hits a resonator, it will resound, and the resulting sound will not fade away immediately, but more or less slowly. In a piano string, which can be regarded as an extreme type of resonator, the decay is extremely slow. In the vocal tract, the decay is much more rapid, but still it is sometimes possible to hear how a sound in the vocal tract decays. If one flicks one's neck above the larynx with a finger while the glottis is kept closed and the mouth is kept open, one can hear a quick decay; it sounds as if one had hit an empty bottle or tin, which, incidentally, are other examples of resonators.

Another characteristic* of a resonator is that it allows sounds to pass through it under certain conditions depending on the frequency of the sound. This is illustrated schematically in figure 2.5. Sounds having certain frequencies pass through the resonator very easily, so that they are radiated with a high amplitude from the resonator. These specially transmitted frequencies which fit the resonator optimally, so to speak, are called the *resonance frequencies* or, if the resonator is the human vocal tract, *formant frequencies*. If a tone with a frequency different from a formant frequency passes through the resonator, the tone will be transmitted with a reduced amplitude; the resonator damps it. One could also say that a resonator *resonates* at certain frequencies, or that it possesses *resonances* (*formants* in the case of the vocal tract) at certain frequencies. Thus, the ability of the vocal tract to transmit sound is greatest at the formant frequencies. Most resonators possess a number of resonance frequencies. In the vocal tract the four or five lowest formants are the most relevant ones. The two lowest formants determine most of the vowel color; all of them are of great significance to voice timbre. These aspects will be considered in greater detail in chapter 5.

Why Do the Vocal Folds Vibrate?

When an airstream is forced through a sufficiently narrow glottis, the vocal folds start to vibrate. In this process, the so-called Bernoulli force[†] plays an important role. The Bernoulli force is activated when an object prevents a flowing substance, such as air, from streaming freely, so that certain layers of the stream have to travel a longer distance than the rest of the stream. Under these conditions the velocity is greater in that layer which is forced to travel the longer way than in the freely streaming part. Such a difference between the layers' velocities generates an underpressure, which is greatest in a direction perpendicular to the direction of the freely travelling stream. In the glottis, the middle layer of the airstream goes undisturbed through the slit. The lateral layers of the airstream are deflected by the vocal folds, so that they have to travel a longer distance than the middle layer. Thus, the condition for generating the Bernoulli force is met, and hence an underpressure results along the vocal folds. This underpressure strives to

---

*To tell the truth, this is *not* another characteristic, but a different manifestation of the same characteristic as the one just described.

†Bernoulli was a Swiss physicist in the eighteenth century who described this phenomenon in physical terms.

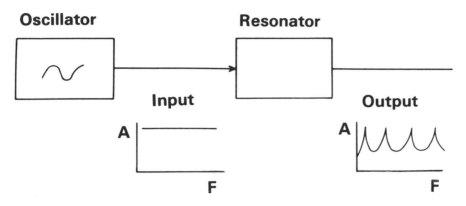

Figure 2.5. Schematic illustration of the vocal tract resonator; it transmits sounds from the glottal end to the lip opening with a variable efficiency, depending on the frequency of the sound to be transmitted. If a tone sweeping from low to high frequency at a constant amplitude is introduced in the glottal end, the amplitude measured at the lip opening varies as a function of frequency. The regions of high amplitude are resonances that are called formants in the vocal tract, and the center frequencies at which the resulting amplitude culminates are the center frequencies of the formants, which are called the formant frequencies.

move the vocal fold tissues toward the midline of the glottis slit. This is equivalent to saying that the Bernoulli force strives to close the glottis as soon as there is a transglottal airstream. A schematic illustration is provided in figure 2.6.

Just for fun, let us here mention some other well-known applications of the Bernoulli force. One example is a sailboat beating to windward. On the leeward side the wind layer closest to the sail has a longer distance to travel than the layers further away from the sail, because the sail is bending toward the leeward side. Thus, the Bernoulli force strives to pull the sail forward, or, in other words, it helps the boat to move forward. Another application is found in the airplane. The wings are flat on the underneath side and vaulted on the upper. The airstream layer closest to the upper surface has a longer distance to travel than the layer further up in the air. The Bernoulli force strives to lift the plane upward or, in other words, to keep it in the air.

After this little digression, let us return to the glottal aspects of phonation. In the glottis, the Bernoulli force strives to pull the vocal folds toward each other. Furthermore, the Bernoulli force arises as soon as an airstream passes the glottis. This means that as soon as the glottis opens, a Bernoulli force is activated again, and the glottis closes. But when the glottis is closed, the air pressure is higher below the glottis than above it. If the vocal folds are adjusted for phonation, they cannot resist this air pressure difference. Instead, they open and allow a new air pulse to escape. Then the Bernoulli force comes again and again shuts the glottis. This description is a simplified version of the process, which in practice is far more complicated. The nonlinear properties of the vocal fold mechanism play a decisive role. For instance, it is important that the entire vocal fold does not move

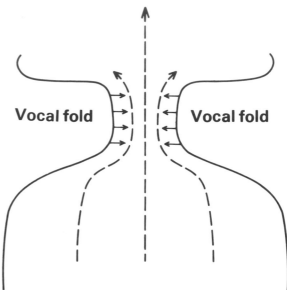

Vocal fold **Vocal fold**

Figure 2.6. Schematic illustration of the Bernoulli effect. The layer of the airstream in the center between the vocal folds travels a shorter distance than adjacent layers, which are forced to bend around the vocal fold contours. The difference in traveling distance generates an underpressure, or a sucking force, as shown by the small arrows. This sucking force strives to close the glottis as soon as an airstream passes.

as a unit; instead, the lower part must be a bit ahead of the upper part in the cycling movement; otherwise, there will be no vibration. But as this is a complicated matter, we will content ourselves with the above description.

The Bernoulli force is not the only factor contributing to the closing of the vibrating glottis. There are, as mentioned, a number of adducting muscles; by contracting they can adjust the glottal width so that the vocal folds can vibrate. Also, the vocal folds are elastic, a condition that contributes a force in the same direction as the Bernoulli force. But without the Bernoulli force we would not be able to produce voiced sounds. Our muscles for adduction, and also our nerve signals, are much too slow to produce contractions as frequent as several hundred per second.

Not long ago, there were many people who believed that this was indeed possible. It was assumed that our brain, via nerve signals, determined the instant at which the vocal folds part and approach. In other words, it was believed that there was one nerve impulse per glottal vibratory cycle. The man behind this hypothesis, later proven untenable, was the Frenchman Raoul Husson. His hypothesis was appealing from the point of view that it explained how singers may produce a given pitch directly, without any initial error. Instead, we seem to develop this ability to predict directly which muscles to contract and how much, in order to achieve the movement needed. For instance, we can learn to play the piano without looking at the movements of our fingers and hands. Also, most of us can bring our hands together so that the thumbs meet without looking. The realization of a previously imagined pitch is no more inexplicable than these other examples of our capability to predict when and what muscles to contract. Nevertheless, Husson's view, extensively presented and defended in scientific articles, had a great positive impact on our understanding of the glottal mechanism. Many researchers apparently felt challenged by Husson's claims, and this generated a great number of investigations, which substantially improved our understanding of the glottal mechanism.

Abduction and Adduction

The terms *abduction* and *adduction* were mentioned above. Adduction is required for phonation to take place, and abduction is necessary both for taking a breath and for producing voiceless sounds. The muscles controlling abduction and adduction are therefore significant in the control of phonation. Adduction is executed by contraction of the lateral cricoarytenoid and the interarytenoid muscles.* Their course and effect are illustrated in figure 2.7. They pull the anterior processes of the arytenoid cartilages forward, so that

Adduction and Abduction

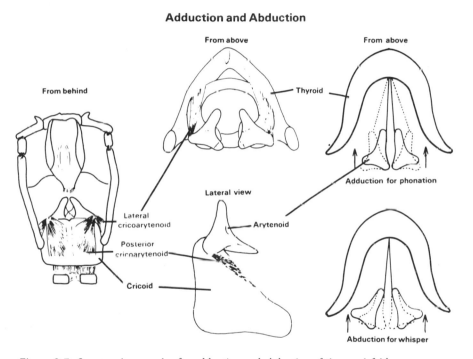

Figure 2.7. Some major muscles for adduction and abduction of the vocal folds. Contraction of the lateral cricoarytenoid muscles adduct, or approximate the vocal folds, and contraction of the posterior cricoarytenoid (also called the posticus) muscles abduct, or separate, the vocal folds. The left figure shows the larynx as seen from behind, the upper part of the center figure shows the larynx as viewed from above (not showing the vocal folds), and the lower figure shows the cricoid cartilage from the side. The right figures illustrate the result of a contraction of the lateral cricoarytenoid muscles without (above) and with (below) a concomitant contraction of the interarytenoid muscles; these muscles, not shown in this figure, connect the posterior parts of the arytenoid cartilages, and by contraction, they close the posterior part of the glottis. (After Zemlin, 1968.)

---

*As a rule there is law and order in the medical names of muscles. They are named after the structures they join. The rule is that the more stable attachment structure supplies the initial muscle designation. As an example, the thyroarytenoid muscles run between the more stable structure of the thyroid cartilage and the more mobile arytenoid cartilages.

the vocal folds approximate. Abduction is executed by the posterior crico-arytenoid muscles, also called the posticus. Their course and effect are illustrated in the same figure. They pull the lateral processes of the arytenoid cartilages posteriorly, so that the vocal folds part. Other muscles also have a certain abduction effect when they contract. However, the interarytenoid and the lateral cricoarytenoid muscles and the posterior cricoarytenoid muscles are the main agents in adduction and abduction, respectively.

Control of Vocal Fold Vibration

It was mentioned before that the frequency of the note generated by the vocal fold vibrations equals the vibration frequency of the vocal folds; if one sings the note A4, which has the frequency of 440 Hz, the glottis opens and closes 440 times per second. We can all change the pitch of the sounds we generate with our voice. This is very essential not only in singing but also in speech, where the melodic changes of pitch, or the *pitch contour,* carry quite a lot of information. For example, in many languages, question and statement are identical with respect to wording and spelling (disregarding for the moment question marks and periods), and the distinction is maintained primarily in the pitch patterns. Any change in the pitch of a voiced sound evidently corresponds to a change in the vibration frequency of the vocal folds. Next we will see how such changes in the vibration frequency can be achieved; but before going into that, let us introduce another term, together with its definition. Henceforth, the term *phonation frequency* will be used rather than the vibration frequency of the vocal folds. Phonation frequency is given in Hz, and it is the physical correlate of the pitch of the note sung.

By what means do we control phonation frequency? Two factors affect it: the overpressure of air in the lungs, which is called the *subglottic pressure,* and the *laryngeal musculature* which determines the length, tension, and vibrating mass of the vocal folds. The influence of the subglottic pressure is straightforward; if subglottic pressure is raised, phonation frequency rises, although not very much. However, the major effect of a rise in subglottic pressure is not so much the increase in phonation frequency but rather an increase in the intensity of phonation. If one wants to increase the pitch, but not the intensity of the vowel produced, one should not change the subglottic pressure very much. Instead, one has to give the main responsibility to the muscles manipulating the properties of the vocal folds. What happens mechanically is simply that the vocal folds are stretched to different degrees, depending on the intended phonation frequency. The longer, the thinner, and the more tense they are, the higher the phonation frequency becomes. The vocal fold tension is achieved by increasing the distance between their terminating structures, or in other words, between the thyroid (anteriorly) and the arytenoid cartilages (posteriorly). Normally this is the result of a contraction of the cricothyroid muscles (see figure 2.8).

When these muscles contract, the cricoid cartilage is tilted, so that its anterior portion approaches the thyroid cartilage. If the arytenoid carti-

Cricothyroid muscles

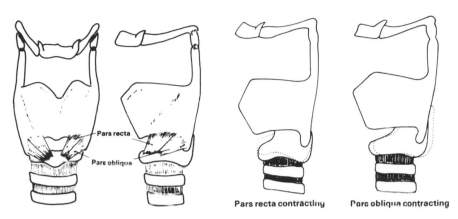

Figure 2.8. Illustration of function of the cricothyroid muscles, which by contraction lengthen the vocal folds. They consist of two parts: the pars recta and the pars obliqua. Contraction of the pars recta tilts the cricoid cartilage, thus reducing the distance between the thyroid and cricoid cartilages, so that the distance between the thyroid and arytenoid cartilages is increased and the vocal folds are stretched. Contraction of the pars obliqua slides the cricoid cartilage forward, thus increasing the distance between the thyroid and the cricoid cartilages, and this also results in a stretching of the vocal folds.

lages, in which the vocal folds insert, are stabilized so that they do not yield, a contraction of the cricothyroid muscles will result in a lengthening of the vocal folds. The slit between the anterior parts of the thyroid and cricoid cartilages is narrowed when we increase phonation frequency; if one puts a finger on this slit while varying phonation frequency, one can feel this slit change in width. Also, the distance between the epiglottis and the arytenoid cartilages increases when phonation frequency is raised. By means of a fiberscope or a laryngeal mirror, one often can see how the distance between the epiglottis and the arytenoid cartilages is increased when phonation frequency is raised; the entrance to the larynx tube seems to widen. In some subjects, high-pitched phonation causes the entrance to the larynx tube to look like the beak of a hungry nestling. When phonation frequency is low, on the other hand, the entrance is generally very narrow indeed. For this reason patients are often asked to avoid phonating at too low a pitch during examination of the vocal folds by means of a laryngeal mirror.

By means of electromyography (EMG), the nerve signals that tell the muscle to contract can be picked up and recorded. Some EMG measurements have been made on laryngeal muscles. It is in this way that evidence has been obtained for the pitch-raising role of the cricothyroid muscles. It is remarkable that it is still unclear which muscles are used to lower phonation frequency. It is likely, but not yet shown, that the lateral cricoarytenoid muscles (also called the thyromuscularis muscles) have this function. They run parallel to the vocalis, but more laterally, as can be observed in figure 2.9. This muscle continues upward and narrows

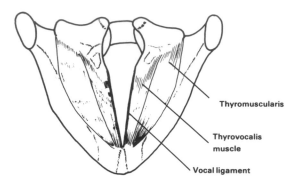

Figure 2.9. Illustration of the two bundles of the thyroarytenoid muscles: (1) the medial thyrovocalis, or simply vocalis, muscles and (2) the external thyromuscularis muscles. When the vocalis muscles contract, the vocal folds are tensed; and when the thyromuscularis muscles contract, the vocal folds are shortened, as for low phonation frequency. The thyromuscularis muscles continue upward, so that by contraction they also narrow the larynx tube. (After Zemlin, 1968.)

the larynx tube opening when it contracts. Thus, if it is correct that the lateral cricoarytenoid muscles lower phonation frequency, the narrowing of the larynx tube opening associated with low-pitched phonation would be explained.

Phonation frequency is determined partly by the laryngeal muscles, partly by subglottic pressure. If this pressure is raised, the intensity of phonation is also increased, as mentioned. Indeed, an increase of the sub-glottic pressure is the normal way to increase intensity of phonation, as we will see in the next chapter. Now, if the pitch is supposed to remain constant while intensity is supposed to increase, or, in other words, if a swelling tone is supposed to be produced, it is necessary to compensate by means of the pitch-regulating muscles for the rise in the phonation frequency generated by the increased subglottic pressure. Considering these and other complicated interrelations between various laryngeal muscle functions, it is indeed rather amazing that it is not only possible but even easy to sing a swell tone with constant pitch without extensive voice training. This is only one out of a great multitude of proofs of our virtuosity in handling our voice organ. We do not need to bother about the extremely complicated maneuvers we perform. We just perform them unconsciously, and what catches our attention is the end result, the sound.

From Air Stream to Sound

Regarded from a purely physical point of view, sound consists of microscopic and quick variations of the air pressure. In order to be perceived as a sound by human hearing, these variations must be more rapid than 20 per second, or, in other words, the frequency must be above 20 Hz and less rapid than 20,000 per second; that is, the frequency must be lower than 20,000 Hz. When we grow older and lose some hearing ability, the upper limit, in particular, may drop considerably. Furthermore, these air pressure variations must neither be too small (because then we do not hear anything at all) nor too large (because then we do not hear as much as we feel pain in our ears).

Provided that the air pressure is forced to vary in an adequate way, we can hear such variations as sound. Consequently, the voice organ generates air pressure variations. It is not too difficult to imagine why this must be so. Simplifying a bit, the process can be described in the following way. Every time the vocal folds separate and allow a small amount of air to enter into the larynx tube, the air pressure in that cavity rises somewhat. This increase in the air pressure then rapidly propagates upward in the vocal tract, so that the air pressure in the larynx tube drops again. When the vocal folds separate the next time and pass the next air pulse into the larynx tube, it again rises. The result then is an air pressure that varies in synchrony with the vocal fold vibrations. This is equivalent to the generation of sound, as was just mentioned.

This primary sound generated by the vocal fold vibrations is called the *voice source*, as mentioned before. By and large, the voice source is similar for all voiced sounds produced at the same frequency and intensity of phonation. As there may be huge differences between different voiced sounds, which are equal in pitch and loudness, we conclude that what we hear is not the sound coming directly from the vocal fold oscillator. Something very essential happens to the sound on its way from the glottis to the lip opening.

It was mentioned that the vocal tract is a resonator. This implies that its ability to transfer sound is strongly dependent on the frequency of the sound to be transferred. Tones with frequencies equal to the formant frequencies are most favored; they are carried without any problems, or are even helped. There are four or five formants of significance in the human vocal tract. If the glottal oscillator emits a tone having a frequency equal to a formant frequency, this tone will be radiated with a much greater amplitude than other tones whose frequencies do not match a formant frequency.

During phonation, our glottal sound generator, that is, the vibrating vocal folds, does not give rise to one single tone. Instead, an entire family or *spectrum* of tones is generated. The lowest tone in a spectrum is called the *fundamental* and the other tones are called *overtones*. The fundamental plus these overtones are called *partials*. All of them have different frequencies, otherwise they would not be different tones. Their frequencies form a *harmonic series*. This means that partial number N has a frequency N times the frequency of the lowest partial, which is the fundamental. The second partial has a frequency twice that of the fundamental, the third partial has a frequency three times that of the fundamental, and so on. The frequencies of the partials are simply integer multiples of the frequency of the fundamental.

Thus, the glottal oscillator delivers an entire bouquet of harmonic partials to the vocal tract to be forwarded to its open end, which is the lip opening. The vocal tract treats these partials in various ways because they have different frequencies. The partials lying closest to a formant frequency are helped on their way out, so that they are stronger in the sound radiated from the lip opening than other partials lying further away from a formant frequency. This is illustrated in a schematic way in figure 2.10.

The timbral properties of a note (regarding both vowel quality and voice color) depend on the frequencies at which there are strong and weak partials. In vowel sounds, this depends on the formant frequencies, as we have

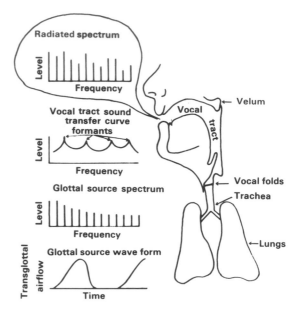

Figure 2.10. Schematic illustration of the generation of voice sounds. The vocal fold vibrations result in a sequence of voice pulses (bottom left) corresponding to a series of harmonic overtones, the amplitudes of which decrease monotonically with frequency (second from bottom). This spectrum is filtered according to the sound transfer characteristics of the vocal tract with its peaks, the formants, and the valleys between them. In the spectrum radiated from the lip opening, the formants are depicted in terms of peaks, because the partials closest to a formant frequency reach higher amplitudes than neighboring partials.

just seen. This allows us to correctly conclude that *vowel quality and a good deal of voice color are determined by the formant frequencies of the vocal tract.* This is a most important point to remember. As we will see in a moment, it is the shape of the vocal tract that determines the frequencies of the formants; therefore, vowel quality and voice color ultimately depend on the shape of the vocal tract.

Formant Frequency Control

As the formant frequencies are of a decisive significance to the vowel quality and the voice color, it is interesting to ask what controls these formant frequencies. The question could almost be formulated in this way: what is it that determines the voice color? This formulation is not entirely equivalent, however, since part of the voice color depends on the voice source, the sound from the vibrating vocal folds. We will return to this later on.

The formant frequencies depend on the length and the shape of the vocal tract, as mentioned. The length is defined as the distance from the glottis to the lip opening. This distance will be referred to as the *vocal tract length*. The shape of the vocal tract normally varies along its longitudinal axis. Another way of saying the same thing is that the cross-sectional area varies with the distance to the glottis. Thus, we could describe the vocal tract shape with a curve where the horizontal axis represents the distance to the glottis and the vertical axis represents the cross-sectional area. Such a description of the vocal tract shape is called an *area function*. Some examples are given in figure 2.11.

The vocal tract length is determined by the individual morphology. For instance, children have shorter vocal tracts than adult females, and adult females have shorter vocal tracts than adult males. In adult males the vocal

Area functions

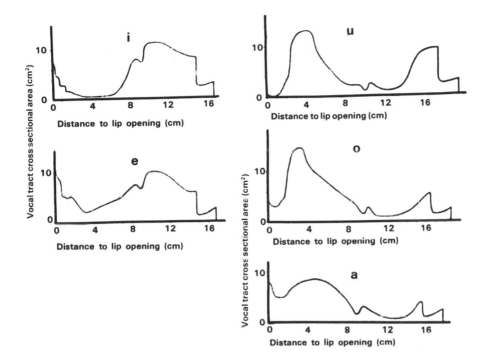

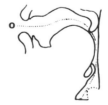

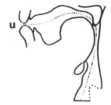

Figure 2.11. Upper graphs: Area functions for some vowels describing the shape of the vocal tract in terms of its cross-sectional area as function of the distance from the lip opening. This shape is determined by the positioning of the articulators as shown in the vocal tract profiles: the lip and jaw openings, the tongue shape, the velum, and the larynx. (After Fant, 1960.)

Vocal tract profiles

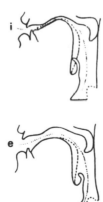

tract length is about 17 to 20 cm. In children the length is strongly dependent upon the age, as we would expect, and may be as short as 7 to 10 cm.

We can modify our vocal tract length to a certain extent. For one thing, the larynx can be raised and lowered. Also, a lowering of the larynx increases the vocal tract length, of course; in addition, we can lengthen our vocal tract by protruding the lips; and if we smile so that we retract the mouth corners, the vocal tract length is, no doubt, reduced. When we speak or sing, the vocal tract length is continuously varied, because not only do we change the position of the mouth corners, but we also move the larynx up and down, depending mainly on the pitch and the vowel, at least in normal speech.

The effect of the vocal tract length on the formant frequencies is quite straightforward: the longer the vocal tract, the lower the formant frequencies, other things being equal. The effect of the vocal tract length on vowel quality and voice color is easy to experience. Try to pronounce the vowel /i:/ (as in the word *beat*) with normal and then with protruded lips; with protruded lips the vowel is changed toward the vowel /y:/ (as in the French word *tu*). A similar effect is obtained if we lower the larynx instead.

The dependence of the formant frequencies on the area function is more complicated. The same change of the area function affects different formants to different extents and often in different directions. However, a certain systematic relationship can be discerned, if the phenomena are regarded from an articulatory point of view. What, then, are the tools we can use in order to change the area function? The main tools are the lips, the jaw opening, the tongue, the velum, and the larynx, which will be referred to as the *articulators*.

The lips can be rounded and spread as when we smile. The lower mandible can be moved upward and downward and also, to some extent, anteriorly and posteriorly. The tongue can be given a number of different shapes. It can bulge upward and forward, so that it reaches the hard palate, or upward and backward, so that it approaches the velum, or downward and backward, so that it constricts the pharynx cavity. The velum can be raised and lowered. When it is raised, it shuts the connection between the vocal and nasal tracts; and when it is lowered, the passage between the nose and mouth cavities is open. Not only can the larynx be raised and lowered, but it can also assume different shapes, particularly because of the very mobile arytenoid cartilages.

A movement in any of the articulators generally affects the frequencies of all formants. As a rule of thumb, we can say regarding these effects that almost all formants are lowered in frequency both by a narrowing of the lip opening and by a lengthening of the vocal tract. As for the individual formants, the first formant frequency is particularly sensitive to changes in the jaw opening; an increase in the jaw opening tends to raise the first formant frequency. The second formant is particularly sensitive to the shape of the tongue. When the tongue constricts the anterior part of the vocal tract (that is, in palatal vowel articulation), the second formant frequency is raised maximally. If the tongue constricts the vocal tract in the velar region, the second formant frequency is low. It is lowered to a lesser degree if the tongue constricts the pharynx. The second formant reaches its lowest value if the tongue constricts the velar region while the lips are protruded, as for the vowel /u:/ (for example in the German word *Buch**). In most vowels, the third formant is particularly sensitive to the position of the tongue tip, or, more accurately, to the size of the cavity immediately behind the incisors. If this cavity is large, the third formant frequency tends to be low.

By moving the articulators, we can change the lower formant frequencies in particular. The following are approximate values: in male adults the first formant can vary between 250 and 1,000 Hz, the second formant can vary between 600 and 2,500 Hz, and the third formant can be varied between 1,700 and 3,500 Hz. The higher formants, the fourth and the fifth, are less mobile. They are much more dependent on the vocal tract length than on the positioning of certain articulators, and the fourth formant is very dependent on the shape of the larynx tube.

Most of us probably intuit that a given vowel sound is associated with specific pattern of articulator adjustments. For example, the vowel /ɑ:/ (as in *father*) is usually pronounced with a more or less widened jaw opening, and the vowel /i:/ is associated with a narrower jaw opening. In reality, this applies to all vowels; each vowel sound corresponds to a characteristic pattern of articulator adjustment. Some examples are shown in figure 2.11 in terms of the mid-sagittal profile of the vocal tract as recorded by means of lateral X-ray pictures.

Furthermore, each articulation also corresponds to a combination of formant frequencies characteristic of that vowel. This really becomes self-evident if we recall that it is the area function that is determined by the articulation and which, in turn, determines the formant frequencies. Because of this factor's great importance, let us repeat it in concentrated form: Each vowel sound is associated with a specific articulatory profile, producing a specific area function that in turn gives a specific combination of formant frequencies (special cases notwithstanding). As previously mentioned, it is the two lowest formant frequencies that are most important to the vowel quality. Figure 2.12 shows the frequencies of the two lowest formants for some vowels. The "islands" in the figure imply that the vowel marked will result, provided the frequencies of the first and second formants remain within the island. For example, if the first and second formants are between 350 and 500 and 600 and 800 Hz, respectively, the vowel will be an /o:/. Note that the vowels are scattered along a triangular contour, the three corners of which are the vowels /i:/, /a:/, and /u:/. The vowel /ə:/ (as in *heard*) is located in the center of the triangle.

As previously mentioned, the formant frequencies determine the vowel

---

*It may seem farfetched to refer to this German vowel rather than to its English equivalent, which is the vowel in *moon*. However, there are typical vowel quality (and hence formant frequency) differences between the German and the English versions of this vowel.

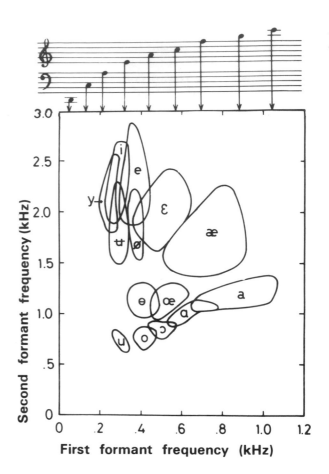

Figure 2.12. The two lowest formant frequencies for some long Swedish vowels. At the top of the graph, the frequency of the first formant is also given in terms of musical notation.

quality, as well as a good deal of the voice color. This necessarily implies that different individuals tune their formant frequencies a bit differently for the same vowel. For instance, it would be completely impossible for small children to bring their formant frequencies down to the values typically used by adult males, children's vocal tracts simply not being sufficiently long. This is the reason why the vowels are represented by islands rather than dots in figure 2.12. The exact position of the two lowest formant frequencies for a given vowel depends on the individual morphology of the speaker's vocal tract, among other things, and also on the habits of pronunciation. The exact location on the vowel island also contributes significantly to the voice color. However, as we will discuss later, the third and higher formants are still more decisive to the voice color than the two lowest formants.

3

Breathing

According to pedagogical experience, respiration is immensely important to the function of the voice organ. A phonatory problem can often be solved by changing the habits of respiration.

Viewed acoustically, the importance of respiration to phonation is something of a mystery. The only thing the vocal folds require from the respiratory mechanism is that it provide an overpressure of air in the lungs, which we will henceforth refer to as a *subglottic pressure.* Such a pressure may result from the contraction of a few out of several muscle groups, and different persons seem habitually to use different muscular strategies. To take a concrete example, one can phonate with the abdominal wall both expanded or pulled in. The muscle group responsible for generating the subglottic pressure could not possibly affect the functioning of the vocal folds, and therefore the choice of muscles used in order to generate the pressure should not affect phonation.

Instead, the way in which the vocal folds vibrate at a given subglottic pressure is entirely determined by the laryngeal musculature. However, subglottic pressure is significant for the amplitude and also, to some degree, for the frequency of phonation. These are two parameters over which a singer needs excellent control. It is possible that different methods of respiration allow different degrees of such control. This is one way of explaining the importance of breathing strategy to phonation.

Taking into account the apparently paramount practical importance of respiration to phonation, another explanation perhaps seems more likely: the way in which the subglottic pressure is controlled by the respiratory muscle system may generate reflexes that affect the activity in the laryngeal musculature. After all, the larynx and the lungs are closely interrelated systems; for instance, the former works as the gatekeeper of the latter. Hence, there may be some reflex-based interrelations between breathing and phonation habits.

The fact that so much attention is given to respiration in voice training and therapy may also to some extent be the result of the simple fact that the functioning of the respiratory system can be observed by the naked eye. This is in contrast to the laryngeal function, which neither the speaker nor the listener can see; it can be observed indirectly, only, in terms of the acoustic output.

In this chapter, we will not be able to offer any verification of the above speculations, unfortunately; but some facts about breathing in speech and singing will be presented, which will, one hopes, convey some concrete ideas.

What is Pressure?

Before starting to think about how the breathing apparatus works, we might review what pressure is. If a gas such as air is compressed in an enclosure such as a rubber balloon, the pressure within the enclosure is raised. This pressure exerts a force on the surface of the balloon, so that the rubber expands. This force may be so strong that it breaks the enclosure, and the balloon explodes. If we open the outlet of the balloon, the pressure will drive out air through this aperture. The resulting air-stream through this hole will be strong as long as the pressure inside the enclosure is high.

What we are considering here is overpressure, which means that the pressure is higher than the atmospheric pressure. Air pressure can be lower than the atmospheric pressure also. If air is sucked out of an enclosure with rigid walls, such as a tank, the pressure inside the tank is reduced, and an underpressure or negative pressure is generated. If the aperture is opened, air will stream into the tank at a rate determined by how low the under-pressure is.

Air pressure values are generally expressed in centimeters of water (cm H_2O), because they are normally measured by means of a manometer, a U-shaped tube partly filled with water. One end of it is opened to the free air, and the pressure to be measured is applied to the other end. The pressure generates a level difference between the water columns in the two shanks. This level difference is used as a measure of the pressure, and it is referred to as cm H_2O. A pressure of 1 cm H_2O is equivalent to 100 Pascals, 1/1000 of normal atmospheric pressure.

In quiet breathing through an open glottis, the quantity of air contained in the lungs is determined by the lung volume. In that case, the air pressure in the lungs is almost the same as in the air outside. When we exhale and inhale, we establish a very slight subglottic overpressure and underpressure in the lungs, respectively.

A closing of the glottis does not change the air volume in the lungs, of course, but an overpressure will be established if the lung volume is reduced by an activation of expiratory muscles. In other words, when the glottis is closed, the subglottic overpressure is determined by the forces exerted on the structures surrounding the air in the lungs. If the glottis is not entirely closed, as during phonation, subglottic overpressure is also affected by the resistance against flow of air through the glottis. During phonation we normally use an overpressure in the lungs (phonation during inhalation is possible but exceptional). For this reason we will henceforth use the term *subglottic pressure* as a synonym for subglottic overpressure.

The Mechanism

The lungs consist of a spongy structure. If a lung is taken out of the body and suspended in free air, it shrinks drastically; it assumes a volume that is actually about as small as the smallest possible volume it may assume within the rib cage. This means that the lungs are always attempting to shrink when hanging inside the rib cage. However, they are prevented from shrinking by the fact that they are hanging in a vacuum. In this respect, the lungs can be said to be similar to rubber balloons. When they are filled with air, they attempt to exhaust this air with a force which is determined by the amount of air contained in them. This means that the lungs exert an entirely passive expiratory force that increases with the amount of air inhaled. After a maximum inhalation, this pressure may amount to around 20 cm H_2O, according to Proctor (1980).

The rib cage is another elastic system of relevance to subglottic pressure. Two types of muscles, called the *intercostal muscles,* join the ribs. The inspiratory intercostals function so that a contraction leads to an increase of the rib cage volume. They provide an inspiratory muscle force, and they are frequently used in normal respiration. When the contraction activity is terminated, the rib cage strives to return to its smaller, nonexpanded volume. Thus, a nonmuscular, passive expiratory force is generated as soon as the inspiratory intercostal muscles are relaxed after contraction; this pressure may amount to some 10 cm H_2O after a very deep inspiration. The second type of intercostal muscles, the expiratory ones, has the opposite effect, that of decreasing the rib cage volume. If we use these muscles for exhalation, a passive inspiratory force is generated; after a very deep exhalation this force may produce an underpressure of about -20 cm H_2O.

To summarize: we have both inhalatory and exhalatory elasticity forces, and their combined effect depends on the lung volume. As a consequence, there is a particular lung volume value for the respiratory mechanism, at which the passive inspiratory and expiratory forces are equal. This lung volume value is called the *functional residual capacity* (FRC). As soon as the lungs are expanded or contracted beyond the FRC, passive forces try to restore the lungs to it. We conclude that there are both passive and active forces for inspiration and for expiration.

The act of respiration is handled by two major muscle groups which, by contracting, expand and compress the lungs. One group is constituted by the inspiratory and expiratory intercostals, which we have just presented. The second group is constituted by the muscles in the *abdominal wall* and *diaphragm*. The diaphragm is an important breathing muscle. When relaxed, it assumes a shape somewhat similar to an upside-down salad bowl. Its edge inserts into the lower contour of the rib cage, as is shown in figure 3.1. When the diaphragm muscle contracts, its form is flattened, similar to a plate. Consequently, the floor in the rib cage is lowered, so that the volume in the rib cage is increased and the lung volume is expanded. This lowers the subglottic pressure, and the air streams into the lungs, provided

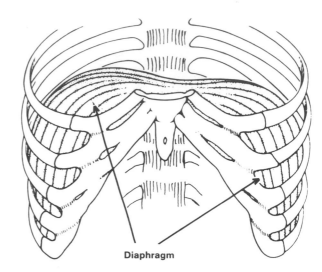

Figure 3.1. The position of the diaphragm muscle in the rib cage. When relaxed, it is dome-shaped, somewhat similar to an upside-down bowl; when contracted, its shape is flattened. The edges are fastened to the lower contour of the rib cage.

Diaphragm

the airways are free. As all this happens as a result of a contraction of the diaphragm, the diaphragm is a muscle specifically for inhalation.

The volume of the abdominal content cannot easily be altered appreciably. Therefore, by contracting, the diaphragm presses the abdominal content downward which, in turn, presses the abdominal wall outward. Actually, this offers an eminent means of observing one's diaphragmatic activity: if the abdominal wall expands during inspiration, the inspiration involves an activation of the diaphragm muscle. Another sign of a diaphragmatic inspiration is an expansion of the lowest part of the rib cage (Strohl and Fouke, 1985).

With the body in an upright position, the diaphragm muscle can be restored to its upward-bulging shape only by means of the muscles in the abdominal wall. By contracting, these muscles press the abdominal content back again and upward, into the rib cage, so that the diaphragm, the floor in the rib cage, moves upward and the lung volume is decreased. From this we conclude that the abdominal muscles are muscles for exhalation. The abdominal wall and the diaphragm constitute a pair of muscle forces by means of which we can both inspire and exhale. The other pair of muscle forces, the intercostals, may assist or replace the diaphragm and abdomen in their roles as respiratory agents; and they can, in turn, be helped or replaced by the diaphragm and the abdominal wall muscles.

To summarize: We have a number of respiratory muscles plus passive elastic forces, all of which affect the lung volume and, hence, also the subglottic pressure. What, then, determines the air pressure inside the lungs during phonation, when the glottis is closed? As we have just seen, important contributions must come from the activities in the diaphragm and abdominal muscles, but the passive recoil forces in the lungs and in the rib cage are also relevant. The magnitude of these recoil forces depends on the amount of air contained in the lungs, or the *lung volume*. The system is described schematically in figure 3.2.

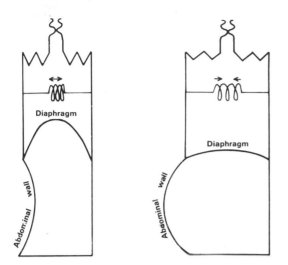

Figure 3.2. Schematic illustration of the breathing apparatus; the rib cage is represented by a bellows with a spring inside corresponding to the total passive recoil forces of the lungs and the rib cage. The left and right figures represent the cases of maximum exhalation and inhalation, respectively. When the expiratory intercostal muscles contract, the rib cage and the lungs are compressed; then, the springiness of the rib cage strives to expand the lungs. When the expiratory intercostals contract, the rib cage and the lungs are expanded, and the springiness of the rib cage strives to compress the lungs. When the abdominal wall contracts, the abdominal content is pressed upward, so that the diaphragm is forced into the rib cage; when the diaphragm contracts, the abdominal wall is pressed outward.

The muscular activity required for maintaining a constant subglottic pressure is dependent on the lung volume because the elastic forces of the lungs and the rib cage strive to raise or to lower the pressure inside the lungs, depending on whether the lung volume is greater or smaller than the functional residual capacity, FRC. When the lungs are filled with a large quantity of air, the passive exhalation force is great, and it generates a high pressure. If this pressure is too high for the intended phonation, it can be reduced by a contraction of the muscles of inhalation. The need for this activity then gradually decreases as the lung volume decreases, and it reaches zero at a volume above FRC where the passive exhalation forces are insufficient for generating the pressure needed. Beyond this point the muscles of exhalation must take over more and more, so that one compensates for the increasing inhalation force of the increasingly compressed rib cage.

Figure 3.3 illustrates this. The curves therein show the changes in the passive expiratory and inspiratory forces due to the recoil effects from the lungs and from the rib cage as the air volume in the lungs is consumed. This part of the figure also shows two typical values of subglottic pressure needed for producing a pianissimo (*pp*) note and a fortissimo (*ff*) note. It is evident that the demands for compensatory activity of inspiratory muscles are quite high when a note is to be sung *pp* after a maximum inhalation, and conversely, that a good deal of muscular expiration activity is required if a note is to be sung *ff* with lungs that contain only some small proportion of their full capacity.

The requirements for maintaining a given subglottic pressure depend on body posture. For instance, in an upright position the diaphragm is pulled downward by gravity for hydraulic reasons: the abdominal content can be said to hang from the diaphragm, provided that the abdominal wall is passive. In supine position, on the other hand, gravity will strive to push the abdominal content back into the rib cage; if one hangs upside down, this effect will be enhanced.

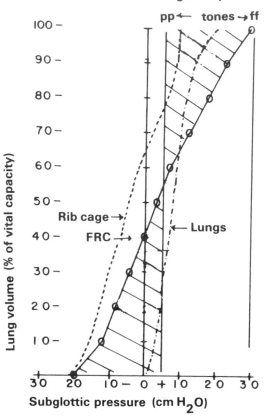

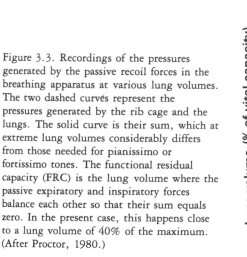

Figure 3.3. Recordings of the pressures generated by the passive recoil forces in the breathing apparatus at various lung volumes. The two dashed curves represent the pressures generated by the rib cage and the lungs. The solid curve is their sum, which at extreme lung volumes considerably differs from those needed for pianissimo or fortissimo tones. The functional residual capacity (FRC) is the lung volume where the passive expiratory and inspiratory forces balance each other so that their sum equals zero. In the present case, this happens close to a lung volume of 40% of the maximum. (After Proctor, 1980.)

An overpressure in the lungs is transmitted downward through a relaxed diaphragm. Hence an increase in the subglottic pressure, produced in order to sing a high or loud note, for instance, will exert an increase in the pressure on the abdominal wall. If the abdominal wall is not supposed to expand as soon as subglottic pressure is raised, then the muscular contraction of the abdominal wall must increase in synchrony with the subglottic pressure: a singer would need to increase the contraction of the abdominal wall continuously with a continuously changing subglottic pressure.

We conclude from the above that the demands placed on the respiratory system in singing must be very high. They arise as a consequence of both the need for a continuous adaptation of the muscular forces to the ever-changing lung volume necessarily accompanying phonation and the need for producing rapid and yet precise changes in subglottic pressure. What are the respiratory strategies that singers use in order to meet these severe demands?

One apparent difference among singers in breathing technique is in the positioning of the abdominal wall. While some singers sing with their abdominal wall expanded ("belly out"), others sing with the abdominal wall pulled in ("belly in"). The arguments used in favor of these strategies are sometimes quite entertaining. For instance, one voice teacher found support for the "belly in" method in the fact that this strategy is apparently used by barking dogs; it is thought-provoking that such arguments can be taken seriously in spite of the striking dissimilarities between the voice sound of a good singer and the voice sound of a barking dog.

Hixon and Hoffman (1978) analyzed the advantages and disadvantages of these two strategies. They point out that a muscle contraction pays off better when the muscle is stretched than when it is already contracted and therefore conclude that in the "belly in" method, the expiratory intercostal as well as the diaphragm muscles are stretched and can thus be efficiently recruited in order to promptly increase subglottic pressure. At the same time, the abdominal wall muscles are contracted, a situation that must reduce their efficiency in producing expiratory force. The "belly out" method is generally combined with an elevated and outward positioning of the rib cage wall. If so, this strategy offers the same advantage as the "belly in" strategy, since the intercostal muscles are stretched, as are the abdominal wall muscles. The disadvantage is in the contracted condition of the diaphragm; on the other hand, the diaphragm will certainly be pressed upward as lung volume is decreasing. It will return to a more stretched condition at small lung volumes, when inspiratory efforts are likely to be needed.

In normal speech, the compensatory inspiratory work required in order to balance the passive expiratory forces of the rib cage and the lungs is handled primarily by the inspiratory intercostal muscles; most researchers have found that in speech the other main inspiratory muscle, the diaphragm, is passive (Draper et al., 1959).

The role of the diaphragm muscle in compensating for the considerable expiratory elastic force of the rib cage and the lungs at large lung volumes was thoroughly examined in an excellent, pioneering investigation of singing by Bouhuys et al. (1966). They compared the pressure above and below the diaphragm in nonprofessional singers. Their results showed that in singing a long, soft, sustained tone at high lung volume, three of their five subjects used the diaphragm for reducing the expiratory recoil forces.

Together with collaborators, this author studied aspects of the respiratory behavior in four singers who performed phonatory tasks not only involving a steady subglottic pressure but also a rapidly changing subglottic pressure, such as when singing octave intervals (Sundberg et al., 1983). The focus of the investigation was the activity in the diaphragm muscle. Two different strategies were found. In one of the singers, a diaphragmatic activity lasting throughout the phrase was observed during long, sustained vowels. In the remaining three singers, the diaphragm was entirely flaccid throughout the phrase and was activated during inspiration only. However, these last-mentioned singers recruited their diaphragm for the purpose of rapidly reducing the subglottic pressure at high lung volumes, for instance, when they suddenly switched from a high tone to a low tone; at those times, the diaphragm apparently contracted suddenly and for a short moment only. The singer showing a diaphragmatic activity throughout the phrase increased his diaphragmatic activity when he was singing at a high subglottic pressure. Thus, his abdominal wall generated an excessive pressure that was reduced to the target value by an increased activation of the diaphragm.

The reason for this last-mentioned strategy may appear mysterious, but it seems likely that there are certain advantages connected with it. For instance, it is possible that a high degree of concomitant contraction of the diaphragm and the abdominal wall muscles, together enclosing the abdominal content, will reduce the displacement of the viscera and, hence, minimize the influence of their inertia on subglottic pressure when it is rapidly changing. Also, in tasks requiring rapid and precise movements of structures, it seems to be a generally applied strategy to activate both the muscles accelerating the structure and the muscles that will arrest the movement of the structure (Rothenberg, 1968).

To summarize: It seems that the diaphragm may play a more prominent role in singing than has been generally assumed, and also that the role of the diaphragm varies in different singers. We will return to these questions and their relevance to phonation later on.

Lung Volume in Speech and Singing

After this presentation of the mechanism for respiration, we now will see how it is used in speech and singing. The lungs contain a certain amount of air when they have been maximally filled; this amount of air is called the *total lung volume.* In an adult man it amounts to something in the neighborhood of 7 litres. After a maximum exhalation, a small amount of air will always remain; this is called the *residual volume.* In an adult male this volume is about 2 litres. The difference between the total lung volume and the residual volume corresponds to the amount of air we can use for breathing and phonation. It is called the *vital capacity,* approximately 5 litres in an adult male.

The vital capacity varies with the size of the body, of course. By and large, this relationship can be described by means of a formula. According to Baldwin et al. (1948), the vital capacity (VC), measured in litres, for males is

$$VC_{male} = (2.8 - .011A)L$$

and for females

$$VC_{female} = (2.2 - .01A)L$$

where L is the body length in meters and A is the age in years. A sufficiently careful contemplation of this formula tells us that females tend to have smaller vital capacity than males, that short people tend to have smaller vital capacity than tall people, and that vital capacity decreases with age. The influence of these factors is illustrated in figure 3.4

When no breathing activity is going on, it is the equilibrium of the passive forces of exhalation and inhalation in the breathing system that determines the quantity of air in the lungs. We mentioned before that this quantity of air, which consequently will remain in the lungs even after

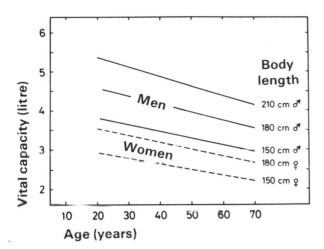

Figure 3.4. The vital capacity depends on age, sex, and body length. Men have greater vital capacity than females, young adults have greater vital capacity than older people, and tall persons have greater vital capacity than smaller persons.

death, is called the *functional residual capacity* (FRC). It is generally slightly less than half of the vital capacity.

In normal breathing one exhales and inhales about 0.5 litres, twelve times per minute, that is, every five seconds. Then, the amount of air escaping the lungs per time unit, or the *airflow*, is quite low, only about 0.1 litre per second. Moreover, one uses only a small portion of one's vital capacity; 0.5 litres out of the available total of 5 litres in male adults corresponds to no more than 10%. In normal passive breathing the act of inspiration is active, whereas expiration is passive. This means that in quiet breathing, the lung volume is varied within a very small range, located just above the functional residual capacity. The fact that expiration is normally a completely passive act is noteworthy, as we will see below.

In speech, the situation is different; it is mostly initiated at about 50% of the vital capacity, or just slightly above the FRC. In other words, we seem to take some advantage of the passive exhalatory forces in establishing the subglottic pressure required for normal speech. As can be seen in figure 3.5, during spontaneous speech, a subject used a range of lung volumes from 55% down to 10% of the vital capacity; his FRC was about 35% and most of the time he used lung volumes below this value. If one reads loudly, a higher subglottic pressure is used and often the air consumption is higher. Then, the phonatory range of vital capacity used is expanded upward, as can be seen in the same figure. This subject used vital capacity values between 10 and 70% in loud reading, and between 15 and 95% in very loud reading.

Figure 3.5 also shows that, in normal reading, the subject tended to take a breath when his lung volume was close to FRC. The same holds also for loud and very loud reading, but not for spontaneous speech. This means that, in reading, this subject tended to take advantage of the passive forces of exhalation in maintaining a suitable subglottic pressure for phonation. Probably, this is typical of many speakers. In any event, we feel physically more comfortable at lung volumes near to or above the functional residual capacity (FRC), according to Proctor (1980).

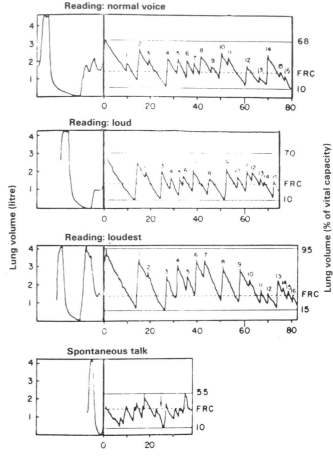

Figure 3.5. The lung volume in litres and in percentage of vital capacity (left and right scales, respectively) of a subject reading a text at different degrees of loudness. The numbers refer to breaths, and the dashed horizontal lines represent the functional residual capacity (FRC). At the arrow in the graph pertaining to spontaneous talk, the subject laughed. At the left of each diagram, the subject made a maximum inhalation followed by a maximum exhalation. (After Bouhuys et al., 1966.)

Longer phrases occur in singing than in normal speech. Phrases extending over 10 seconds are not rare in singing, while in normal speech we tend to take a breath about every five seconds. Thus, the opportunities to take a breath are much more rare in singing than in speech, so that it is essential to avoid overconsumption of air in singing. As demonstrated in figure 3.6,

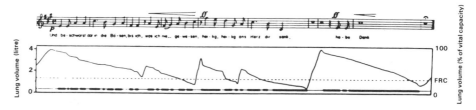

Figure 3.6. Lung volume, given as in figure 3.5, in a subject singing the song shown at the top. The horizontal line at the bottom shows the sound produced. (After Bouhuys et al., 1966.)

long phrases are begun at very high lung volumes, close to 100% of the vital capacity. Also, the range below FRC is taken into use; values as low as 10% or even 5% of the vital capacity occur. This means that the range used in singing is quite similar to that used in very loud reading (cf. figure 3.5).

We conclude that a considerably larger portion of the vital capacity is used in singing and in loud reading than in normal speech. It would then be natural for professional singers or actors to expand their vital capacities somewhat. Gould (1977) has shown that singers possess a vital capacity about 20% greater than the average for nonsingers. This expansion does not take place by an increase of the total lung volume, but rather by a reduction of the residual volume. Thus, voice training seems to have the effect, among others, of teaching one to take advantage of a greater portion of one's total lung volume. It seems that one simply learns how to squeeze one's lungs more efficiently.

Subglottic Pressures in Speech and Singing

When the abdominal muscles contract after inspiration, the air pressure in the lungs, or the subglottic pressure, is raised. How much this pressure is raised depends on the degree of contraction and also on the resistance against airflow provided by the glottis. Next we will examine the magnitudes of the subglottic pressures occurring in speech and singing.

It is not difficult to imagine that subglottic pressure and loudness of phonation must be interrelated. However, before going any further, we need to make a distinction concerning the loudness of phonation, because our subjective impression of loudness does not correspond in a simple way to the physical sound level that we can measure in decibels (dB). For instance, while the perceived loudness of a tone may remain constant when its pitch is changed, its physical level may change by several dB. For these reasons, we must distinguish between subjective loudness and physical loudness. Henceforth the subjective loudness will be called *loudness of phonation,* and the physical loudness will be referred to as the *sound level.*

Rather few measurements of subglottic pressure have been published. The reason for this would be the difficulties associated with this type of measurement. The most reliable results are obtained if a thin needle is inserted into the trachea through the tissues below the cricoid cartilage. Some speakers and a few singers have submitted themselves to this inconvenience. There is, however, another, indirect method of measurement. When the lips are closed and the glottis is open, the subglottic pressure is equal to the pressure in the mouth cavity, as has been mentioned. Therefore, the subglottic pressure can normally be accurately determined from the oral pressure during the production of the consonant /p/.

In order to change loudness of phonation, we need to change subglottic pressure. This is illustrated in figure 3.7 showing measurements from a tenor who sang the tones of a chromatic scale in *piano, mezzoforte,* and *forte.* It can be seen that the pressure is raised with rising loudness. It is also evident that pressure is increased with phonation frequency. In the author's

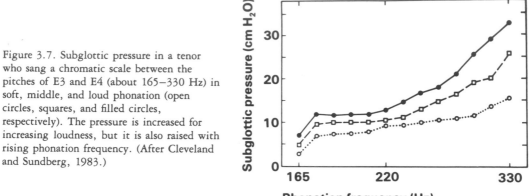

Figure 3.7. Subglottic pressure in a tenor who sang a chromatic scale between the pitches of E3 and E4 (about 165–330 Hz) in soft, middle, and loud phonation (open circles, squares, and filled circles, respectively). The pressure is increased for increasing loudness, but it is also raised with rising phonation frequency. (After Cleveland and Sundberg, 1983.)

experience, this is typical for all voices, particularly in the upper part of the phonation frequency range.

The air pressures used in phonation are rather low, at least if we compare them with what is possible. Subglottic pressure can be raised up to 150 cm H_2O, or more. Such values occur when one carries a very heavy weight, for example. In such cases the expiratory musculature is forcefully contracted. At the same time the glottis is firmly closed, so that the air in the lungs is prevented from simply escaping, with a forceful exhalation as the result. Instead, a high subglottic pressure is generated, thus stabilizing the rib cage. A note played *forte* on a reed instrument such as the oboe may need a pressure of 65 cm H_2O, and similar values seem to hold for lip reed (brass) instruments. Navra'til and Rejsek (1968) measured a subglottic pressure of no less than 195 cm H_2O in a trumpet player.

In normal speech at normal loudness of phonation, the subglottic pressure is much lower than these values, generally in the neighborhood of 6 cm H_2O, and values above 15 cm H_2O are rare in loud speech. In singing, however, higher subglottic pressures have been found. In loud singing, 20 or 30 cm H_2O are not exceptional; the record pressure in published studies seems to be 70 cm H_2O, which was reported to be quite exceptional (Proctor, 1974). However, this author has measured similar values in soprano and tenor singers singing strong notes at high pitches. It seems that different singers use highly varying subglottic pressures, and that voice category and type of voice (or singing technique) are important factors.

Most of the recordings of subglottic pressure in singing have concerned sustained phonation. However, in reality, subglottic pressure is a rapidly varying parameter and often changes between adjacent notes because, as we might guess, the pressure must adapt to both the loudness and the frequency of phonation. In figure 3.8 we can study the undulating pressure in *coloratura* singing. It is apparent that this type of singing requires virtuoso handling of the breathing apparatus. There is a continuous pulsation of the subglottic pressure in synchrony with phonation frequency, so that there is one increase-decrease gesture in pressure per tone. The tempo in a rapid *coloratura* passage may be as fast as 7 notes per second, so the changes in

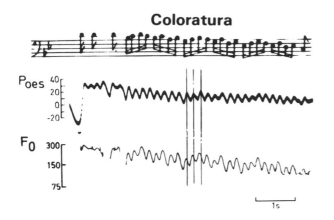

Coloratura

Figure 3.8. The pressure in the esophagus (P_{oes}), approximately corresponding to subglottic pressure and phonation frequency (F_O) in a professional baritone singer performing a coloratura passage. Both pressure and frequency increase and decrease once for each tone, or approximately 6 times per second.

subglottic pressure must be very quick indeed. In a study of subglottic pressure during the production of the consonant /p/, Leanderson et al. (1983) found that subjects occasionally reduced their subglottic pressure only during the /p/-occlusion, that is, for about 100 milliseconds. In the beginning of the phrase this reduction was mostly realized by means of a sudden activation of the diaphragm. Thus, the control of subglottic pressure must be very quick and precise in singing.

Airflow in Speech and Singing

It is clear that the airflow depends on the subglottic pressure, among other things. Figure 3.9 shows airflow values recorded from three speakers

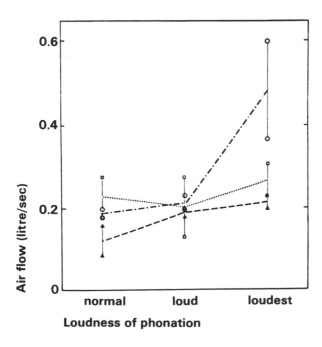

Figure 3.9. Average airflow recorded from three speakers reading a text at different loudnesses. Symbols refer to subjects. The curves represent the averages, and the vertical bars show extreme values. The dependence of airflow on loudness of phonation varies between subjects.

reading a text at various loudnesses. We observe that airflow values between 0.1 and 0.6 litres/sec occur, and that generally airflow increases with loudness, although the differences between individuals are great. Similar values have been measured in singing. These values should be compared with those for normal breathing, which generally lie in the neighborhood of 0.1 litres/sec, which is not very different from what occurs in normal speech. This suggests that we get the necessary ventilation in our lungs when we speak. Therefore, we can speak for a very long time (which one often regrets when listening to boring speeches).

In singing, the pauses where the singer can take a breath are sometimes very short. Let us assume a tempo of a quarter note per second, corresponding to a metronome value of 60 (MM = 60), which is a very slow *lento* tempo. In that tempo a sixteenth-note should have a duration of 0.25 sec. If this is the time available for refilling the air supply in the lungs from 10% to 100% of a vital capacity of 5 litres, then 90% of 5 litres (= 4.5 litres) must be inhaled in 0.25 sec. This would correspond to an airflow of no less than 18 litres/sec! In practice we rarely seem to inhale such a great portion of our vital capacity in such a short time. An airflow as high as 18 litres/sec would also dry the mucosa in the glottal region, thus generating a risk of phonatory disorders. In reality, rapid inhalations in singing have been found to give airflow values of 5 litres/sec or less.

A minimum airflow is often considered a quality criterion for good singing: the less air consumption, the more skilled the singer. This is true to the extent that constant glottal leakage is a sign of poor voice technique. However, the principle—the less air consumption, the better—does not represent the entire story. As we will see in more detail below and also in the next chapter, a simple but certainly unhealthy way of reducing air consumption is to press the vocal folds together and then to raise subglottic pressure high enough to overcome this firmly closed glottis. Under such conditions the airflow can be reduced to very small values indeed.

Glottal Resistance

An increase in subglottic pressure leads to an increase in the airflow. However, this is true only if a third factor is kept constant, namely, the so-called *glottal resistance,* which is the resistance against airflow through the glottis. Glottal resistance is defined as the ratio between subglottic pressure and transglottal airflow, and it varies considerably. For instance, if the glottis never closes completely, air will escape through the glottis over its entire vibration cycle, even during its quasi-closed phase. Such "leaky" or "breathy" phonation is an instance of low glottal resistance, and it results in a breathy voice quality and a comparatively high air consumption. But we all know that the transglottal airflow may be reduced to zero even under conditions of extremely high subglottic pressure, such as when we carry a heavy weight. Then, the glottal resistance is evidently extremely high. We conclude that the glottal resistance can be varied considerably.

The glottal resistance is determined mainly by the degree of adduction activity in the laryngeal muscles.* If glottal adduction is increased, the glottal resistance increases. Certain types of phonation, which we will call "pressed" or "tense," are characterized by high subglottic pressure and low transglottal airflow, or, in other words, by high glottal resistance. In such cases, the voice sounds strained. In the opposite case, when the glottal resistance is very low, the vocal folds fail to make contact, so air consumption becomes high and phonation becomes "breathy." We will return to these matters in the next chapter.

Pressure, Airflow, and Sound

As mentioned above, an increase of subglottic pressure leads to an increase in loudness and, to a certain extent, also in the frequency of phonation, other factors being equal. (We recall that the frequency of phonation corresponds to the vibration frequency of the vocal folds.) The relationship between subglottic pressure and loudness of phonation is rather straightforward in practice. On the average, a doubling of the subglottic pressure yields a 9 dB increase in the sound level of phonation, as can be seen in figure 3.10. However, it can also be seen in the same figure that the data points, collected from four subjects, are considerably scattered.

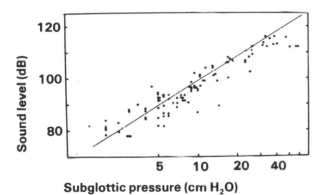

Figure 3.10. Illustration of the significance of subglottic pressure to loudness of phonation. The data points were collected from four subjects, some of whom had trained voices, phonating at different loudnesses. A doubling of the subglottic pressure yields about 9 dB increase of the sound level. (After Bouhuys et al., 1966.)

Incidentally, it is quite interesting that we need to increase the sound level by the same amount—9 dB, on the average—in order to perceive a doubling of the loudness of a sine wave signal. If we really perceive a doubling of the subglottic pressure as such, this suggests the possibility that the voice sometimes serves as a reference even when we are hearing sounds other than those produced by the voice.

Turning to the influence of subglottic pressure on fundamental frequency, we also find a quite simple relationship. If this pressure is raised by

*This description is likely to trigger vigorous emotional reactions among some acousticians. In fact, the unwillingness of the glottis to allow an airstream to pass varies during the vibration cycle. For instance, in the beginning of the open phase of the glottal vibratory cycle, the glottal area is small, and the airflow has to accelerate. The consequence is that the glottis is, in a way, unwilling to let the air stream pass. For such reasons it is more appropriate to use the term "impedance" rather than "resistance."

1 cm H_2O, the phonation frequency is increased by about 3 to 4 Hz in normal phonation. If we take into consideration the fact that 7 cm H_2O is a common subglottic pressure in normal speech and that 100 and 200 Hz are typical average phonation frequency values for males and females, respectively, we realize that the resulting 4 Hz change for such a considerable increase as from 7 to 8 cm H_2O is not very much. We conclude that the subglottic pressure has a very small effect on the frequency of phonation, and accordingly we do not seem to use subglottic pressure for changing phonation frequency in normal speech. Of course, if subglottic pressure is raised by a considerable amount, the resulting increase in fundamental frequency will be substantial. For instance, a rise of the subglottic pressure from 7 to 14 cm H_2O will produce an increase in fundamental frequency of about 28 Hz, which corresponds to something in the vicinity of a major third in the speech of an average male adult.

Pressure and flow are evidently important to phonation. The pressure is controlled by means of the breathing apparatus, but it also depends on the glottal resistance. The flow is determined by the pressure and by the glottal resistance, which, in turn, is tuned mainly by means of the adduction muscles in the larynx. Let us now find out how the three major agents— pressure, flow, and resistance—are used at various frequencies and loudnesses of phonation. In a classic investigation, Rubin et al. (1967) studied the interaction between variations in phonation frequency and loudness on the one hand and airflow and subglottic pressure on the other. Their results, obtained with professional singers, were as follows.

An increase in the loudness of phonation was always found to be accompanied by an increased *subglottic pressure,* regardless of phonation frequency. The loudness of phonation seemed to be controlled by means of subglottic pressure, as might be expected. An increase in subglottic pressure was also generally observed when the frequency of phonation was raised, even when the loudness of phonation was kept constant; in other words, a high tone was generally sung with a higher subglottic pressure than a low tone with the same loudness of phonation. In this author's experience, this is typical of singing, particularly in the upper part of the phonation frequency range. In the lower part of the range, the difference in subglottic pressure for various pitches is very slight.

Returning to the Rubin et al. investigation, the *airflow* was usually (but not always) found to increase when both phonation frequency and loudness were increased simultaneously. Thus, as a rule, more air was consumed for a higher and louder tone than for a lower and softer one. On the other hand, a crescendo with constant pitch may be associated with either constant or increased airflow. Similarly, trained singers often performed a rising glissando with constant loudness of phonation without any substantial increase in airflow; on the contrary, the flow was sometimes observed to decrease under these conditions. Therefore, higher tones do not necessarily consume more air than lower tones; but if the loudness of phonation is increased for a high tone, an increase in air consumption generally occurs.

It may appear mysterious that an increase in the frequency of phonation is not necessarily associated with an increase in airflow. For example, if phonation frequency is increased by one octave, the fundamental frequency is doubled. This implies that the glottis will open twice as frequently as with the lower tone. Intuition may suggest that airflow would also be doubled under these circumstances, but this is not the case. The fact is that the time during which the glottis is open within each vibration cycle is approximately halved when the phonation frequency is doubled, provided that everything else is kept constant. Thus, the glottis allows only about half the air volume to pass in each vibration cycle in the case of the higher tone as compared to the case of the lower tone. The end result is that approximately half the air volume passes the glottis twice as frequently, so that the air consumption for the higher tone is similar to that of the lower tone. In other words, the airflow does not necessarily depend on phonation frequency.

These matters become more complex as soon as the subglottic pressure or the glottal resistance is altered by changes in phonation frequency because they affect the airflow. Such changes are likely to occur; certain muscles engaged in raising the frequency of phonation probably have an effect on the degree of adduction of the vocal folds. For instance, the vocalis muscles, which are often active in pitch rises, tend to increase adduction. In some singers, a high pitched note is often sung with a less relaxed, or more "pressed," voice than a low note. This would reflect a change in the adduction activity, as suggested previously. A change in the glottal adduction activity during phonation implies a change in glottal resistance. For these reasons we cannot expect any simple relationship between airflow and phonation frequency.

In the falsetto register of untrained voices, there is a stable relationship between phonation frequency and flow, according to Isshiki (1964): phonation frequency is almost exclusively controlled by means of airflow in this register so that phonation frequency is increased by increasing the airflow. However, it can be assumed that several differing types of phonation are included in what is called "falsetto"; for instance, some types of phonation in the falsetto register use a complete closure in the glottal vibratory cycle and some do not, and the type of falsetto singing used by countertenors is probably different from other types of falsetto. The fundamental frequency control may very well differ between such different types of phonation in falsetto register.

To summarize: Loudness of phonation is primarily controlled by subglottic pressure, while phonation frequency is primarily controlled by laryngeal muscles. Still, in the highest part of a singer's pitch range, subglottic pressure typically rises with rising phonation frequency. Airflow (which, of course, determines air consumption) is entirely determined by subglottic pressure and glottal resistance, the latter of which, in turn, reflects the degree of adduction activity. In normal speech, airflow is often increased when loudness of phonation is raised. In professional singers, the airflow does not show a simple dependence, either of frequency, or of loudness of phonation. In untrained voices, airflow has been found to increase with phonation frequency in falsetto register.

Let us now consider some measurement data. Figure 3.11 shows a recording of airflow, subglottic pressure, and sound level in a professional singer performing a rising scale and a descending glissando. The graphs illustrate the observations just mentioned. Airflow remains essentially constant in the vicinity of 0.10 to 0.13 litres/sec for all the tones in the scale, while subglottic pressure is raised from about 7 cm H_2O for the lowest tone to about 23 cm H_2O for the highest tone in the scale. At the same time the sound level increases by several dB. Also, we can observe that the airflow and the sound level exhibit small and rapid undulations that mirror the vibrato. It may be mentioned here that vibrato-free tones are sung with about 10% less airflow than vibrato tones, according to Large and Iwata (1971). We will return to this later. Corresponding observations can be made for the glissando.

In the glissando we also note that the sound level shows a rather irregular pattern, in contrast to the smooth curves for airflow and subglottic pressure. This is a typical observation, so let us digress here for a moment and explain the reason, which is quite simple. Generally, the sound level is determined almost entirely by the amplitude of the strongest spectrum partial. In most vowels the strongest spectrum partial is the partial closest to the first formant. When pitch is continuously lowered, such as in a glissando, the overall sound level will rise, as long as the strongest spectrum partial is approaching the center frequency of the first formant from above, and the level will then drop again after the same

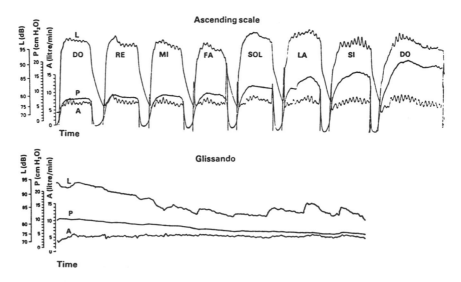

Figure 3.11. Recording of airflow, subglottic pressure, and sound level (curves marked A, P, and L) in a professional singer performing an ascending scale (upper graph) and a descending glissando (lower graph). Airflow is kept essentially constant, while subglottic pressure rises with pitch. (After Rubin et. al., 1967.)

partial passes the formant frequency and increases its frequency distance from it. However, soon this partial will no longer be the strongest one in the spectrum, for the pitch is constantly lowered in the glissando. Consequently, the same story will be repeated with regard to the next highest partial in the spectrum.

Curiously enough these changes in sound level are rather hard to detect by ear. This is one more good argument for the distinction previously made between perceived loudness and physical sound level. Actually, there are almost always good reasons for separating acoustic data from what we can perceive.*

Let us return to subglottic pressure in singing. Up to now, we have mostly considered the pressure during long, sustained notes. However, in real singing, changes—sometimes even very rapid changes—are not only normal but even mandatory. It was mentioned above that subglottic pressure generally varies considerably with pitch, at least in the upper part of a singer's range. This raises the question of how the subglottic pressure looks in real singing, when the pitch is changing. Figure 3.12 shows some

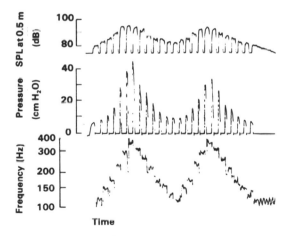

Figure 3.12. Simultaneous recordings of sound level (SPL), subglottic pressure, and phonation frequency in a professional singer singing an ascending major triad followed by a descending dominant-seventh chord with each tone beginning with a /p/. As higher tones are sung with higher pressure, the pressure has to be changed in accordance with pitch. Pressure regulates loudness, and the musically most stressed note is the one that follows the highest pitch. This stressed note is given the highest pressure.

recordings of this. Here, the subglottic pressure was estimated from the oral pressure during the occlusion of the mouth for the consonant /p/. The singer was singing an ascending triad to the duodecim and then a descending dominant seventh triad. This pitch contour can be clearly discerned in the subglottic pressure contour. This means that the singer produced a carefully planned subglottic pressure for each individual note in this simple tone sequence.

Figure 3.13 shows some pressure data collected when the subject sang a sequence of alternating rising and falling octave intervals. Here, the

---

*This is not to say that acoustic data are more "real" than what we perceive. Both are, of course, equally real, in a sense. But often acoustic data are easier to deal with, because they can be defined and specified much more easily than what we perceive. Also, they are not so dependent on subjective factors as our perception.

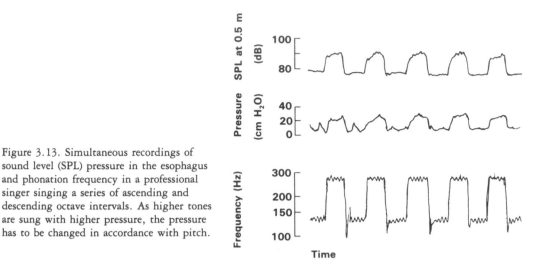

Figure 3.13. Simultaneous recordings of sound level (SPL) pressure in the esophagus and phonation frequency in a professional singer singing a series of ascending and descending octave intervals. As higher tones are sung with higher pressure, the pressure has to be changed in accordance with pitch.

pressure in the esophagus was measured instead of the subglottic pressure. These pressures are equal except for the effect of the recoil force from the lungs, which can be regarded as approximately constant for adjacent tones. (It will be recalled that this recoil force decreases with lung volume, which, however, is practically the same for two short tones produced in succession.) Since the higher note in the octave was in the upper part of this singer's range, he had to raise his subglottic pressure for the high note and then lower it for the low note. The figure shows that these changes are executed very rapidly and very precisely.

It is interesting here to recall the effect of subglottic pressure on phonation frequency. The changes in subglottic pressure associated with an octave interval may be substantial, according to figure 3.13, and must be associated with considerable effects on phonation frequency. The singer needs to take these effects into account—most often unconsciously—in order to arrive at the intended pitch when performing a wide pitch interval. Because subglottic pressure affects phonation frequency, a mistake is likely to result in singing out of tune.

For the sake of comparison, some corresponding data concerning nonsense speech produced by untrained voices are shown in figure 3.14. The subglottic pressure changes slowly and by no means in synchrony with fundamental frequency. This suggests that the demands on control of the breath apparatus determining subglottic pressure are much higher in singing than in speech. However, we probably need a rather precise control of subglottic pressure in speech as well: subglottic pressure determines loudness of phonation, which is relevant to the meaning of what we want to say. Still, it seems likely that the demands on precision in the control of subglottic pressure are much higher in singing than in speech, though we would need more experimental data on this topic.

It is interesting to observe some details in the curve representing the intraoral air pressure in figure 3.14. As we mentioned before, this pressure

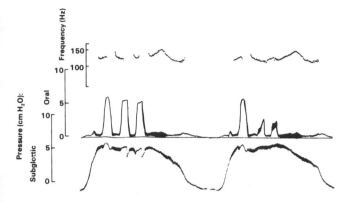

Figure 3.14. Oral and subglottic pressures and phonation frequency (top, middle, and bottom curves, respectively) in Swedish nonsense speech /ja sɑ pɑpa ijen, ja sɑ bɑba ijen/. The oral pressure rises during the production of stop consonants such as /b/ and /p/. The subglottic pressure momentarily drops during the voiceless consonants /s/ and /p/, which were pronounced with aspiration. (After Löfqvist, 1975.)

is raised to the subglottic pressure when we pronounce certain consonants in which the free outlet of air is prevented by a constriction in the mouth. It can be seen that an aspirated /p/ causes a perturbation of the subglottic pressure. ("Aspirated" here means that a short /h/ sound follows the release of the noise burst of the stop consonant.) *Stop consonants* are pronounced differently in different languages. The consonants /p/, /t/, and /k/ are not aspirated in some languages—for example, Italian, French, and Finnish—while these consonants are aspirated in other languages, such as German, English, and Swedish. Because of the significance of subglottic pressure to phonation, these differences are probably relevant to singing. One suspects that singers more or less unconsciously handle their supraglottic air pressure with greater care than nonsingers in order to avoid disturbances of the subglottic pressure and hence also of the vocal fold vibrations.

Finally, figure 3.15 shows some graphs published by Rubin et al. (1967) representing the sound level, the subglottic pressure, and the airflow as recorded under conditions of varied types of phonation. Some interesting observations can be made. For instance, a tone can be sung at a given sound level using a higher or a lower subglottic pressure combined with a lower or a higher airflow, respectively; this implies differences in the glottal resistance. It can be seen that an untrained voice may have to expend a higher subglottic pressure than a singer in order to produce a tone at a given sound level.

Particularly interesting are the curves pertaining to the situation when the air supply in the lungs is almost exhausted, as might occur toward the end of a long phrase. While airflow and sound level are kept constant, subglottic pressure rises. This means that the glottal resistance is increased, or, in other words, a seemingly desperate increase in the adduction activity is resorted to when the air reservoir is nearly depleted. The phonatory consequence of this would be a change in voice quality toward "pressed" phonation. We might speculate: Is it the absence of such instances of increases of glottal resistance that voice and singing teachers call "support"? Do such increases occur even for other reasons than a failing air supply, such as during the production of difficult tones? And how much time does the larynx need in order to restore the initial adduction

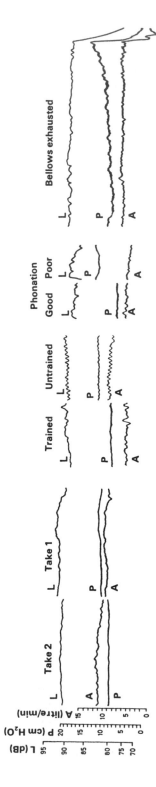

Figure 3.15. Recording of airflow, subglottic pressure, and sound level (curves marked A, P, and L) in subjects sustaining a tone in various ways. The three pairs of curves to the left in the figure present different instances of the fact that the same sound level may be produced with different subglottic pressure and airflow values. The lefthand pair of graphs pertain to a tone sung by a subject on two occasions; the second pair from the left compare tones sung by a well-trained singer (left) and a poorly trained singer; the third pair on the right stem from a singer who sang a tone optimally (left) and then tensely (right curve). The righthand edge of the figure shows what happened when the subject ran out of air: sound level and airflow remain constant, even though pressure is increased, indicating that the subject increased his adduction activity when the air supply was about to be exhausted. (After Rubin et al., 1967.)

activity? No concrete answers can be given at present, but, presumably, the singer's confidence that the air supply in the lungs will suffice is important to an undisturbed, steady phonation. In any event, more experimental work may help to clarify the matter.

Breathing and Phonation

Earlier in this chapter, it was mentioned that we may phonate both with a retracted and an expanded abdominal wall (the "belly in" and the "belly out" methods) and that these techniques reflect differences in the use of the respiratory muscles. With the "belly in" method, the abdominal wall is contracted so that the diaphragm is vaulted into the rib cage. With the "belly out" method, the diaphragm is flatter. We have also seen that some singers contract the abdominal wall against a forcefully contracted diaphragm, while others do not show any diaphragm activity at all except when subglottic pressure must be quickly lowered in the beginning of a phrase. The question then arises as to whether these different strategies lead to different types of control of subglottic pressure and phonation, a question that many singing teachers discuss with ardor.

In a series of experiments in which the author participated, the role of the diaphragm during singing and the significance of the diaphragm activity to phonation was analyzed (Leanderson et al., forthcoming). Singers and nonsingers performed the same phonatory tasks with a passive and with a contracted diaphragm. This voluntary control was facilitated by displaying the diaphragmatic activity on an oscilloscope screen in front of the subjects. We will return to this investigation in the next chapter, but it should be mentioned here that these different conditions turned out to have an effect on the voice source that was similar in most of the subjects.

Now, has this chapter on breathing explained why, according to all experience, adequate breathing is the key to a desirable type of phonation? Hardly! But perhaps some parts of an answer have emerged, which we will summarize.

The vital function of the larynx is to act as the watchdog of the lungs; the larynx should prevent solid objects and liquids from falling into the lungs. The glottis automatically opens when we take a breath, and during exhalation there tends to be a faint adductory gesture—in other words, an activation of the mechanisms for abduction and adduction is associated with the mechanism for respiration in quiet breathing. As we will see in greater detail in the following chapter, the mechanism for adduction and abduction is important to phonation. There is no evidence that these associations between laryngeal adjustment and breathing are equal in quiet breathing and during phonation. However, it is still possible that certain methods of inhalation performed for the purpose of phonation tend to be associated with a particular posturing of the larynx. In any event, we may safely assume that certain types of laryngeal posturing are adequate for a relaxed type of phonation while other types are not. Thus, there are certain ties between the musculature used for respiration and that used for phonation.

If these ties exist even for phonatory breathing, they offer the explanation, according to the last-mentioned investigation, for the effect on the voice source of a change in the muscle strategy used for maintaining subglottic pressure—or, in other words, why the method of breathing is decisive to the voice function.

There may be other reasons why breathing technique is important to phonation. Subglottic pressure is decisive to loudness and also, to some extent, to frequency of phonation. Both pitch and loudness must probably be handled with a greater precision in singing than in speech. This implies a demand for a well-controlled subglottic pressure. As this pressure is controlled by means of the muscles of respiration, it follows that a good control of these muscles is important to good control of the voice.

Probably, a very important difference between normal speech and singing is that in normal speech the passive expiratory recoil forces of the breathing apparatus habitually tend to play a more important role in establishing the needed subglottic pressure, while in singing active muscle forces are more important. The singing teacher may have to exert considerable energy to draw the beginner's attention to such breathing habits and to teach the singer how to change them.

The Voice Source

The voice source is what we call the sound that is generated when the vocal folds are set into vibration by an airstream from the lungs. The voice source very significantly contributes to the voice timbre, even though important contributions are provided by the vocal tract resonator as well. Why the vocal fold vibrations occur and why sound is thereby generated has been explained in chapter 2, which also presented the anatomy and physiology of the voice organ. In the present chapter we will see how the voice source is affected when certain parameters are changed, and how it varies under different conditions.

If we want to arrive at a good description of voice source characteristics relevant to the voice timbre, we need to define the source in at least three dimensions: fundamental frequency, amplitude, and spectrum, or using somewhat less acoustical terms, pitch, loudness, and timbral characteristics. We recall that phonation frequency equals the vibration frequency of the vocal folds which is controlled mainly by the laryngeal musculature and determines the pitch of the tone produced. The loudness of phonation reflects another property of the vocal fold vibration, as we will see in this chapter. It is controlled by the subglottic pressure, which, in turn, is controlled by the respiratory apparatus. The timbral characteristics of the voice source also depend on properties of the vocal fold vibration, which, in turn, depend on both the laryngeal musculature and the subglottic pressure.

These matters, particularly the voice source spectrum, are closely related to the somewhat hazy notion of register. For instance, we saw in the previous chapter that phonation frequency seems to be controlled differently in the various registers. Let us therefore start by trying to find out what is meant by the term *register*.

Register

Unfortunately, there is no generally accepted clear definition of the term *register*. The most common description is that a register is a phonation frequency range in which all tones are perceived as being produced in a similar way and which possess a similar voice timbre. Hollien (1974) defines register in the following way: "a vocal register is a totally laryngeal event; it consists of a series or a range of consecutive voice frequencies which can be produced with nearly identical phonatory quality; . . . there will be little overlap in fundamental frequency and . . . the operational definition of a register must depend on supporting perceptual, acoustic, physiologic and aerodynamic evidence."

The picture may become clearer if we take a concrete example. In the male voice one often distinguishes between normal, or *modal,* register, which is used for lower phonation frequencies, and *falsetto* register, which is used when males attempt to imitate the female voice character. When phonation is changed from one register into another, a *register break* may occur. Such a break can be described as a sudden shift in phonation frequency and voice timbre. Presumably, voice breaks in the male voice correspond to short excursions into the falsetto register. Corresponding phenomena may occur in the female voice.

The terminology used for the various registers is confusing. Many authors speak about two main registers in the male voice and three in the female voice. The names used for these registers differ greatly. As it may be fully normal to use the falsetto register in a male voice, for instance, in laughing or as a sign of great surprise, the term *modal* is often regarded as more appropriate than the term *normal* for the register chiefly used for lower phonation frequencies. As much as possible, we will use the former term henceforth. (This will, however, be impossible in the description of research results that have been presented in a different terminology.)

As to the female voice, the literature generally distinguishes between three registers: *chest register, middle register, head register.* Henceforth, we will try to adhere to this terminology wherever possible.

There are some other, more unusual, registers as well. One is used for producing very low notes in the male voice; it is typically used in singing the lowest voice in certain Eastern European and Russian choir music, such as that performed by the "Don Cossacks"; in German this register is called "Strohbass" (straw bass). In normal speech, both male and female, phrases are often terminated on an extremely low frequency of phonation, in such a way that we can perceive each individual voice pulse. This type of phonation is often regarded as a special register, and it has been called *vocal fry* or *pulse register.* Many authors identify a special register in the top range of the female voice and call it *whistle register.*

It should be realized that the chaos in register terminology merely reflects a regrettable lack of objective knowledge; voice research has not developed to the point of any complete understanding of the glottal mechanism and its voice quality aspects, even though significant advances are being made. As a typical and seemingly unavoidable consequence of this lack of objective knowledge, strong emotions enter the discussions; and it is not always realized that only objective knowledge can restore peace. Seen from outside, the disputes on register terminology may appear rather picturesque, particularly when the emphasis is placed on the choice of terms rather than on what they mean in terms of glottal functions. In order to solve such disputes, it is sometimes useful to replace the traditional terms by something else, such as numbers, which are generally free from emotional connotations; but, of course, this would not help solve the real problem. To be on the safe side, the author wants to state explicitly that he does not favor any particular terminology; rather, he was forced to choose one and then try to be consistent.

A register covers a certain phonation frequency range, but the various registers overlap, so that a person may phonate at a given phonation frequency in different registers. The range of overlap between male modal and falsetto registers is in the vicinity of 200 to 350 Hz (pitches G3–F4, approximately). In the female voice, the ranges of overlap are found in the neighborhood of the following phonation frequencies: chest–middle: 400 Hz (pitch G4), and middle–head: 660 Hz (pitch E5). These ranges of register overlap, and the register boundaries vary substantially among individuals.

Generally, it is easy to determine the register from the voice timbre. However, a classic aim of singing pedagogy is to reduce or even eliminate timbral variation between registers; it is generally regarded as optimal that shifts into a different register be accompanied by the smallest possible timbral differences. This means that not only register breaks but also clearly audible register shifts can be eliminated by training. Under such conditions the differences in the register of a skilled singer will be hard to define perceptually, although they may, of course, still exist at a laryngeal level.

The description of register given above suggests that the variations in voice timbre in different registers occur because of changes in the voice source. Therefore, we may expect differences in the way the vocal folds vibrate in different registers.

Control

We know that the voice source is controlled partly by means of the airstream from the lungs, which in turn is controlled by the musculature for respiration, and partly by means of the adjustment of the vocal folds, which in turn is controlled by means of the laryngeal musculature. Three audible voice source properties exist that are controlled by these means: (1) the pitch of the sound produced, corresponding to phonation frequency; (2) the loudness of phonation; and (3) certain voice timbre characteristics corresponding to certain aspects of the voice source spectrum.

Let us first describe in some detail how the frequency of phonation is controlled. Phonation frequency is mainly determined by the tension (that is, the elasticity) and the thickness (the vibrating mass) of the vocal folds. The tension is varied by stretching the folds, that is, by manipulating the vocal fold length; this length, therefore, helps to control phonation frequency. Thus, when a low-pitched sound is produced, the vocal folds are relaxed, thick, and short. For high-pitched sounds they are tense, thin, and long. Figure 4.1 illustrates how the vocal fold length varies with phonation frequency. The upper graph shows that there is a similarity to the behavior of rubber bands in the sense that the application of a slight force leads to a

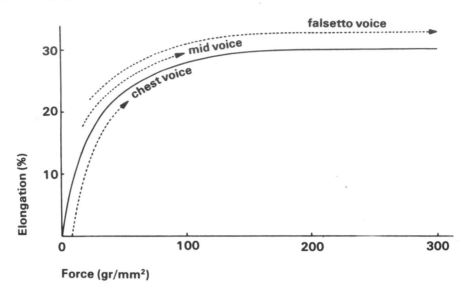

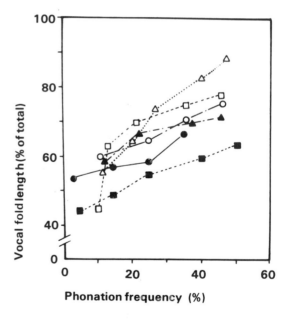

Figure 4.1. Upper graph: Response of the vocal fold length to a longitudinal tension force. A minor force results in a great elongation when the vocal folds are short and lax. When the folds have been stretched, a longitudinal tension will fail to lengthen the folds appreciably. The dotted lines illustrate the elongations used in the main registers; in falsetto register, the vocal folds cannot be lengthened at all, because they are as long as they can be. (After van den Berg, 1962.) Lower graph: Vocal fold length observed in 6 speakers, represented by symbols, at various phonation frequencies. In the middle (50%) of the subject's range, the folds assume between 60% and 90% of their maximum length. (After Hollien and Moore, 1960.)

substantial length increase only when the vocal folds are short and relaxed. When they are long and tense, they need a greater force in order to be still more lengthened and tensed. To cite results and terminology from van den Berg (1968), we may say that chest register is characterized by the first-mentioned situation with relaxed and thick vocal folds, while in falsetto the folds are maximally lengthened.

The variation of the vocal fold length is brought about partly by means of the muscles for vocal fold lengthening and shortening, partly by the muscles for vocal fold tension. The lengthening is handled by the cricothyroid muscles, as we may recall from chapter 2. If the cricothyroid muscles contract, they move the anterior part of the cricoid cartilage upward and backward, so that the slit between the thyroid and cricoid cartilages is narrowed, see figure 2.8, p. 17. We also recall that it is easy to experience these movements if one puts a finger on this slit while changing phonation frequency. The arytenoid cartilages, in which the posterior end of the vocal folds are inserted, are situated on the posterior upper part of the cricoid cartilage. The vocal folds originate close to the angle of the thyroid cartilage. If the cricothyroid muscles contract, the result is an increase in the distance between the posterior and anterior attachments of the vocal folds, which implies that the vocal folds are lengthened. A prerequisite for this result is, however, that the arytenoid cartilages are stabilized, so that they do not merely yield and slide anteriorly when the cricothyroid muscles contract.

The vocal folds are capable not only of being stretched (by contraction of the cricothyroid muscles), but also of being stiffened (by contraction of the vocalis muscles), and this stiffening also contributes to a raising of the phonation frequency, as mentioned. Therefore, an increase of the phonation frequency is obtained by an activation of both the cricothyroid and vocalis muscles. However, it turns out that the vocalis muscle activity is also connected with registers.

Hirano et al. (1970) measured EMG signals from the cricothyroid, vocalis, and lateral cricoarytenoid muscles in singers. EMG signals are obtained by inserting thin electrodes into the muscle under observation. The signals thus recorded are representative of the contraction of that particular muscle: when the signal is strong, the muscle is contracting vigorously. Let us review the main results of this investigation.

Another word on register terminology is required, however. In the investigation of Hirano et al. (1970), the following registers were designated (listed in order from heavy to light): chest, mid, head, light head, and falsetto. The mid and light head were noticed only in the female subjects. We observe that these authors found reasons to introduce the adjectives *heavy* and *light* in order to describe a relevant quality in the functioning of the laryngeal muscles. As we will see more clearly in the following paragraphs, the reason for this is that there are differences in the muscular behavior between the female chest and middle registers, which are similar to those found between the female middle and head registers, as well as between the male modal and falsetto registers. Thus, when phonation frequency is raised beyond a certain point, it seems that the entire control apparatus is in some way reset, so that the values used for the bottom range of the lower register can again be used for the bottom tones of the next higher register, almost as in shifting the gears of a car. However, we are unfortunately still far from a complete understanding of the physiology of register function.

As the singer changed from a heavy to a lighter register, a reduction of the activity in the vocalis and cricothyroid muscles was always observed. Even the (adduction) activity in the lateral cricoarytenoid muscles was often observed to be less in a lighter register than in a heavier one. A transition from modal register to falsetto was never observed to be associated with an increase in the activity of any of the cricothyroid, the vocalis, or the lateral cricoarytenoid muscles. The vocalis muscles were considered particularly important in regard to register. As long as these muscles are active, the voice is kept in modal register, but the voice switches to falsetto as soon as the vocalis muscles cease tensing the vocal folds.

In the same investigation of Hirano et al. (1970), the control of phonation frequency was shown to differ between registers. During phonation in heavy register, phonation frequency was always raised by an increase in the activity of the cricothyroid, vocalis, and lateral cricoarytenoid muscles, while in a light register the activity in these muscles was not seen to vary in synchrony with phonation frequency. In this type of register, phonation frequency control is apparently taken care of either by some other muscle, or by the air flow, as Isshiki (1965) found. The general picture seems to be in agreement with that proposed by van den Berg (see figure 4.1); the cricothyroid muscles, assisted by the vocalis and the lateral cricoarytenoid muscles, keep increasing their contraction as long as possible. When they can no longer manage to increase the length and tension of the vocal folds, they may simply give up. Then, phonation switches over to a lighter register, such as falsetto; and the control over phonation frequency is taken over by some other mechanism.

The role of the lateral cricoarytenoid muscles in this connection would be to prevent the vocal folds from abducting. The abducting force may stem from the contraction of some laryngeal muscles engaged in the pitch-raising maneuver. This force must be taken care of by means of adductor muscles, such as the lateral cricoarytenoid muscles.

Though these results seem quite clear and neat, there is no reason to feel content, since contradicting evidence was later published by Shipp et al. (1979). These authors analyzed the EMG signals from laryngeal muscles in male subjects who phonated in the range from 90 to 550 Hz and found no correlation between vocalis (thyroarytenoid) activity and phonation frequency, even though the subjects must have been using falsetto register for the top pitches. The reason that the results from the investigation of Shipp et al. differed from those of the Hirano et al. study is unclear. Perhaps falsetto register can be produced in different ways.

Various investigations have revealed that nonsingers can lower phonation frequency at a greater speed than they can raise it. In trained singers, on the other hand, this author found no significant difference in this respect, as can be seen in figure 4.2 (Sundberg, 1979). One possible interpretation of these data is that phonation frequency is lowered passively just by reducing the contraction of the cricothyroid and vocalis muscles. This view is defended by many researchers (for instance, Fujisaki, 1981). Another possible interpretation is the opposite one: there is some muscle function which, by contraction, actively lowers phonation frequency. Results from EMG measurements have suggested the sternothyroid muscle as a candidate for bringing phonation frequency from mid to low (Erickson et al., 1983).

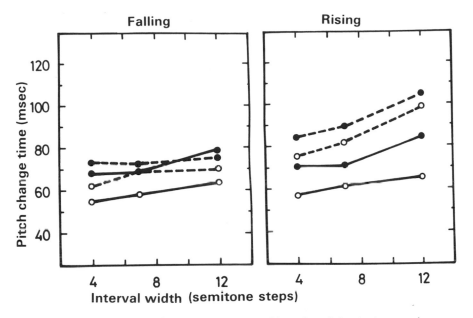

Figure 4.2. Maximum rate of pitch change measured in male and female singers and nonsingers. The singers (solid lines) show a greater rate in rising intervals than nonsingers (dashed lines), and female subjects (open circles) show greater values than male subjects (filled circles). In nonsingers, pitch rises are performed more slowly than pitch drops. (After Sundberg, 1979.)

This muscle originates at the sternum and inserts in the thyroid, and by contracting, it causes the thyroid cartilage to move and to tilt forward slightly. According to Sonninen (1956), a contraction of this muscle can lower the pitch.

The lateral thyroarytenoid (also called the thyrovocalis) is a muscle pair which runs parallel to the vocalis muscle but more laterally (see figure 2.9, p. 18). It originates at the posterior surface of the thyroid cartilage, near the angle, and inserts in the vocal process and lateral surface of the arytenoid cartilage. If the lateral thyroarytenoid muscles can contract independently from the vocalis muscles, the result would be a shortening and relaxing of the vocal folds.

It can be noted that the lateral thyroarytenoid muscles serve the vital purpose of protecting the lungs. When they contract, the entire larynx tube narrows or even closes. The larynx tube typically narrows considerably as phonation frequency is lowered, supporting the hypothesis that a drop in pitch results from a contraction of the lateral thyroarytenoid muscles. Indirect support for this supposition can be found in the discovery that the maximum rate of phonation frequency lowering was not greater in singers than in nonsingers, whereas singers were found to be able to raise phonation frequency more rapidly than nonsingers (Sundberg, 1979). In other words, if there is a muscle actively lowering phonation frequency, the action of this muscle is fast and strong in all voices, regardless of training. This is consistent with the assumption that the muscles involved in pitch-lowering can be assumed to serve a vital purpose, such as shutting the larynx tube when a foreign object is on its way down to the lungs.

Hirano et al. (1970) also studied the activities in the cricothyroid, vocalis, and lateral cricoarytenoid muscles when loudness of phonation was changed. In the heavy registers, they found an increase in vocal effort associated with increased activity in the vocalis and lateral cricoarytenoid muscles. Evidently, this means that we have a tendency to increase both vocal fold tension and adduction activity when we increase loudness of phonation. We recall that the main tool for raising loudness of phonation is an increase in subglottic pressure. When subglottic pressure is raised, an increased adduction may be required for continuing the vocal fold vibrations. In any event, as we will see later in this chapter, different subjects make different laryngeal adjustments when increasing loudness of phonation by raising subglottic pressure. Thus, the acoustic interpretation of the increased activity of the cricothyroid, vocalis, and lateral cricoarytenoid muscles observed by Hirano et al. is not evident.

The study by Hirano et al. (1970) also showed a decrease in the cricothyroid activity during a crescendo. This result is probably another laryngeal response to the increased subglottic pressure underlying a crescendo. As has been mentioned, an increase in subglottic pressure leads to a small increase of phonation frequency, if everything else is kept constant. Therefore, if phonation frequency is supposed to remain unchanged in a crescendo, there is a need for compensation in the system regulating phonation frequency, presumably a reduction in the cricothyroid activity. We know that the effect on phonation frequency of an increase in subglottic pressure is small, only about 4 Hz per cm H_2O, but also that the increase in subglottic pressure producing a crescendo may be quite great. If it amounts to 10 cm of H_2O, the resulting pitch change to be compensated for is no less than 40 Hz, which at 100 Hz fundamental frequency corresponds to an augmented fourth, approximately.

The results of the Hirano et al. (1970) investigation of EMG activity in the laryngeal muscles of singers can be summarized as follows. Register, phonation frequency, and loudness of phonation are by no means independent at a laryngeal level. Still, certain muscles seem to be the primary agents in controlling each of these voice parameters. Thus, *register* is dependent on the vocalis activity from the beginning; in a heavy register the vocalis activity is greater than in a lighter register. In a heavy register it is the cricothyroid muscles that mainly control *phonation frequency,* although a change in phonation frequency is generally associated also with increases in the activity of the vocalis and lateral cricoarytenoid muscles. In a high falsetto register, phonation frequency seems to be controlled in a different and as yet undetermined way, perhaps by airflow. *Loudness of phonation* is controlled by subglottic pressure, although increases in loudness of phonation are associated with increases in the activities of the vocalis and lateral cricoarytenoid muscles in a heavy register.

The investigation just described concerned professional singers. Are the results also representative of nonsingers? They probably are, but one would suspect that the individual differences are greater among nonsingers; a singer must arrive at an optimal control over frequency and loudness of phonation as well as register function, while all this is not needed for normal speech. Therefore the singer can be assumed to have mastered the system more efficiently than the nonsinger, and this would imply an optimization of control. While nobody would object if a nonsinger allowed changes in loudness of phonation to be always accompanied by a change in phonation frequency, such a covariance would be totally unacceptable in a professional singer. The professional must learn to control each of these three voice dimensions separately and independently insofar as is feasible. Only in this way can the singer develop access to the wide phonatory variability which great musical and emotional expression requires.

From what has been said above, it is clear that the understanding of the muscular control of the larynx is still incomplete, to say the least. This is not surprising if we consider the difficulties involved. First of all, EMG measurements are invasive and may easily disturb the subjects, so that they behave atypically during the experiments. Second, both the instruction of the subjects and the reporting on the experimental findings may be obscured by the lack of generally accepted terminology. Third, the individual differences between subjects may lead them to devise different strategies for utilizing their laryngeal muscles. Fourth, as demonstrated by Shipp and coworkers (Shipp et al., 1983), the muscular control of laryngeal function is also influenced by lung volume.

Control System

We have just seen how the voice source is controlled by means of the respiratory and laryngeal muscles. We have observed that a singer needs to control subglottic pressure skillfully and accurately, and also that each change in subglottic pressure and in cricothyroid muscle activity (for the purpose of changing loudness and frequency of phonation, respectively) requires compensatory adjustments in the activity of laryngeal muscles. Next, we shall see what allows the singer or the speaker to continuously make such adjustments during phonation. In other words, what is the nature of the *neural control system* for phonation? Wyke has written several articles about this (see, for instance, 1974), and the following paragraphs present an overview of his ideas.

During normal breathing, the vocal folds are of course abducted; and for phonation they must be adducted. What is the timetable for this change in laryngeal adjustment? Investigations using EMG technique have revealed that muscle activity develops in the adduction muscles (the lateral cricoarytenoid muscles) 50 to 500 msec before the phonation is initiated. At the same time, the activity is reduced in the antagonistic muscles for abduction (the posterior cricoarytenoid muscles). About 50 to 100 msec after the adduction has been initiated, the raising of the subglottic pressure starts, as demonstrated by aerodynamic studies of speech and singing.

In other words, the first thing we do is adduct the vocal folds, and thereafter we raise subglottic pressure. This order of things is appropriate, since a substantial rise in the subglottic pressure presupposes a closed airway, for instance, a closed glottis; otherwise, the air would simply escape the lungs and stream out into free space. After subglottic pressure has been raised, the activity in the muscles for abduction and for adduction is continuously varied in a way determined by the frequency and loudness of phonation and by the sounds produced. Behind this regulatory activity there are two control systems, one voluntary and one reflexive.

Wyke points out that the *voluntary control system* seems to include the prephonatory adjustments of switching from abduction to adduction activity and of raising the subglottic pressure. Probably this prephonatory voluntary activity also involves the positioning and the tuning of the vocal fold mass, length, and inner tension. The values given to these vocal fold and subglottic pressure parameters are determined by which type of sound is intended. From experience and practice we have acquired a solid knowledge about our voice function, so that we know (though unconsciously) how to adjust our larynx and breathing apparatus in order to produce the voice sounds we want. To describe this ability in a terminology familiar to singers, we would probably refer to "hearing the next tone in advance" rather than speaking about voluntary prephonatory adjustments.

Singing and speech would not be singing and speech if the voice parameters did not change continuously in various respects. In the preceding sections we have seen that, if the result is going to match our intentions, a change in one parameter often necessitates a change in others. For instance, a change in subglottic pressure seems to require compensatory changes in the activity of certain laryngeal muscles if phonation is going to continue. Similarly, a change in the activity of one laryngeal muscle generally presupposes activity changes in other laryngeal muscles. According to Wyke (1974), some of these compensatory adjustments are reflexive. As they happen during phonation, they are called *intraphonatory reflexes*. In the tissues within and below the larynx, there are certain sensors, called *mechanoreceptors,* which generate reflexes. These reflexes are probably responsible for the continuous changes in the laryngeal muscles that occur completely unconsciously during phonation.

Three different systems of mechanoreceptors generate such reflexes. One is constituted by the *stretch-sensitive myotatic mechanoreceptors,* which can be found in each of the intrinsic laryngeal muscles. During phonation these receptors are continuously stimulated by the variations in the stretching force on laryngeal muscles. The resulting signals continuously affect the musculature for adduction and abduction, and the result is that the vocal folds maintain the intended posture and characteristics.

Another reflex generating system is constituted by the *mucosal mechanoreceptors,* which are located in the subglottal mucosa. They are stimulated to generate signals by the subglottic pressure. Their significance for the control of the laryngeal muscles during phonation is demonstrated by the effects that can be observed when they are anaesthetized. Before continuing the account of Wyke's ideas, we will pause to describe these effects.

The result of anaesthetizing the receptors is that they need more stimulation than normal before they react, for instance, by sending "status reports" to the brain. If the mechanoreceptors in the subglottal mucosa are anaesthetized, they require a higher-than-normal subglottic pressure before they react. Gould and Okamura (1974) carried out an experiment in which this receptor system was anaesthetized. They found that both glottal resistance and subglottic pressure showed higher values than normal, as soon as other than trivial phonatory tasks were to be performed. This is in agreement with experiences reported by Proctor (1974); when the subglottal mucosa was anaesthetized, it was difficult to sing, but he had no trouble speaking normally. Gould and Okamura also found that, prior to the initiation of phonation, the abdominal muscles contracted during a longer-than-normal period of time when the receptors had been anaesthetized.

A possible interpretation of these results would be the following: First, the brain sends an order to the appropriate muscles to adduct the vocal folds and to raise the subglottic pressure. Then it waits until reports have arrived that the intended values have been reached. While anaesthetized, a higher-than-normal pressure is required before the receptors send such a report. Therefore, the abdominal muscles keep contracting for a longer-than-normal period of time. These experiments demonstrate that there is a close reflexive interrelationship between the activity in the abdominal wall muscles and the receptors in the subglottic mucosa, or, in other words, that the receptors in the subglottic mucosa are important for the control of the laryngeal muscles during phonation.

After this digression concerning the significance of the mechanoreceptors in the subglottal mucosa, let us return to the account of Wyke's view of the reflexive control system. Apart from the stretch receptors in the laryngeal musculature and the subglottal mechanoreceptors mentioned before, there is a third group of relevant receptors, namely, the *articular mechanoreceptors*, in the fibrous capsules of the intercartilaginous joints of the larynx. These receptors sense motions occurring in the laryngeal cartilages, particularly in the cricothyroid and cricoarytenoid joints.

How are these reflex generating systems used, then? First, the singer or speaker starts by tuning the laryngeal musculature so that the next sound to be produced will match the intentions, according to previous experience and practice. The respiratory system raises the subglottic pressure. That starts a transglottal airflow, which, in turn, generates the sound. Then, the system for automatic phonatory control is switched on. The stretch receptors in the laryngeal muscles, the mechanoreceptors on the subglottic mucosa, and the articular mechanoreceptors in the cartilage joints continuously send status reports to the brain about the conditions in their domains. On the basis of these reports, the brain decides what muscle to contract, how much, and at what moment; and all this happens subconsciously, by reflex.

However marvelous this system may seem, it parallels other systems in the body that enable us to move various parts without looking. For example, skilled musicians do not have to look at their fingers in the highly complicated patterns required for piano or violin playing. In another, less complicated act, we can reach and scratch an itching place on our back. The computations performed by the brain under such conditions are most impressive. By looking at the status reports from receptors, conclusions are drawn as to the present position of the finger; and on the basis of this, decisions are made as to which, when, and to what degree muscles should be contracted. Of course, we have other control systems to check what happens when we contract our muscles. In the case of limb movement we often use our vision; in other words, visual feedback is helpful. In phonation, our sense of hearing may offer the brain useful information in terms of auditory feedback.

The practical role of prephonatory tuning, intraphonatory adjustments, and listening to one's own voice, or auditory automonitoring can, according to Wyke (1974), be described in the following way. The *prephonatory adjustment* is voluntary. It concerns, besides the intrinsic laryngeal muscles, the diaphragm, the intercostal muscles, the extrinsic laryngeal muscles, and the middle ear muscles (a function that reduces the sensitivity of the ear just before the initiation of phonation), as well as the muscles of articulation. This prephonatory adjustment is initiated as soon as one takes a breath during phonation and can be improved by practice.

The *intraphonatory reflex system* involves reflexes generated by mechanoreceptors in the intrinsic laryngeal muscles, in the subglottic mucosa, and in the joints between laryngeal cartilages. This system comes into operation as soon as the subglottic pressure has started to rise. The efficiency of this reflex system can be increased by training at a young age, and it deteriorates as one grows older. Interestingly, these reflexes are also influenced by barbiturates and certain other tranquilizing drugs. If the function of the reflex system deteriorates, it is not hard to guess the effect. The system serves the purpose of providing the brain with the information needed in order to give the right command to the proper muscles at the proper moment. If the system does not work accurately, the muscles will contract a bit too much or too little, so that, e.g., phonation frequency is not adjusted with the usual precision. This causes instability in intonation, or even singing off pitch. In contrast to the prephonatory adjustment, the intraphonatory reflex system does not necessarily deteriorate with advancing age.

Auditory automonitoring contributes to the control of the phonatory musculature. We depend heavily on this feedback channel when we learn to speak or sing; this is the main reason that deaf children do not develop speech very easily. However, once we have learned to speak or to sing, we do not seem to need the auditory feedback continuously. This is demonstrated by the effects obtained when this feedback channel is distorted or eliminated. If an adult loses the sense of hearing, there will be no effects on this person's normal speech for a long time. However, difficulties in performing unfamiliar tasks that depend on auditory feedback will appear immediately; for example, a singer who is hard-of-hearing might have problems in hearing the pitch from the accompaniment. Even though we are apparently not dependent on auditory automonitoring for producing and singing, it still offers a means to improve the control of the musculature for breathing and phonation.

To summarize: The control of the voice source is dependent on three reflex-generating systems coupled to mechanoreceptors which are located (1) in the intrinsic laryngeal muscles (telling how stretched these muscles are); (2) in the subglottic mucosa (telling how high the subglottic pressure is); and (3) in the joints of the laryngeal cartilages (telling about the relative positions of these cartilages). These reflex generating systems are particularly important when phonation deviates from normal.

An experiment carried out by Ward and Burns (1978) strikingly demonstrated that, for phonation frequency control, the importance of the receptor systems just described is much less than the importance of the auditory feedback. Trained and untrained singers sang rising and falling scales with and without a noise in their ears. The noise was loud enough to prevent them from hearing what they were singing. The results are shown in figure 4.3. There was no clear difference between singers and nonsingers as long as the subjects could hear the sound of their own voices. But when the auditory feedback was eliminated by the noise, the subjects started to sing out of tune, the nonsingers more than the singers. The most interesting point here is that the hardest task was to perform a slow *staccato* scale, that

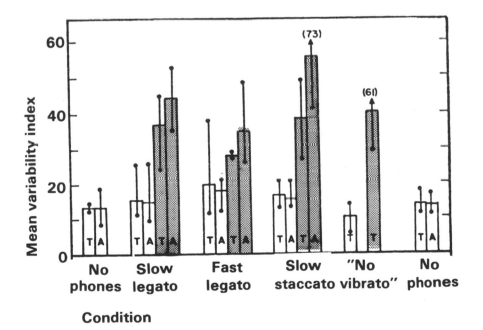

Figure 4.3. The average phonation frequency error in cents observed when 4 trained singers (T) and 4 amateur singers (A) sang different types of ascending and descending scales under various conditions. White and hatched columns refer to singing with and without auditory feedback, respectively. Absence of auditory feedback disturbs the amateur singers much more than the more trained singers, and slow staccato singing was the most difficult task. (From Ward and Burns, 1978.)

is, a scale with silent intervals between each note. When the auditory feedback was eliminated, the nonsingers made errors of no less than 55 cents* (=3.2% from correct frequency), while the singers' corresponding values were significantly lower, namely, 40 cents (=2.3%). This experiment demonstrates that the receptor systems sensing subglottic pressure, the tensions in laryngeal muscles, and the positions of laryngeal muscles do offer more valuable help to singers than to nonsingers in the fine control of phonation frequency. Thus, one of the results of a singer's successful education is the development of a proprioceptive memory, which is useful in performing intended shifts in phonation frequency. Sometimes this memory is called "muscle memory for pitch" by singers. If trained to an appropriate accuracy, the singer would find frequent use for this kind of memory, for instance, when the accompaniment is so loud that it occasionally masks the singer's auditory feedback.

Vocal Fold Vibration

Various techniques are available for monitoring the vibrations of the vocal folds. A laryngeal mirror alone is insufficient because the vibrations are too fast to be followed by the naked eye. One technique is to take a motion picture of the laryngeal mirror's view using a very high film speed (a couple of thousand frames per second compared to the normal 16). When the film is viewed at normal speed, one can see the vocal fold motions quite clearly in slow motion. If phonation frequency is constant, it is also possible to view the vocal fold vibrations in slow motion by means of stroboscopic technique; the glottis is illuminated by a light flashing at a frequency that deviates only slightly from the phonation frequency. The technique is illustrated schematically in figure 4.4. Thus, if phonation frequency is 100 Hz, the flash will light, say, 94 times per second. Such an asynchrony between the rate of vibration and the rate of the light flashes results in an image similar to that of slow motion, where the cycle derives from a long sequence of adjacent cycles.

By means of such photographic techniques, it has been revealed that the vocal folds vibrate according to different patterns at low and high phonation frequencies. When phonation frequency is low, the glottal closure is initiated far down in the glottis, in the lower part of the thick vocal folds. Then, the closure rolls upward toward the upper part of the vocal folds. The collision of the uppermost part of the folds generates surges on their upper surfaces which travel away against the flanks of the thyroid cartilage. The vocal folds appear very lax and loose. The rolling motion along the medial parts of the vocal folds is referred to as the *mucosal wave,* illustrated in figure 4.5.

When phonation frequency is high, on the other hand, the vocal folds are

---

*Cent is a measure for musical intervals. For instance, 100 cents correspond to a semitone step, and 700 cents correspond to a fifth in the equally tempered scale. One cent is defined as the interval obtained between two frequencies having the ratio of $(2:1)^{1/1200}$.

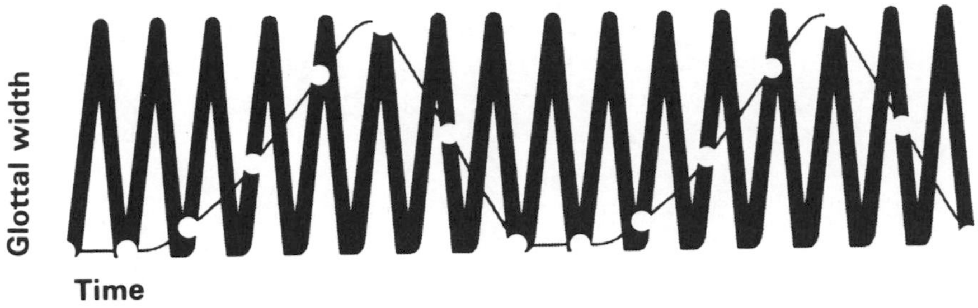

Figure 4.4. The principle for stroboscopy. The heavy curve shows how the glottal area varies during phonation. A flashlight illuminates the glottis, which is thus filmed at each point marked by the open circles. When this movie film is played, the slowed-down version represented by the thin line can be seen. (From Kitzing, 1985.)

long, thin, and tense, and no clear glottal wave can be seen; the long and thin folds appear to close simultaneously along the entire depth of the glottal chink. Nor can any surges be seen on the upper surface of the folds. In falsetto, the complete glottal closure nearly disappears; the vocal folds merely increase and decrease the glottal area but never let it reach zero.

Depending on the glottal conditions, other types of vocal fold vibrations also occur. In one type of breathy phonation, the glottis assumes a Y-shaped form, so that a triangular opening remains even during the quasi-closed phase. This type of breathy phonation is caused by a failing contraction of the interarytenoid muscles. (As we know, these muscles originate from the posterior surface of one arytenoid cartilage and insert into the corresponding surface of the other. They adduct the vocal processes of the arytenoid cartilages.) The phonation resulting from this glottal configuration is characterized by a harmonic spectrum that is mixed with a constant, hissing, high frequency noise emanating from the leaking air. When the vocal folds fail to make contact along their entire length, a different type of breathy phonation results; it is similar to a slightly voiced whispering. In the more common type of whispering, the vocal folds are partly abducted, so that the slit is widest at the posterior end of the glottis, between the arytenoid cartilages. The glottis then assumes the shape of a Moselle wine bottle, as was shown in figure 2.7, p. 15. Under these conditions, the vocal folds are so tense and abducted that they cannot be brought to vibration by the airstream from the lungs. Instead, the airstream becomes turbulent, so that it generates a noise sound.

Spectrum

We have repeatedly mentioned the important fact that the voice source is the sound generated by the chopping of the airstream by the vibrating vocal folds. It has also been mentioned that the voice source is constituted of a number of harmonic partials, the frequencies of which form a harmonic series: $f_1 = 1 \cdot f_1$, $f_2 = 2 \cdot f_1$, $f_3 = 3 \cdot f_1$, which is a complicated way of saying that the frequencies form a multiplication table. The timbral characteristics of

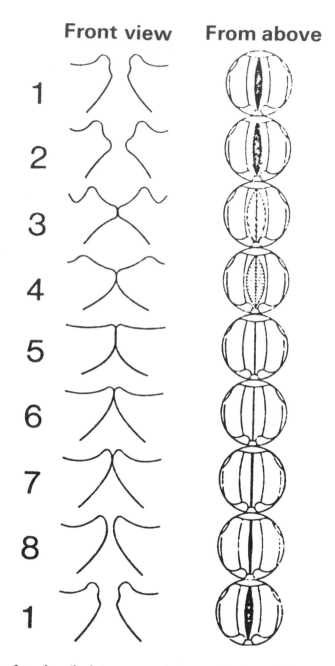

Front view   **From above**

1
2
3
4
5
6
7
8
1

Figure 4.5. Schematic illustration of the vibrating vocal folds: a series of snapshots seen in frontal section (left) and from above, as seen through a laryngeal mirror (right). The series covers one vibration cycle. The glottal closure starts in the lower part of the glottis when the mucosa is sucked into the glottal midline by the Bernoulli force. The bulging of the mucosa then propagates upward, constituting the so-called *mucosal* wave. (After Schönhärl, 1960.)

the voice source are often described in terms of the amplitudes of these partials, or, in other words, in terms of the *voice source spectrum*.

It can be shown theoretically that the sound levels of the harmonic components constituting the voice source spectrum can be expected to decrease by about 12 dB/octave. This implies that each partial is about 12 dB weaker than the partial which is one octave below and, hence, has a half frequency. Figure 4.6 illustrates this. It shows that the *source*

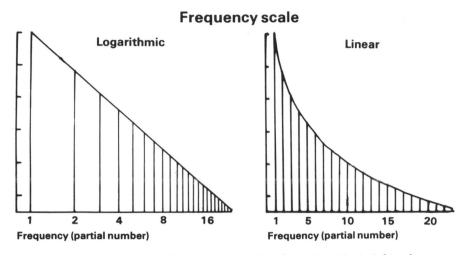

Figure 4.6. Idealized spectrum of the voice source plotted on a logarithmic (left) and linear (right) frequency scale. When the frequency scale is logarithmic, a constant frequency ratio corresponding to a musical interval like an octave is represented by a certain distance; in this case, the typical source spectrum slope of − 12 dB/octave comes out as a straight line. When the frequency scale is linear, a constant number of Hz, such as the frequency distance between adjacent partials, is represented by a certain distance; in this case, the − 12 dB/octave slope comes out as a curve.

spectrum envelope, which is a curve smoothly connecting the harmonics in a spectrogram of the source, falls off at a rate of 12 dB/octave. However, it should be kept in mind that this is merely a theoretically based approximation. In practice, substantial deviations from this approximation occur, as we will soon see.

Before presenting some source spectrum data, we will first mention how such data may be obtained. The procedure applied is based on the theory of voice production as presented in chapter 2. Let us recapitulate: The ability of the vocal tract to transport sound from the glottis to the lip opening, or the *sound transfer function,* is strongly dependent on the frequency. This ability culminates at the formant frequencies and is also heavily influenced by their density. If the frequency interval between two adjacent formants is halved, the ability to transport sound increases by 6 dB at these formant frequencies and by 12 dB midway in the valley between them. The curve showing the sound transfer ability is often referred to as the *transfer function.*

The important thing here is that, given the formant frequencies, this transfer function is essentially *predictable.* For instance, rather accurate predictions can be made with the aid of a digital computer. It is also possible to construct electronic equipment that provides the same transfer function as the vocal tract, a device that is often referred to as a *formant synthesizer.* It is built up by a series of electronic resonance circuits, one for each formant. The resonance frequencies of these circuits can be tuned so that they agree with the formant frequencies of a specific vowel. The synthesizer then possesses the same transfer function as the vocal tract when it produced that vowel. The only difference is that while the input to the vocal tract is acoustic, or sound, the input to the synthesizer is the electric equivalent of the sound, or an electrical signal.

The predictability of the transfer function offers an opportunity to determine the nature of the voice source. One way is as follows: An electrical signal representing an idealized voice source with a spectrum falling off at exactly 12 dB/octave and with a fundamental frequency equal to that of the real vowel to be analyzed is fed into the formant synthesizer. The synthesizer converts this signal into a synthesized vowel. The spectrum of this vowel will look exactly like the spectrum of the real vowel only if the input spectrum to the synthesizer was exactly the same as the spectrum of the voice source of the real vowel. This implies that the differences observed between the real and the synthesized spectrum can be entirely ascribed to the difference between the idealized source spectrum and the real source spectrum. In this way, the source spectrum of a given vowel can be estimated. This method of analyzing something by trying to synthesize it has been used with great success in speech research; it is generally referred to as *analysis by synthesis*. In the case of estimates of the source spectrum of vowels it is generally called *spectrum matching*.

Another version of essentially the same idea is used in so-called *inverse filtering*. The main idea here is that the vowel sound itself is fed to an electronic circuit which simply compensates for the uneven sound transfer function curve that characterized the vocal tract when producing the vowel.

An inverse filter consists of a series of filters, ideally, one for each formant, the transfer function of which is the *negation* of the transfer function of a formant. Therefore, if formants are considered as resonances of the vocal tract, these filters should be described as *antiresonances*. If we know that a vowel sound has a first formant at, say, 470 Hz, we tune the first antiresonance of the inverse filter to that frequency. Then, the filter compensates for the resonance in the vocal tract at that frequency, and the influence of that formant on the spectrum is eliminated. In the same way, the influence of other vocal tract resonances, or formants, can be eliminated. What is obtained as the output of an inverse filter, therefore, is a signal corresponding to the real voice source. If care is taken to preserve the original waveform of the vowel produced (for instance, by using a frequency modulation tape recorder instead of the normal amplitude modulation tape recorder), the output will have not only the correct spectrum but even the true waveform of the voice source. It will show the airflow past the glottis versus time. We will call such recordings *flow glottograms*. We will return to flow glottograms later in this chapter.

Particularly prior to the digital-computer era, both spectrum matching and inverse filtering were very time-consuming. Also, in cases where the frequency of the fundamental is high and that of the first formant is low, both methods give unreliable results. Consequently, rather few reliable studies of the voice source have been published, and those published do not convey any complete picture of reality. Moreover many of these investigations are based on very few subjects so the results are merely tentative. Nevertheless, we will review what has been published in this area. Let us start by looking at the *source spectrum* in different types of voices. The question is how many of the timbral variations between different voices are due to the voice source. But before we answer it, we need to put down some words on the plotting of source spectrum data.

As it turns out, it is a bit inconvenient to examine source spectra if they are plotted just as they are, because the source spectrum characteristic that tends to catch the reader's eye is then the steep slope of the curve, which is really uninteresting. More significant are the deviations from a standard slope, such as −12 dB/octave. For this reason, all source spectra shown here have been normalized with respect to this −12 dB/octave slope, so that the curves merely show the deviations from this slope. Also, the curves have been so arranged that the mean deviation of the partials above 1,000 Hz equals 0 dB.

Part of the voice timbre differences between the male and the female voice seems to be due to the voice source. Figure 4.7 gives an example. It compares source spectra obtained from one male and one female subject pronouncing the same vowel in the same word. Both voices were those of untrained speakers. The male subject had a weak fundamental while the female subject had a strong fundamental. Apart from this difference, the deviations from the −12 dB/octave slope shown seem unsystematic in the case of the male subject, while the voice source spectrum of the female subject seems to fall off at a higher rate than −12 dB/octave.

The author participated in a study (Ågren and Sundberg, 1978) in which the source spectra of two alto singers were compared with those of two tenor singers. Here, not only the vowel and the word were the same but

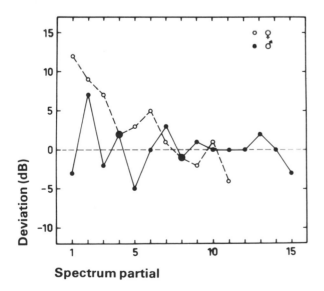

Figure 4.7. Source spectra from a male (filled circles) and a female voice (open circles). The spectra are represented by a curve showing how the spectrum contour deviates from the standard slope of −12 dB/octave. (After Karlsson, 1976.)

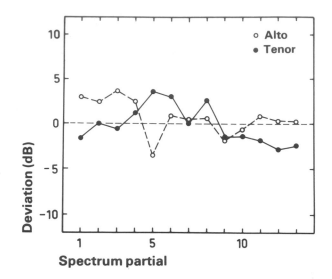

Figure 4.8. Average source spectra from two alto (open circles) and two tenor (filled circles) singers singing at identical pitches. The spectra are given as in figure 4.7. (After Ågren and Sundberg, 1978.)

also the fundamental frequency. The results are shown in figure 4.8. Even though the fundamental frequency is the same here, one can see that the fundamental is stronger in the alto voices. This supports the assumption that a strong fundamental is typical also of female singers' voices, if vowels with the same fundamental frequency are compared. This last-mentioned condition may be significant to the results, though. It means that a tone in the lower part of the alto's range is compared with a tone in the higher part of the tenor's range. With respect to the overall source spectrum slope, there is no clear difference between these trained voices; if we disregard the lowest partials for the moment, both can be roughly described as falling off at a rate of -12 dB/octave.

It is important to note that these two investigations considered the source spectrum of so few voices that no generalization whatsoever can be made. On the other hand, the voices examined represented typical examples of male and female voice quality. Therefore it seems fair to conclude only that the differences in voice timbre between these subjects could not be explained without postulating source spectrum differences regarding the amplitude of the fundamental.

A comparison between untrained speakers and professional singers is shown in figure 4.9. This figure shows results from two different investigations, which, however, used the same method of analysis (Carr and Trill, 1964; Cleveland, 1977). The curves shown in the figure represent the average obtained from the vowels /u:, i:, ɑ:/. The fundamental frequency of the untrained voices was lower than that of the trained voices. The deviations from the -12 dB/octave slope seem small and unsystematic, but a difference in the amplitude of the fundamental, clearly stronger in the voices of the professional singers, can be observed again. However, this difference was to a great extent due to the data obtained from the vowel /i:/.

Earlier, we quoted the rather hazy definition of *register:* tones belonging

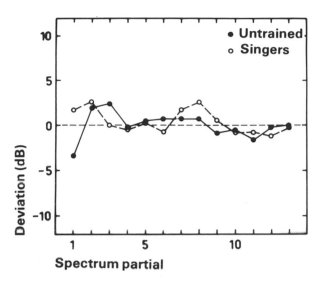

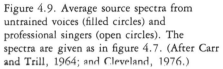

Figure 4.9. Average source spectra from untrained voices (filled circles) and professional singers (open circles). The spectra are given as in figure 4.7. (After Carr and Trill, 1964; and Cleveland, 1976.)

to the same register sound similar and, during phonation, feel as if they are produced in a similar way. If we think about what this may mean, we suspect that register differences must refer to voice source differences. And if one examines the voice source characteristics in different registers, one becomes convinced that they are. Figure 4.10 shows averaged source spectra for three trained male singers pronouncing the vowel /ɑ:/ on the same fundamental frequency in modal and falsetto register. Once more, we must state that the main difference is found in the amplitude of the fundamental. It is about 5 dB stronger in the falsetto register.

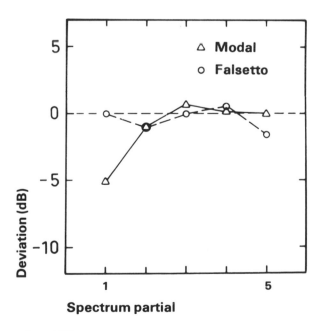

Figure 4.10. Average source spectra for three trained male singers pronouncing the vowel /ɑ:/ on the same fundamental frequency in modal register (triangles) and falsetto register (circles). The spectra are given as in figure 4.7.

The author compared source spectra in a trained, but not professional, female singer, who sang the same two vowels on the same fundamental frequency in two different registers: chest and middle (Sundberg, 1977d). The results are shown in figure 4.11. The most apparent difference concerns the amplitude of the fundamental, once again, which in this case is no less than 10 dB stronger in the middle register, or about twice as great as what we have seen in most of the previous graphs. The singer, who was a music teacher in a school, often demonstrated these register differences to her pupils. In the present experiment she exaggerated the differences in the same way as in her teaching. For instance, her phonation in chest register would have been nearly impossible to use in a traditional concert, the tones sounding too tense. Hence, the data shown in figure 4.11 would be representative of exaggerated source spectrum differences between chest and middle registers. Still they seem representative; Schoenhard et al. (1983) reported similar results from a spectral analysis of tones sung in these two registers by eight subjects.

Disregarding this difference for a moment, we also observe that for both middle and chest register the overall spectrum slope is about −20 dB/octave in this subject; this is considerably more than the classical −12 dB/octave, but not too dissimilar to the slope we found for the untrained female voice (cf. figure 4.7). Such a steep source spectrum slope was not found for the professional alto singer, as shown in figure 4.8. One interpretation is that alto voices possess stronger source spectrum overtones than soprano singers. However, this interpretation is not supported by spectrum data on

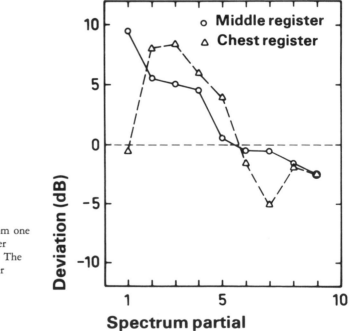

Figure 4.11. Average source spectra from one female singer phonating in chest register (triangles) and middle register (circles). The spectra are given as in figure 4.7. (After Sundberg, 1977d.)

a professional soprano (Sundberg, 1975); here the source spectrum fell off at the rate of approximately −12 dB/octave. Therefore, it is more plausible that the steep source spectrum fall in figure 4.11 is atypical of a professional soprano.

Figure 4.12 offers an example of personal voice timbre differences. It compares averaged source spectra from two voices with great voice timbre differences; one voice had an extremely dark color, typical of a deep bass singer, while the other voice had a lighter color, more like that of a baritone. Apart from formant frequency differences between these two voices, there were also voice source differences, as shown in the figure. In the low frequency part of the spectrum (below 1 kHz), the partials show higher average amplitude in the case of the dark voice. We may conclude that part of the differences in voice quality between different singers stem from the voice source.

To summarize: This issue of source spectrum appears to be rather confusing. In the comparisons we have made, a major difference was found primarily in the amplitude of the fundamental. The source spectrum of a male voice had a weaker fundamental than the source spectrum of a female voice; modal and chest registers showed a weaker fundamental than falsetto and middle registers, respectively; untrained speakers had a weaker fundamental than trained singers.

To some extent, these observations would match our experiences with voice timbre. For instance, a female voice certainly sounds more similar to male falsetto phonation than to male modal register phonation. This is in agreement with the observation that the female voice and the falsetto voice are both characterized by a strong source spectrum fundamental. However, as we will see later, the main similarity stems from likeness of the formant frequencies between male falsetto and the female voice. On the other hand, a male singer's voice does not necessarily sound more female than the voice of an untrained male speaker, and still, the singer's voice is more similar to the female voice with respect to the amplitude of the source spectrum

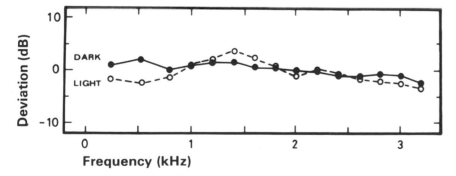

Figure 4.12. Average source spectrum differences between two singers, one with a very dark voice color (filled circles) and the other with a light voice color (open circles). (After Sundberg, 1973.)

fundamental. We can safely conclude that the amplitude of the source spectrum fundamental does not tell the whole story about the difference between male and female voice quality.

In comparing source spectra it is also important to observe that the voice source spectrum of a person is far from being constant. The voice source generally varies considerably when the most important voice parameters, loudness and frequency of phonation, are changed.

As far as untrained voices are concerned, there seem to be no explicit source spectrum studies published. On the other hand, it is possible to infer source spectrum changes from vowel spectrum changes under certain conditions. When loudness of phonation is increased, the amplitudes of the spectral overtones increase considerably more than the amplitude of the fundamental, according to Fant (1960). For instance, if the loudness of phonation is increased so that the sound level of the vowel is increased by 10 dB, the amplitude of the source spectrum fundamental generally increases by no more than 4 dB. Also, the higher overtones tend to increase more than the lower overtones. This is in agreement with the typical observation that the lower source spectrum partials are much more dominant when the loudness of phonation is low than when it is high.

Does this apply also to singers? The author studied the effects on the source spectrum of changes in loudness and frequency of phonation in professional male singers (Sundberg, 1973). Figures 4.12 and 4.13 show

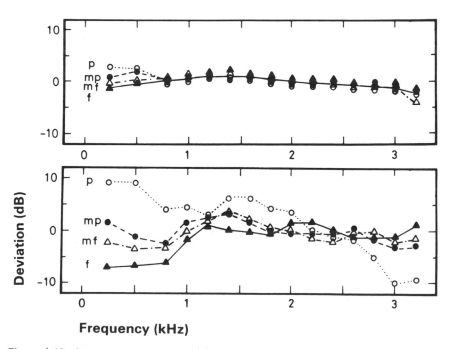

Figure 4.13. Average source spectrum differences of the singers in figure 4.12 singing various vowels at various pitches in different degrees of loudness: p = soft, mp = medium soft, mf = medium loud, f = loud.

averaged source spectra obtained when the intensity and frequency of phonation were varied. Note that the spectra have been normalized with respect to the standard −12 dB/octave slope, so that the loudness differences are hard to see. Both voices, like those in figure 4.12, show the same trend. Speaking relatively, the lower source spectrum components (below 1 kHz) are more dominant in soft phonation than in loud phonation. Moreover, we can see that above 1 kHz the source spectrum can be roughly described by the classical −12 dB/octave slope, except for the softest phonation of the light voice. The differences accompanying these changes in loudness of phonation are considerably greater in the case of the light voice. Most of these effects are similar to those reported for nonsingers. We conclude that there seems to be no great difference between singers and nonsingers with respect to the influence of loudness of phonation on the voice source.

Generally, changes in phonation frequency are also associated with source spectrum changes in untrained voices, according to Fant (1968); when frequency of phonation is raised, the source spectrum overtones tend to lose in amplitude. Figure 4.14 compares averaged source spectra with differing fundamental frequencies as sung by the same two professional singers. The effects are rather small and limited to the lowest spectrum partials, which become somewhat less dominating when the phonation frequency is high. It is possible that this is the same effect as that just observed under

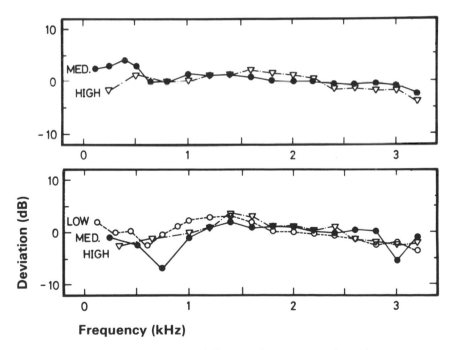

Figure 4.14. Average source spectrum differences of the singers in figure 4.12 singing various vowels in different degrees of loudness at various pitches: low (open circles), medium (filled circles), and high (triangles). (After Sundberg, 1973.)

conditions of varied intensity of phonation. High notes are often sung with greater loudness of phonation than lower notes. We just observed that the lower source spectrum partials tended to be more dominant in soft phonation than in loud phonation. The physiological background of this might be that singers tend to sing high notes with slightly higher subglottic pressure than low notes, as was mentioned in the chapter on breathing. Returning to figure 4.13, there is no clear tendency in these singers to reduce the dominance of the source spectrum overtones above 1 kHz when phonation frequency is raised; all curves lie rather parallel to the horizontal line that represents the spectrum slope of -12 dB/octave. In untrained speakers this is not so, as was mentioned, suggesting that the source spectrum variability is less in singing than in normal speech.

This variability is probably an important difference between singing and speech. In normal speech the source spectrum is allowed to vary freely with pitch and/or loudness changes, because such variations would do no harm to spoken communication. In singing, on the other hand, there is a demand for "equalization," which probably means "similarity in voice quality even under conditions of changing pitch." In other words, the voice source is probably not allowed to shift very much in character just because the pitch or the loudness is raised or lowered. The singer would need a source spectrum, the overtone content of which is, if not constant, at least well-controlled. It may be a difficult task in vocal education to eliminate such voice source habits; they are perfectly acceptable in normal speech but unacceptable in singing.

Before leaving these aspects of the voice source spectrum variability, it might be interesting to see what the consequences are in terms of the radiated vowel spectrum. They are illustrated in figure 4.15, which shows the sound levels of the fundamental, the first formant, the second formant, and the formants in the frequency range 2 to 4 kHz of a singer and a nonsinger who both phonated the vowel /ae:/ at different loudnesses but with constant fundamental frequency. The graph illustrates a basic aspect of increases in phonatory loudness: the louder a vowel is phonated, the more dominating the overtones become in the spectrum. This is very important and often overlooked, so it is worth repeating: when loudness is increased, the higher spectrum overtones gain more in amplitude than the lower ones.

Waveform

Next we will focus our attention on the waveform of the voice source. Since we have dealt with the spectral characteristics above, it might be appropriate to recall what the relationships are, in general terms, between the waveform and the spectrum of a signal.

Sounds correspond to microscopic air pressure oscillations. The air particles move backward and forward in the direction of sound propagation. They approach or move away from their neighboring air particles; and as a result, the density of the air particles varies. When the density is increased, the air pressure rises; and when the density is reduced, the pressure drops.

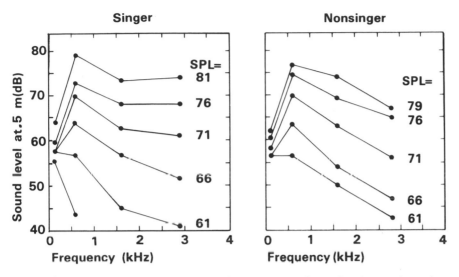

Figure 4.15. Typical spectral implications of a change in loudness of phonation observed in a singer and a nonsinger who sang the vowel /ae:/ at different loudnesses, specified by the sound pressure level (SPL) at 0.5 m, while keeping phonation frequency constant. The curves show the level in equally wide spectral bands, the center frequency of which is plotted on the horizontal axis. In soft phonation, the fundamental is the strongest partial in the spectrum. At moderate loudnesses, the strongest partial is that which is closest to the first formant, and the overall sound level is almost identical with that of the first formant at 0.6 kHz. As loudness is increased, the higher spectrum partials gain more in amplitude than the lower spectrum partials.

The air pressure variations that we perceive as sound are very small in amplitude. Their repetition rate mirrors the frequency. If the frequency is, say, 220 Hz, the air pressure in a given point in the sound field varies from maximum to minimum 220 times per second. These air pressure oscillations move our eardrums by a microscopic amount by sucking them outward and pressing them inward toward the middle ear, and the result is that we hear sound. One normally speaks of *sound pressure* rather than air pressure in cases of oscillations causing perception of sound.

One way to describe a sound is to specify the amplitudes of its spectrum partials. This is how spectrum analysis works, as we have just seen previously in this chapter. An equally efficient description is to show how the *sound pressure* varies with time. Sounds that possess the quality of pitch correspond to sound pressure variations that are periodic. This means that they can be described as a repetition of a small pattern of variation. This pattern of variation is equivalent to the *waveform* of the sound. We conclude that the waveform of a sound actually shows how the sound pressure varies with time.

The spectrum and the waveform of a sound are, of course, closely related to each other; both tell the same thing about the sound, but in two different ways. The spectrum tells us at which frequencies there are partials in the signal and how strong these components are. Each of these partials corresponds to a sine wave. The waveform of a signal, on the other hand, is simply the sum of the sine waves constituting the sound. This means that the relationship between spectrum and waveform is no more complicated than this: if one adds the sine waves of all partials shown in the spectrum to their appropriate amplitudes, one obtains a waveform corresponding to this spectrum. As a sequel to this, a rule of thumb emerges regarding the relationship between the spectrum and the waveform; the smoother and more sinusoidal the waveform is, the softer the higher partials are; and, conversely, the more abrupt the changes are in the waveform, the richer in strong, high partials the spectrum will be.

To be exact, the same spectrum may correspond to several waveforms. The reason for this is that the result of the summation of the waveforms depends on the phase relations between the sine waves, that is, how they are synchronized in time. Fortunately, this will cause us no headache here. We can safely concentrate on one particular waveform, because, as a moment's reflection will tell us, it must be the waveform of the airflow through the glottis—that is, the *transglottal airflow*—that is the primary information about the voice source; this waveform is the first consequence of the fact that the airstream from the lungs is chopped into a sequence of air pulses by the vibrating vocal folds. The source spectrum offers only a description of a certain aspect of the voice source, that is, its composition of partials.

To be precise once more, the direct equivalent of the spectrum that specifies the sound pressure values of the partials cannot really be equated with the waveform of the transglottal airflow. Instead, it should be equated with the waveform of the corresponding sound pressure. In order to arrive from the airflow to the sound pressure, we just need to make a very simple correction, namely, to highpass filter the signal with a filter characteristic of +6 dB/octave. This means that the spectrum envelope slope is reduced by 6 dB/octave, so that it becomes flatter. But these are technicalities that do not concern us here. One more thing should be added for the sake of exactness. In a spectrum, the amplitudes of the partials are generally given in the logarithmic and relative dB units rather than in pressure units. The dB unit reduces the differences between large and small amplitudes. In a waveform, on the other hand, the amplitude is normally given in the actual unit itself, such as Pascal for sound pressure, litres/sec for airflow, or whatever the waveform really shows.

What conclusions can one draw from the spectrum and waveform of the voice source, then? The spectrum is closely connected with timbre, in the sense that the voice source spectrum is important to the voice timbre we perceive. Indeed, there are important voice source properties that can be observed only in a spectrum with the dB unit, namely, the amplitudes of the high frequency partials, because these partials happen to be at the same time of small amplitude and highly relevant to the personal voice timbre. We will see more about this in the next chapter. But the spectrum does not tell us much about the behavior of the vocal folds. This information is contained in the voice source waveform. Therefore, the waveform is significant from the point of view of vocal fold function. We arrive at the conclusion that not only the spectrum but also the waveform of the voice source deserves our interest. As a sign of its importance we will give the glottal waveform a name of its own; henceforth the waveform of the voice source will be called a *flow glottogram*. In this way its close relationship to the glottal function is noted.

How can the voice source waveform be measured so that glottograms can be obtained? One method is to put light on the glottis and to measure the amount of light that passes the glottis. This is possible if light is sent through the skin underneath the glottis and is picked up in the pharynx by means of a fiber-optic sensor inserted through the nose. The glottograms thus obtained show how the glottal area varies with time and are often referred to as *optic glottograms*. However, the variations in glottal area do not correspond exactly to the variations in glottal airflow (see Rothenberg, 1981).

Another method is to use the *inverse filtering* technique mentioned earlier. This method provides correct glottograms only if the sound-processing equipment accurately reproduces the waveform. Among other things this requirement necessitates the use of a so-called FM tape recorder rather than a conventional tape recorder. Inverse filtering is a classic method for measuring the voice source. It was formerly very tedious to use, but it was simplified in an ingenious way by Rothenberg (1973). The voice sound is picked up by a special microphone mounted in a mask, which the subject holds over the nose and mouth. Holes are drilled in the mask and are covered with a fine mesh. The microphone measures the pressure difference across this mesh, and the signal thus obtained corresponds to the airflow. This arrangement substantially simplifies the technicalities of the inverse filtering.

Let us now find out how a flow glottogram should look, just by thinking about what this type of graph actually shows. The voice source is a pulsating flow of air passing between the vibrating vocal folds. The flow glottogram obtained from inverse filtering shows the resulting transglottal airflow, or, more specifically, how this airflow varies with time. One axis of a flow glottogram represents the transglottal airflow in litres/sec, and the other represents time in milliseconds. It is then easy to imagine that normally a flow glottogram must be a curve that repeatedly returns to the value of zero litre/sec, because this must be the transglottal airflow under conditions of a closed glottis. In between these values of zero flow, the curve must reach another maximum value, which would result from an open glottis.

Figure 4.16 shows a schematic flow glottogram. When the glottis is closed, no airflow is generated, so the curve goes to zero. The length of the horizontal portion of the flow glottogram corresponds to the time during which the vocal folds make contact, or the duration of the closed phase. When the glottis opens again, the airflow gradually increases, and it then gradually decreases as the glottis closes. Often the slope of the curve in the closing appears to be steeper than it is during the opening of the glottis; in

Flow glottogram

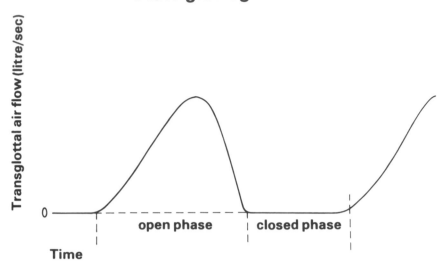

Figure 4.16. Schematic illustration of a flow glottogram.

other words, the *opening phase* seems longer than the *closing phase*. In the figure, the closed phase and the open phase are of approximately equal duration. The resulting curve is constituted by horizontal portions interleaved with triangular figures that are more or less tilted to the right.

The above reasoning was based on the tacit assumption that there is a one-to-one relationship between glottal area and transglottal airflow. As mentioned, this relationship is not at all simple, and this fact is a very strong argument for distinguishing between optical glottograms and flow glottograms. In the beginning of the open phase, the airflow has to accelerate; as a consequence, the airflow is less than it would be if this acceleration phenomenon did not exist. Likewise, at the end of the closing phase, the airflow is greater than the glottal area would permit, because of an effect of the inertia of the airstream. This contributes to the tilting of the triangular pulses in a flow glottogram. This mechanism has been described by Rothenberg (1981).

It was shown above why there must be a close interrelationship between the spectrum and the waveform of a signal. A rule of thumb was mentioned: the sharper the waveform discontinuities, the stronger the high frequency partials in the spectrum. In general, this is about all that can be said except with respect to the voice source. This is due to the fact that the waveform, as represented by the flow glottogram, cannot vary beyond certain limits. For instance, we just found that a flow glottogram should normally be a curve that can be described as a horizontal line with interspersed triangular excursions that correspond to the closed and open phases, respectively.

The relationship between the waveform and the spectrum of the voice source was long a mystery. A number of measures were suggested for the description of flow glottograms, such as open quotient, speed quotient, duty cycle, and others. However, we need not burden our memories with the ways in which these measures were defined, because, actually, no one ever managed to show that they had any acoustical and timbral relevance.

Recently, some light has been shed on how flow glottograms relate to the acoustic properties of the voice. Together with Gauffin, the author examined the voice source in singers and nonsingers (Sundberg and Gauffin, 1979). The analysis included the partials up to about 1,000 Hz. One important conclusion was that the flow glottogram amplitude, in other words, the maximum value of transglottal airflow in a period, is directly related to the amplitude of the voice source spectrum fundamental. The greater the maximum airflow amplitude in the flow glottogram, the stronger the voice source fundamental.

Fant (1979) studied the relationships between the voice source spectrum and waveform from a theoretical point of view. He combined some portions of sine waves and a straight line in such a way that a variety of waveforms similar to typical flow glottograms was obtained. This description of flow glottograms allowed him to study the spectral implications of various waveform changes. He found that the amplitudes of the overtones are directly dependent on another flow glottogram characteristic, namely the closing rate, or, more accurately, the *maximum rate of airflow change* during a period which, in mathematical terms, is called the *peak amplitude of the differentiated glottogram*. However, life will turn out to be unnecessarily short and maybe even a bit empty if we spend too much of it pronouncing and reading very long words. For this reason this flow glottogram parameter will be referred to as the *closing rate*. Generally, the sound level of a vowel is almost entirely determined by the amplitude of the strongest spectrum partial, and normally this partial is the one that is closest to the first formant frequency. Provided that the pitch is not high, this partial is an overtone. This means that the sound level of a vowel is mainly determined by the closing rate of the flow glottogram. It should, however, be kept in mind that other factors also influence the sound level, such as the frequency distance between the first formant and the partial lying closest to it.

In figure 4.15 we saw that the amplitude growth of the higher partials is greater than that of the lower partials; for example, if a partial at 500 Hz increases by 6 dB, the amplitude growth of a partial near 2,500 Hz is about 9 dB. Thus, when the closing rate increases, the dominance of the higher overtones is increased in the spectrum. In other words, a vowel pronounced at a high intensity of phonation possesses more dominating high frequency overtones than a vowel pronounced at a lower intensity of phonation.

To summarize: In the relationship between voice source waveform and spectrum, the amplitude of the fundamental depends on the flow glottogram amplitude; the amplitudes of the overtones depend on the closing rate in the flow glottogram; and an increase of the closing rate pays off more in the amplitudes of the higher overtones than in those of the lower overtones.

It was mentioned that the flow glottogram is closely related not only to the source spectrum but also to the mode of vibration of the vocal folds. An investigation which the author made with Gauffin (Sundberg and Gauffin, 1979) allowed some conclusions regarding these relationships. It showed that the flow glottogram amplitude can be varied within wide limits during phonation, depending on the mode of phonation. If a high subglottic pressure is combined with a high adduction force in the larynx, the flow glottogram amplitude and, hence, the amplitude of the voice source fundamental are low. Inversely, the flow glottogram amplitude is increased if one phonates with a lower subglottic pressure and a lower degree of adduction force; under these conditions the dominance of the fundamental is increased. For the two extremes with respect to these modes of phonation, we proposed the terms *pressed phonation* and *flow phonation,* respectively. Adduction force can be still more reduced, so that the vocal folds fail to make contact during the quasi-closed phase; then, the glottis is no longer completely closed but only nearly so; in this case, phonation turns into what is known as *breathy phonation.* Thus, we end up with a *phonatory dimension* ranging from pressed phonation to breathy phonation. If phonation is changed from pressed toward breathy, it may pass flow phonation where the flow glottogram has the greatest possible amplitude and still retains a closed phase.

The acoustic effects associated with these different phonation types are by no means negligible. The amplitude of the fundamental can be increased by 15 dB or more when the mode of phonation is changed from pressed phonation to flow phonation. It is remarkable that this may happen without substantial changes in sound level. This is due to the fact mentioned previously that the sound level is mainly determined by the amplitude of the strongest partial in the spectrum, normally the partial closest to the first formant frequency. If the fundamental frequency is lower than half of the first formant frequency, it is an overtone that is closest to the first formant and that is hence decisive for the sound level. It is only in very soft phonation and in cases when the fundamental and the first formant are close in frequency that the fundamental is the strongest partial in the spectrum so that it can determine the sound level of the vowel. In other words, as long as the first formant is well above the fundamental, the sound level is mainly determined by the amplitude of an overtone. This explains why the amplitude of the fundamental may vary within wide limits without affecting the sound level.

To summarize: Pressed phonation is characterized by a high subglottic pressure combined with a strong adduction force, while flow phonation has a lower subglottic pressure and a lower degree of adduction force. One may hypothesize that the Bernoulli effect plays a more important role in the closing phase in flow phonation and that adduction activity gains in importance in the closing phase during pressed phonation. The type of phonation that Rubin et al. (1967) observed when the singer subjects were running short of air seems to be an example of a change of phonation type toward pressed phonation (see figure 3.15, p. 46). We also observed that pressed phonation is a rather poor affair in terms of vocal economy; one expends a high subglottic pressure plus strong adduction force without gaining anything in sound level. Flow phonation is preferable from this point of view; a lower subglottic pressure and a more moderate adduction force would yield an unchanged or even increased acoustic output, as we will see soon.

The results of the flow glottogram investigations discussed (Fant, 1979; Sundberg and Gauffin, 1979; Gauffin and Sundberg, 1980) suggest that two glottogram characteristics are acoustically decisive, namely, the glottogram amplitude and the closing rate. These two factors are determined by two phonatory parameters. The position of phonation along the dimension ranging from pressed to breathy is reflected in the amplitude of the flow glottogram, which, in turn, determines the amplitude of the source spectrum fundamental. The sound level of the vowel produced is dependent on the closing rate of the flow glottogram and is closely related to loudness of phonation. Since loudness of phonation is mainly determined by subglottic pressure, subglottic pressure must be important to the closing rate of the flow glottogram. In short, then, the position of phonation along the pressed to breathy dimension determines the amplitude of the source spectrum fundamental and is signaled by the amplitude of the flow glottogram; and the degree of vocal loudness determines the acoustic amplitude of the output and is manifested by the closing rate of the flow glottogram.

Before we turn to the question of how these source parameters vary during phonation, two important things should be stressed. First, pressed and breathy phonation constitute the *extremes* of a phonatory dimension. Between them are an infinite number of gradations. Thus, if a pressed phonation is changed along this dimension, it does not necessarily mean that phonation becomes breathy. Instead, it means only that phonation becomes *less* pressed. Second, if voice source A has a stronger fundamental than voice source B, one cannot infer that source A uses flow phonation while source B uses pressed phonation. The amplitude of the glottogram pulses must depend not only on the adducting forces but also on the glottal dimensions. Longer vocal folds will yield a longer glottis, presumably yielding higher glottogram pulses than a shorter glottis, other things being equal, simply because the glottis area is greater. Therefore, it is difficult to compare different voices in this respect. But if the *same voice* pronounces two vowel sounds with identical formant frequencies and with differing amplitude of the fundamental, we would infer that phonation was closer to the pressed extreme when the vowel with the weaker fundamental was pronounced.

It is also important to stress that the amplitude of the voice source fundamental is not equal to the amplitude of the fundamental of the spectrum radiated from the lip opening. It will be recalled that the spectrum radiated from the lip opening depends not only on the source spectrum but also on the modifications of this spectrum due to the sound transfer characteristics of the vocal tract, which can be described in terms of the formant frequencies. Moreover, the amplitudes of the individual spectrum partials also depend on the fundamental frequency. For this reason, we have always to take into account the formant frequencies and the pitch when we compare two spectra differing, for example, with respect to the amplitude of the fundamental. The source spectrum can be blamed for such a difference between two vowel spectra only if the formant frequencies and the pitch are identical in the two spectra. Interestingly, voice experts seem to distinguish readily between source characteristics and vocal tract transfer characteristics—in other words, between phonation and articulation; voice pedagogues and therapists seem to know whether it is articulation or phonation that needs improvement. What is more remarkable, some voice researchers have *failed* to make the distinction between phonation and articulation when they investigate spectral differences between various phonation types.

Let us now take a look at research results on the voice source regarding the amplitude of the flow glottogram and the closing rate, the two acoustically most relevant glottogram characteristics. The reader will note that the information is incomplete, primarily because the inverse filter technique has been a useful research tool for a rather short time.

Figure 4.17 gives an idea of how the voice source tends to vary with

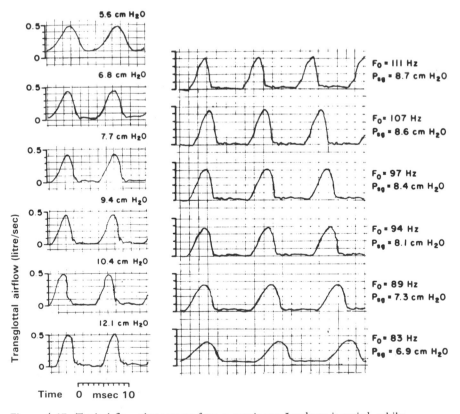

Figure 4.17. Typical flow glottograms from a nonsinger. Loudness is varied, while phonation frequency (F_o) is rather constant in the left series and vice versa in the right series. The numbers above each curve refer to subglottic pressure (P_{sg}). (From Rothenberg, 1973.)

phonation frequency and subglottic pressure under normal phonatory conditions in a nonsinger's voice. The right graphs in figure 4.17 show flow glottograms for various phonation frequencies within a typical male speaking range produced at approximately the same subglottic pressure. We observe that a glottal leakage appears when this subject lowers his phonation frequency far below what he typically uses in normal speech; the glottal airflow does not go down to zero during the quasi-closed phase because some portion of the glottis never closes. The amplitude reaches its maximum value at a phonation frequency of 107 Hz, and it decreases clearly toward lower frequencies. The closing rate seems to increase with rising phonation frequency.

The left graphs in the same figure show a series of flow glottograms where phonation frequency was kept approximately constant while subglottic pressure was varied. We can see that glottal leakage arises also under conditions of very low subglottic pressures; the airflow in these flow glottograms never reaches the zero line. The amplitude is kept reasonably constant until the subglottic pressure is reduced to a value as low as 4 cm H_2O. Then the amplitude is decreased. What really changes is the closing rate which increases with rising subglottic pressure. Subglottic pressure controls loudness of phonation and hence sound level, which depends on the closing rate.

The left series of graphs in figure 4.18 shows flow glottograms for phonations at very low subglottic pressures. The middle graph is an example of a flow glottogram for vocal fry phonation typically occurring when subglottic pressure is very low; the pulses do not appear at equal time intervals, so that every second pulse is sticking closely to its neighbor, so to speak. This effect is assumed to occur when the vocal folds vibrate out of phase with each other.

The right series of graphs in figure 4.18 illustrates the difference between normal and breathy phonation. The more the amplitude increases, the greater the glottal leakage. The physiological background of such a glottal leakage must be an abduction of the vocal folds, because a great flow glottogram amplitude would reflect a low degree of adduction force.

After this survey of flow glottograms of nonsingers, we will continue with a more detailed examination of how the two acoustically most relevant flow glottogram parameters vary under different conditions. Most of the data given will stem from the author's investigation with Gauffin (Sundberg and Gauffin, 1979; Gauffin and Sundberg, 1980).

Figure 4.19 gives a survey of how flow glottograms are affected by change of loudness (left series) and adduction force (right series). The figure also specifies the sound pressure level, the subglottic pressure, and an estimate of the maximum glottis area. For low pressures, the glottis is never closed. As loudness is increased, the closing rate increases and the closed phase becomes longer. When the adduction force is high as in pressed phonation, the glottogram amplitude becomes small, the closed phase long, subglottic pressure is high, sound level is low, and the glottal

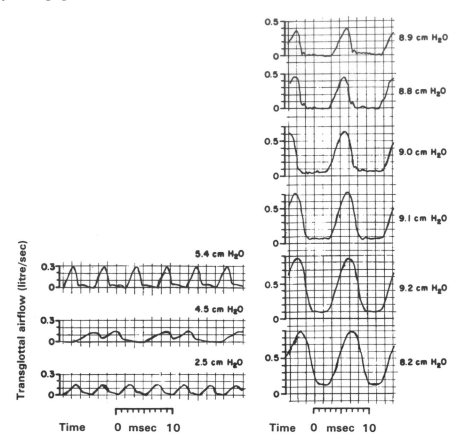

Figure 4.18. Flow glottograms obtained from a nonsinger. The left series shows examples of phonation at very low pressures given in cm H_2O; the middle curve represents vocal fry phonation. In the right series, the adduction force is varied: flow amplitude increases while subglottic pressure remains essentially constant. (From Rothenberg, 1973.)

area is small. In normal phonation the amplitude is higher, the closed phase shorter, pressure is lower, sound level higher, and glottal area wider. In flow phonation the amplitude is high, the closed phase long, pressure moderate, sound level high, and glottal area wide. In breathy phonation and, still more, in a slightly voiced whisper, the glottis never closes, so that airflow never reaches the zero-line, pressure and sound level are both low, and the glottal area is very wide.

After this overview we shall now examine how the two acoustically most relevant glottogram characteristics vary under different conditions. Most of what will be said stems from the author's investigations with Jan Gauffin.

Figure 4.20 shows how the maximum amplitude of the flow glottogram varies with the sound pressure level of the vowel /ae:/ in two male voices, one of them a professional singer, the other an untrained speaker. Each of the curves pertains to different phonation frequencies. We see that the

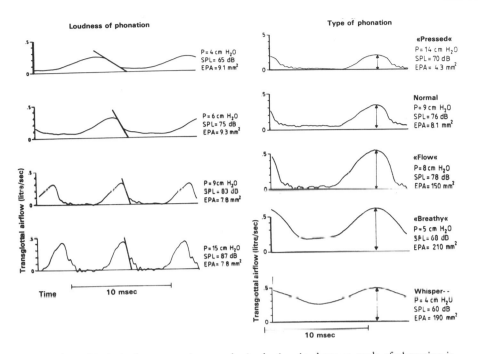

Figure 4.19. Typical glottogram changes obtained when loudness or mode of phonation is changed (left and right series). As loudness of phonation is raised, the closing part of the curve becomes more steep. When phonation is pressed, the glottogram amplitude is low, and it increases as adduction force is reduced. The least adducted, and yet not leaky, phonation is called flow phonation. To the right of the curves are given subglottic pressure (P), sound pressure level (SPL) at 0.5 m, and estimated glottal peak area (EPA). In pressed phonation pressure is high, flow amplitude low, and sound level low, while in flow phonation pressure is moderate, flow amplitude is high, and sound level is high.

amplitude rises with the sound pressure level. We also observe that flow phonation and pressed phonation are characterized by great and small amplitudes as expected. Phonation in falsetto register shows a low sound pressure level compared with phonation in modal register.

Comparing the two voices, we observe that the overall slope of the data points for a given phonation frequency differs. The thin reference line represents the slope to which the curves would adhere if the sound pressure level and the flow glottogram amplitude were to grow at the same rate; to take a concrete example, the line represents a 10 dB increase in sound pressure level associated with a 10 dB increase in the glottogram amplitude. The figure reveals a clear difference between these voices. When the singer increases loudness of phonation, his glottal airflow increases at the same rate as does the sound pressure level; for each phonation frequency curve, the slope is similar to that of the thin reference line. When the untrained voice performs the same maneuver, his flow glottogram amplitude increases *less* than the sound pressure level. This is not astonishing. It merely implies that the nonsinger's phonation changed toward pressed phonation as he increased loudness.

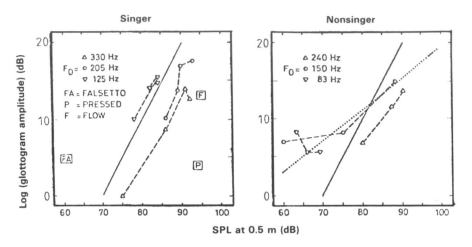

Figure 4.20. Peak amplitude of flow glottograms of a professional singer and an untrained speaker singing the vowel /ae:/ with different loudnesses at a high, a low, and a middle fundamental frequency (F_0). The dashed lines connect adjacent degrees of loudness. The thin solid line is a reference representing the case in which the amplitude of the glottogram increases at the same rate as the sound level. FA, P, and F pertain to falsetto register phonation, pressed phonation, and what the singer called "darkened" phonation, respectively. Pressed phonation is characterized by a very low peak amplitude of the glottogram. (After Sundberg and Gauffin, 1979.)

These results may be typical for male singers and nonsingers; at least the results appear familiar. In untrained voices loud phonation is often more tense than phonation at normal intensities, or, to put it differently, non-singers tend to scream when they phonate very loudly. The habit of changing phonation toward the pressed extreme as loudness is raised can hardly be acceptable in professional singers, who must be capable of singing loudly without necessarily changing phonation mode.

Note also that the singer did not make use of the softest sound pressure levels, produced by the untrained subject. The *piano* of the singer corresponded to a minimum sound pressure level of 75 dB (1/2 m from the mouth in an anechoic chamber) while the untrained voice phonated at sound pressure levels as low as 60 dB. It is also noteworthy that there is no dramatic difference between the two voices regarding their maximum sound pressure level. The untrained voice reaches 90 dB, and the professional singer, 93 dB. What makes the professional singer's voice easier to discern against a loud background sound (an orchestra, for instance) is largely a matter of articulation rather than of voice source, as we will see in the next chapter.

In figure 4.21 the same flow glottogram amplitudes are plotted against phonation frequency while loudness of phonation is the parameter. There is really no military order in the plot; the curves pertaining to the various degrees of vocal effort cross each other. A tone sung in *mezzopiano* may possess a greater flow glottogram amplitude than a tone sung more loudly. As a rule, however, an increase in the intensity of phonation is associated with an

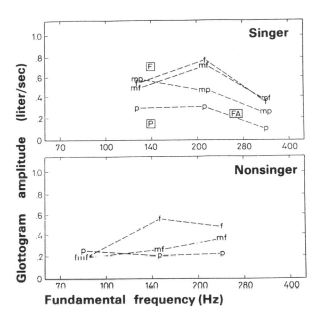

Figure 4.21. The same data as in figure 4.20 plotted against phonation frequency with loudness as the parameter; p = piano, mp = mezzopiano, mf = mezzoforte, f = forte. The range of glottogram amplitude variation is smaller toward the extremes of the subjects' ranges. (From Sundberg and Gauffin, 1979.)

increase in the flow glottogram amplitude. In loud phonation both voices show the greatest flow glottogram amplitude in the middle of their phonation frequency range. This seems to be typical, at least for male voices; it was observed in a number of differing voices. We might speculate about what this means. It is possible that a voice is most remote from the pressed phonation extreme when phonation is loud and neither very high or very low in phonation frequency. If this is correct, it may be of pedagogical interest. It would be a good idea to start with phonation in this nonpressed range and then ask the subject to change phonation frequency without changing the mode of phonation.

We have examined above how the amplitude of the flow glottogram varies in a singer and a nonsinger under various phonatory conditions. Let us now turn to the other acoustically important characteristic of the flow glottogram, namely the closing rate.

Figure 4.22 presents closing rate data from a singer and a nonsinger. The data have been arranged as a function of phonation frequency. Falsetto register and pressed phonation are associated with rather moderate closing rates. We also observe that the curve for the loudest note performed by the untrained voice drops in passing from the middle to the top pitch, but this is not the case for the singer. Pressed phonation is characterized by a low closing rate. As we saw before, the untrained subject lost a bit of his flow glottogram amplitude for his loudest notes, so that we could infer that he phonated these notes in a more pressed mode of phonation than the singer. Thus, it seems likely that the drop in the curve for the top pitch of the untrained subject is a consequence of a shift of phonation toward the pressed extreme.

We observed above that singing in the falsetto register causes a lower

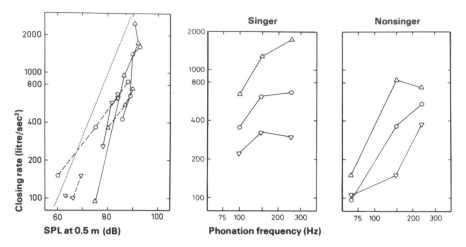

Figure 4.22. Peak amplitude of the differentiated flow glottogram for a singer and a nonsinger. Left graph: The data are shown as a function of sound level, the pitch being the parameter (triangles pointing downward = low; circles = medium; and triangles pointing upward = high pitch: solid line = singer, dashed line = nonsinger). Middle and right graphs: The data are shown as a function of phonation frequency with the loudness of phonation as the parameter (triangles pointing downward = p; squares = mp; circles = mf; and triangles pointing upward = f). Phonation in the modal and falsetto registers is indicated.

closing rate and a higher flow glottogram amplitude than in the modal register. Figure 4.23 compares flow glottograms for falsetto and modal register phonation in three singers. A great intersubject variability can be observed; the flow glottograms for the modal and falsetto registers differ considerably between the subjects. However, in the modal register, all flow glottograms show a reasonably clear closed phase (disregarding the ripple due to a failing cancellation of higher formants), while in the falsetto register, the flow glottograms show a smoother or more nearly sinusoidal

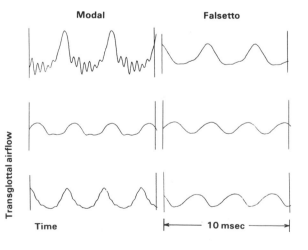

Figure 4.23. Flow glottograms for falsetto and modal register phonation in three singers. The ripple in the glottogram is an artifact. In spite of a great intersubject variability, it can be seen that the glottogram pulses are narrower and the curves switch more abruptly from closing phase to closed phase in modal register.

waveform. The spectral correlate of this flow glottogram difference was found in the dominance of the voice source fundamental. In falsetto register phonation, the amplitude difference between the first and the second partial was much smaller than in modal register phonation. This was true for all of these three voices, even though the magnitude of this difference varied between subjects.

It should also be stressed that falsetto singing seems to include a great variability regarding the voice source. A clear discontinuity indicating a quasi-closed phase can sometimes be observed in flow glottograms of falsetto phonation; this is the case with the top and bottom glottograms in figure 4.23. Therefore, the amplitude of the voice source fundamental in relation to the overtones seems to distinguish the voice source in these two registers.

The closing rate is a highly relevant characteristic of the flow glottogram as it determines the sound level of the vowel and hence reflects loudness of phonation. It is determined mainly by subglottic pressure but is also affected by such factors as mode of phonation and register. Actually, it is being regularly mapped in some phoniatric clinics, but not in its original form. Rather, it is the maximum and minimum sound level that is being measured at different fundamental frequencies. The graphs thus obtained are called *phonetograms,* and these have been found to be useful descriptions of the phonatory status of voices (Schutte, 1980). It should be observed that a phonetogram is closely related to, but not identical with, a graph of closing rate versus fundamental frequency. It will be recalled that the sound level of a vowel is also influenced by the frequency distance between the first formant and the partial lying closest to it. Also, it is influenced by the frequency of the first formant *per se.* Therefore, a phonetogram offers information on the voice source only if the formant frequencies were kept the same throughout, regardless of pitch and loudness. Moreover, the important aspect of phonation mode is not accounted for. On the other hand, it is much easier to obtain a phonetogram than flow glottograms.

Theoretical Models of the Voice Source

The waveform and the spectrum of the voice source are closely interrelated, as we have seen quite clearly in the present chapter. Given a few flow glottogram parameters, we can predict certain voice source spectrum characteristics, and inversely, we can make inferences as to the flow glottogram from spectra, provided that the formant frequencies are the same. As the spectrum is relevant to the timbre, the last mentioned connection is interesting. If our ears tell us that a particular voice has a weak fundamental and loud high frequency overtones, we could infer that the underlying voice source is characterized by a flow glottogram having a low peak amplitude and a high closing rate. Probably this is the type of unconscious analysis that voice teachers make when they determine the problems of a voice needing improvement.

Another interesting aspect of the voice source, not least from a pedagogical point of view, is the physiology behind these flow glottogram and spectrum characteristics. To take a concrete example, how does a contraction of the vocalis muscles affect the voice source?

It is not easy to find the answer to such a question. If we ask a subject to increase the contraction of his vocalis muscles while keeping the contraction of all other muscles constant, the subject will not obey. All laryngeal muscles are closely interrelated, and we cannot normally control the activity in a specific muscle. Therefore, in order to explore the influence of a particular muscle on the voice source characteristics, it is necessary to construct models of the vocal folds.

Two important theoretical models of the vocal folds have been made, one by Ishizaka and Flanagan (1972) and the other by Titze (1973, 1974). The latter is more detailed since the vocal fold is represented by no less than 16 mass elements, each of which corresponds to a portion of the vocal fold. Figure 4.24 shows results from a further development of Titze's model (Titze and Talkin, 1979). It shows the effects on the flow glottogram of changes in certain laryngeal control parameters. The parameter labeled "glottal width" is the separation of the vocal folds in the absence of a transglottal airstream; apparently, it is closely related to abduction and adduction. It affects the flow glottogram amplitude, so it would be related to the pressed-flow-breathy dimension in our terminology. The "ligament parameter" in Titze's model leads to similar flow glottogram consequences, but it also influences phonation frequency. The vocalis parameter also affects phonation frequency, but it primarily concerns the length of the closed phase.

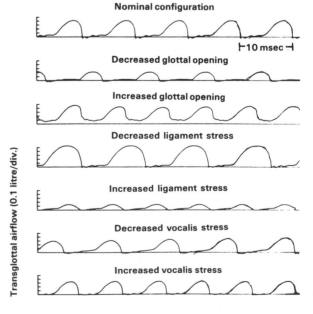

Figure 4.24. Glottograms derived from Titze's theoretical model of the vocal fold mechanism showing the effect of varying different glottal control parameters. "Glottal width" is the separation of the vocal folds in the absence of a transglottal airstream and, hence, apparently corresponds to degree of glottal adduction. (After Titze and Talkin, 1979.)

Much work with models remains before we have arrived at a clear picture of how the various laryngeal muscles interact and how they affect phonation and determine different voice source parameters. And of course, the realism of the model and of the values inserted into it is decisive for the accuracy of the results. Still, theoretical models are indispensable for developing theories that describe reality, particularly when reality is as complex as in phonation.

Voice Source and Vocal Tract

In the present chapter we have regarded the voice source as a fully autonomous system. This is not entirely true, though; a change in an articulatory parameter, which really should influence only the vocal tract shape, and hence the formant frequencies, may sometimes affect the voice source as well. Singers often experience difficulties in the continuity of phonation; the voice timbre changes automatically, as it were, just because the pitch or the vowel is changed, or, in other words, just because the frequency relationship between the fundamental and the formants changed.

It is not only the vocal tract that may disturb phonation; resonance phenomena in the subglottal airways may also have this effect. The lowest resonance in the audible range occurs near 600 Hz in adults. It is tempting to speculate that registers are in fact a glottal response to this subglottal resonance. In male voices the register transition between modal and falsetto registers occurs at about half that frequency, or 300 Hz. This is not very different from the region of the female transition from chest to mid register. The dimensions of the vocal folds and the vocal tracts differ considerably, while the difference in the frequency of the lowest subglottal resonance is much smaller. Recently Titze (1983) presented theoretical evidence supporting the assumption that subglottal resonances give rise to register phenomena.

It was mentioned in the preceding chapter that different singers use different breathing techniques during singing. For example, some singers use their diaphragm only during inspiration and for the purpose of rapidly reducing subglottic pressure at high lung volumes, while others contract it throughout the phrase.

Together with co-workers, this author investigated to what extent these different breathing strategies had any clear effects on the voice source (Leanderson et al., 1987). Five nonsingers and two singers performed pitch changes with and without a contraction of the diaphragm. This was feasible by displaying the transdiaphragmatic pressure on an oscilloscope screen in front of the subject: the oscilloscope beam moved as soon as the subject contracted the diaphragm.

The voice source, analyzed by means of inverse filtering, was then compared for the two conditions. The results showed no behavior that was shared by all subjects. For all subjects except one (a clarinet player) the flow glottogram amplitude was higher under conditions of diaphragm activation. This suggests that phonation was changed away from the pressed extreme in this case. Also, most subjects showed a trend to a longer closed phase and a more stable articulation when they contracted their diaphragm during phonation. These results suggest that breathing strategy tends to influence the voice source and also articulation.

Before leaving the voice source it is pertinent to mention that a change in a voice source property is often associated with a change in the articulatory system. Good examples of such interactions are offered by Estill (Estill et al., 1983), where the relevance of voice source characteristics to various singing styles is also described. Another example is the fact that pressed phonation seems affiliated with a raised larynx position (Sundberg and Askenfelt, 1983). Of course, such interactions do not decrease the importance of separating phonation from articulation in describing voice function.

It should also be pointed out that much of what has been said about the voice source in this chapter is rather recent knowledge, and a reservation is in order as to how much we should generalize from the results, in particular from those derived from the study of only one or two subjects. Much relevant knowledge is lacking. For instance, what are the voice source characteristics of female voices, and what typically distinguishes male from female voices? Do registers originate from physiological or acoustic phenomena, or both? Let us hope that the answers to these and many other open questions regarding the voice source will appear in the near future. In any case, several of them are certainly within reach, thanks to the modern inverse filtering technique and the development of vocal fold models.

Articulation

Articulation is the name for the maneuvers made in order to adjust the shape of the vocal tract during phonation. This is achieved by means of the articulators: the lips, the tongue, the jaw, the velum, and the larynx. A given configuration of articulator positions defines the area function corresponding to a specific shape of the vocal tract. The shape can be described by an area function, which is a diagram showing how the cross sectional area of the vocal tract varies along the longitudinal axis of the vocal tract as a function of the distance to the glottis. This area function determines the sound transfer ability of the vocal tract, which can be specified in terms of a transfer function, a diagram displaying this ability as a function of the frequency of the sound to be transferred. Figure 5.1 gives a simple example. Those frequencies most easily transferred by the vocal tract are called the formant frequencies. Those partials in the spectrum of the voice source, which are closest to a formant in frequency, are radiated from the lip opening with a greater amplitude than other partials. We repeat these facts here because this chapter will deal quite a lot with formants and factors influencing them.

Ultimately, the transfer function depends on articulation, because it is articulation that determines the frequencies of the formants, and once those are given, the entire transfer function curve is more or less defined. In other words, a given combination of formant frequencies is associated with one

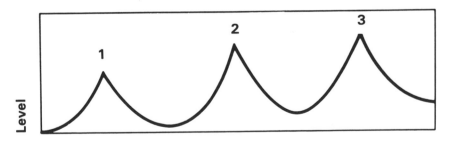

Figure 5.1. Example of a transfer function for a neutral vowel. The peaks represent the formants.

and only one transfer function (we disregard for the moment the details of the curve close to the formant frequencies).

The way in which the formant frequencies determine the transfer function is described by the theory of the sound transfer in the vocal tract resonator (Fant, 1960) and is illustrated schematically in figure 5.2. That figure also illustrates how the transfer function and other relevant factors contribute to determining the spectrum envelope.

The top graph shows the contributions of two factors to the spectrum envelope. One is the voice source spectrum (S) sloping about 12 dB/octave. The other is a correction (HP) implying that the amplitudes of the spectrum

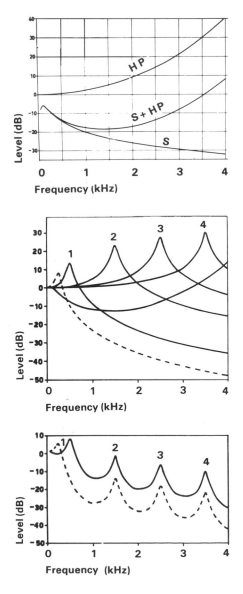

Figure 5.2. Schematic illustration of the factors contributing to the spectrum envelope of voice sounds. Top graph: Factors that do not depend on the vowel. HP is the influence of higher poles, or vocal tract resonances, above 4 kHz; S is the source spectrum slope complemented by +6 dB/octave, taking into account that pressure rather than flow is measured; S + HP is the sum of these factors. Middle graph: Contributions to the sound transfer characteristics from the formants. For the first formant two different frequencies are shown, 250 Hz and 500 Hz (dashed and solid curves). Bottom graph: Resulting spectrum envelopes. The dashed and solid curves refer to the cases in which the first formant frequency is at 250 and 500 Hz. (From Fant, 1960.)

partials are increased as a function of frequency. This correction depends on the sound radiation characteristics of the lip opening and on the higher formants not included in the figure. The curve (S+HP) represents the summed effect of these two factors.

The middle panel in figure 5.2 shows the same (S+HP) curve plus the sound transfer curves for some formants. Each formant gives a contribution of its own to the total sound transfer function. The contribution can be said to be similar for all formants, provided first that we disregard the frequency region closest to the formants, and second that we measure amplitude and frequency in logarithmic units. At every frequency, the resulting transfer function can be seen as the sum of the contributions from each formant's transfer curve at that frequency. Thus, by adding up the values indicated by the individual solid curves at each frequency in the middle graph of figure 5.2, one obtains the transfer function, and by adding the (S+HP) curve to this transfer function one obtains the spectrum envelope shown as the solid curve in the righthand graph of the same figure.

The formant frequencies in the middle panel are at 500 Hz, 1,500 Hz, 2,500 Hz, and 3,500 Hz. The dashed curve in the middle panel shows the case that the first formant is one octave lower, or 250 Hz. Its contribution is greater at low frequencies and smaller at high frequencies so that the spectrum envelope is lowered by more than 10 dB above the first formant frequency, as can be seen in the bottom graph. Such a change in a formant frequency thus affects the *entire* spectrum at low as well as at high frequencies.

It was mentioned that the transfer function at and between two formants increases if the formants approach each other in frequency. If the distance is halved, the sound transfer ability is raised by 6 dB at the formant frequencies and 12 dB midway between them. Actually this is merely the inversion of what was just said; the formants help each other if they come closer in frequency, so to speak. This is of great significance in opera singing, as we will see later.

It should also be stressed here that the ability of the lip opening to radiate sound is *not* dependent on the lip opening area: the voice organ does not produce more sound energy just because the mouth opening is widened. The only effect is that the formant frequencies are changed, and that may affect the sound level to some moderate extent.

Formants and Articulation

How can one determine the articulatory changes necessary to change the frequency of a given formant in a specific way or to determine the formant frequency consequences of a shift in the positioning of one specific articulator? It would not be a good idea to ask a subject to move one articulator and try to keep all other articulators constant, because the subject has no possibility of obeying: we do not have that kind of command over articulation. If we move one articulator, we can take it for granted that all others will move as well. The situation is similar to the one we just met in dealing with the glottal control muscles: they all tend to act together. Also, our awareness of our articulatory activities is generally low. We think of articulation in terms of the sounds we produce rather than in terms of positioning articulators.

A better way to gain insight into these matters is to construct a theoretical model of the articulatory system. A couple of such models have been constructed, and we will briefly review one of them here (Lindblom and Sundberg, 1971).

The Lindblom and Sundberg model was based on measurements on lateral X-ray pictures of a subject pronouncing various long vowels. It included five articulators: jaw, tongue body, tongue tip, lips, and larynx.

All these articulators move according to certain patterns. For instance, if the *jaw opening* is increased, the lower jaw is moved slightly posteriorly, so that the distance from the jaw to the cervical vertebrae is somewhat reduced. This means that an increase of the jaw opening will result not only in a widening of the mouth but also in a narrowing of the pharynx.

If the behavior of the *tongue body* is studied using the mandible as the reference, as in figure 5.3, one can see that many vowels are produced with very similar tongue body contours. The tongue body contour for the vowel /i:/ is almost identical with that used for a great number of other vowels, and the tongue contour for the vowel /ɑ:/ is similar to that in the vowel /o:/. The tongue contour used for the vowel in the (German) /u:/, on the other hand, is not used for any other long (Swedish) vowel.

From figure 5.3 we conclude that the tongue contour may assume very

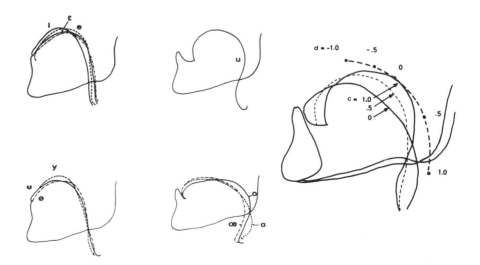

Figure 5.3. Mid-sagittal contours of the tongue body for the vowels indicated, using the contour of the lower mandible as reference. Many vowels are produced with a frontal positioning of the tongue body. The righthand contours illustrate the system used for describing tongue contours in the Lindblom and Sundberg articulatory model: c is the parameter describing the degree of bulging, and d is the parameter describing the direction of bulging. (From Lindblom and Sundberg, 1971.)

different shapes; it may bulge in various directions—such as toward the hard palate, toward the velum, and toward the back pharynx wall—and this bulging may be slight or extreme. This means that tongue shapes must be described by two parameters at least, one specifying the *direction* of the bulging, and the other specifying the *quantity* of this bulging, or in other words, to what extent the tongue is bulging in that direction. These parameters are given in numbers. Thus, direction -1 means "toward the hard palate," as for the vowel /i:/; direction 0 means "toward the velum," as in the vowel /u:/; and direction $+1$ means "toward the lower part of the posterior pharyngeal wall," as in the vowel in /ɑ:/. When the quantity parameter is 1, the degree of bulging is the same as that used for a normal pronunciation of the vowels in /i:/, /u:/, and /ɑ:/. The value of 0 refers to a neutral tongue, which does not bulge at all. With intermediate values of the direction and quantity parameters, intermediate tongue shapes could be described.

The orientation of the *tongue tip* did not vary appreciably between the different vowels included in the investigation. In most vowels it was lying quite passively, just behind the lower incisors. One exception to this was the articulation of the vowel /u:/, where it was retracted, as can be seen in the figure. If the tongue tip seems a bit lazy in the production of long, steady vowels, it makes up for it in consonant articulation. Several consonants require complete or almost complete contact between the tongue tip and the hard palate. Thus, the tongue tip can be lifted upward, but it can also be moved anteriorly and posteriorly.

The *lip opening* is of course mainly dependent on the jaw opening: it generally means hard articulatory work to combine a small lip opening with a wide jaw opening or the reverse. However, the lip opening can be rounded and spread (advanced and retracted mouth corners). The interdependence between the jaw opening and the distance between the mouth corners under neutral conditions, that is neither rounded nor spread, is illustrated in figure 5.4. It is not astonishing that, under neutral conditions, the distance between the upper and lower lips is dependent on the distance between the mouth corners.

The *larynx* can be raised and lowered. In normal speech, the larynx height varies depending on the sounds pronounced. For instance, different vowels are often associated with different larynx positions. The main rule seems to be that the larynx is raised in vowels pronounced with spread lips, such as /i/, and lowered for vowels pronounced with rounded lips, such as /u:/. It seems that our brain-computer is rather competent in dealing with acoustic theory of voice production; it understands, as it were, that the acoustic effect achieved by a change in the position of the mouth corners is very similar to that obtained from a shift in the vertical position of the larynx, or in other words, that if a retraction of the mouth corners is combined with a raising of the larynx, the lip rounding does not need to be very drastic.

In normal speech, the vertical larynx position also varies with phonation frequency; the higher the frequency, the higher the larynx. Indeed, this

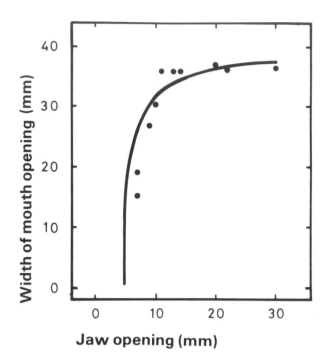

Figure 5.4. Dependence of width of the lip opening on the jaw opening under conditions of neutral (neither spread nor rounded) lips. The dots show measured data; the line is an approximation. (From Lindblom and Sundberg, 1971.)

interrelation has been used for measuring fundamental frequency in speakers; rather than measuring the frequency, which is sometimes a complicated task, one determines the vertical larynx position. The interrelation is illustrated in figure 5.5, which is taken from an investigation of male voices by Shipp and Izdebski (1975). Looking at the left graph we can see that untrained voices behave very differently, but still all subjects raise their larynx somewhat with rising phonation frequency up to 200 Hz,

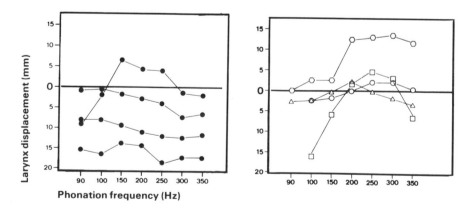

Figure 5.5. Relative vertical larynx position as compared with rest position (0mm) in male singers (left) and nonsingers (right) as a function of phonation frequency. In most singers, the larynx descends slightly with rising pitch, while nonsingers' larynxes tend to rise somewhat. (From Shipp and Izdebski, 1975.)

which corresponds to the entire phonation frequency range used in normal speech. Above this frequency, the subjects behave in different ways. Data for professional singers are shown in the right panel of the same figure. Here the picture looks quite different. The general trend is that the larynx is lowered with rising phonation frequency. We will return to the question of larynx positioning in singers later in this chapter.

After this digression, let us return to the Lindblom and Sundberg articulatory model. As all articulatory parameters were quantified in that model, articulatory configurations that were intermediate to those represented in the X-ray material could be computed. Articulatory configurations of the vocal tract can be converted into area functions; given the position of the articulator contours, the cross-sectional area can be estimated with a fair degree of accuracy. The formant frequencies corresponding to a given area function can be measured, if it is modeled in terms of an acoustic tube resonator. In this way, the formant frequencies associated with any articulatory configuration can be mapped; and the formant frequency effect of a manipulation of one articulatory parameter at a time can be explored, as was done with this model.

Results are shown in figures 5.6, 5.7, and 5.8. From figure 5.6 we can see where the formant frequencies go when the jaw opening is varied. Notice that the first formant is the only one that consistently moves in only one direction, when the jaw opening is increased. It seems that the jaw opening is a very efficient tool to use in order to change the frequency of the first formant. Notice in figures 5.7 and 5.8 that the second formant frequency changes quite considerably when the shape of the tongue body is changed, regardless of whether the direction parameter or the quantity parameter is varied. Consequently, the tongue body shape can be regarded as an articulator that is especially efficient for manipulating the second formant frequency.

From figures 5.6 through 5.8, we may also observe that a rounding of the lips always lowers all formant frequencies more or less. Although not illustrated in these figures, the same is true for a lowering of the larynx. Part of the explanation for this effect of a rounding of the lips is that it lengthens the vocal tract; long tubes have low resonance frequencies. The reader who does not realize the truth of this statement should spend a moment of contemplation in front of an organ prospect: long pipes are needed for low frequencies.

It is a well-known fact that one can speak clearly even if the jaw opening is kept constant, as when a person speaks with a pipe between the teeth. On the other hand, the articulatory model considered here regards the jaw opening as an articulator of great importance both for the lip opening and for handling the first formant frequency.

How does this match the case of the man speaking intelligibly with a pipe between his teeth? Experiments have shown that the formant frequencies produced under such conditions are about the same as those that are pronounced normally. This appears to prove that the jaw opening is irrelevant to the formant frequencies. However, it turns out that we are very

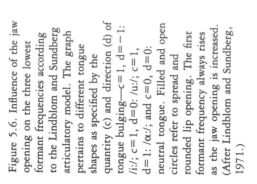

Figure 5.6. Influence of the jaw opening on the three lowest formant frequencies according to the Lindblom and Sundberg articulatory model. The graph pertains to different tongue shapes as specified by the quantity (c) and direction (d) of tongue bulging—c=1, d=−1: /i:/; c=1, d=0: /u:/; c=1, d=1: /ɑ:/; and c=0, d=0: neutral tongue. Filled and open circles refer to spread and rounded lip opening. The first formant frequency always rises as the jaw opening is increased. (After Lindblom and Sundberg, 1971.)

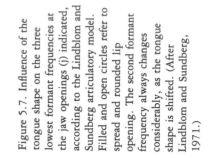

Figure 5.7. Influence of the tongue shape on the three lowest formant frequencies at the jaw openings (j) indicated, according to the Lindblom and Sundberg articulatory model. Filled and open circles refer to spread and rounded lip opening. The second formant frequency always changes considerably, as the tongue shape is shifted. (After Lindblom and Sundberg, 1971.)

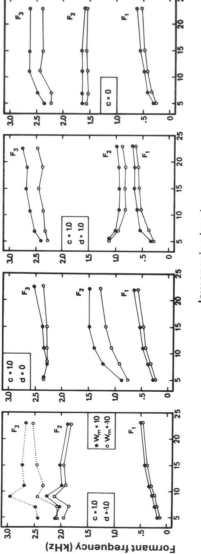

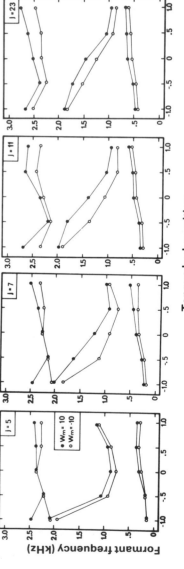

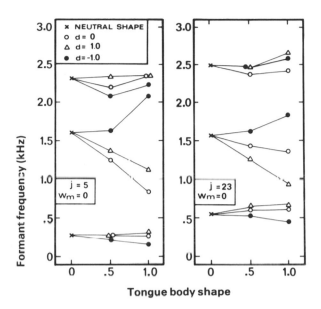

Figure 5.8. Influence of the degree of tongue bulging (d) on the three lowest formant frequencies for three tongue shapes articulated with two jaw openings (j) according to the Lindblom and Sundberg articulatory model. In the graphs the lefthand values refer to a neutral tongue, and the righthand values refer to a fully bulging tongue shape, as in normal articulation of sustained vowels. The second formant frequency always changes considerably, as the tongue shape is shifted. (After Lindblom and Sundberg, 1971.)

skilled in adjusting the vocal tract to that area function which is needed in order to produce the intended combination of formant frequencies. When the jaw is prevented from moving freely, its articulatory work is taken over by another articulator, such as the tongue. Thus, if the jaw does not help the tongue to a frontal position as for the pronunciation of the vowel /i:/, then the tongue simply moves further away than normal from the neutral position (the quantity parameter of the model would then exceed the value of 1.0). The remarkable thing is that we seem to know exactly how much compensation is needed for a failing jaw, even in situations we have never experienced before. It seems that we take in a good deal of help from tactile feedback (we can feel where the tongue is on the palate) under these conditions. From this fact we can draw the important conclusion that the jaw opening is not the *only* means by which the frequency of the first formant is tuned.

The fourth formant is highly relevant to the voice timbre, or, in other words, to the personal component in the sound of the voice. Two factors are particularly important to the frequency of this formant: the vocal tract length and the vocal tract dimensions within and around the larynx tube. Whether one or both of these factors are relevant to a given area function depends on the cross-sectional area of the lower part of the pharynx. If the pharyngeal cross-sectional area is considerably wider (more than 6 times) than the cross-sectional area of the larynx tube opening, then the fourth formant frequency is almost exclusively determined by the area function in the larynx tube, particularly the volume of the laryngeal ventricle which is the cavity located between the vocal folds and the ventricular bands. If the larynx ventricle is appropriately expanded, the fourth formant frequency drops. If, on the other hand, the larynx tube opening is not considerably narrower than the pharynx width, the fourth formant frequency is dependent both on the vocal tract length and the larynx tube configuration (Sundberg, 1974).

Formant Frequencies in Men, Women, and Children

Men, women, and children generally differ with respect to average vocal tract length, which is significant for the formant frequencies, as we know. For this reason, the same vowel is usually represented by different formant frequencies in men, women, and children. Figure 5.9 shows male and female averages for the two lowest formant frequencies, which are decisive to vowel quality. It can be seen in the figure that in most of the small vowel islands the female values are pretty close to the periphery while the male values are closer to the center of the plot. This means that for a given vowel the average male formant frequencies are higher than the average female formant frequencies.

In the same figure, average formant frequency differences between male and female adults are expressed as the percentages by which the three lowest formant frequencies of a given vowel in female adults exceed those in male adults (Fant, 1975). The differences are substantial, and they vary considerably between vowels, particularly for the lowest two formants. On the other hand, these percentage differences occur similarly in various languages. The first formant frequency shows a maximum percentage difference in the open /a:/ vowel of the Italian word *caro*. The second formant frequency shows high values for all front vowels. The difference, averaged over the entire set of vowels, amounts to 12%, 17%, and 18% for the three lowest formants. Children's average formant frequencies are about 20% higher than those for female adults, or 32%, 37%, and 38% higher than those of male adults. Probably most of these differences are due to inequalities in the vocal tract dimensions between the various groups of speakers. Thus, younger children tend to have higher formant frequencies than older children because of their shorter vocal tracts.

If the proportions of the average female and male vocal tracts are compared, one finds that the female vocal tract is not merely a small-scale version of the male vocal tract. According to Nordström (1977), the average mouth length of a female adult is about 85% of that of the average male adult, while the female pharynx length is only 77% of the corresponding male value. In other words, the average female pharynx is much shorter than the average male pharynx, while the average difference is smaller with regard to the mouth.

If one computes the formant frequency differences that would result from these dissimilarities in the mouth and pharynx proportions between adult males and females, one finds a discrepancy between prediction and reality; the differences that have been found in the dimensions do not explain the actual formant frequency differences, according to Nordström (1977). The reason for this is not well understood. The existence of sex dialects, or "sexolects," cannot be excluded; it is possible that females and males use a slightly different articulation of some vowels. The reason may be hidden in

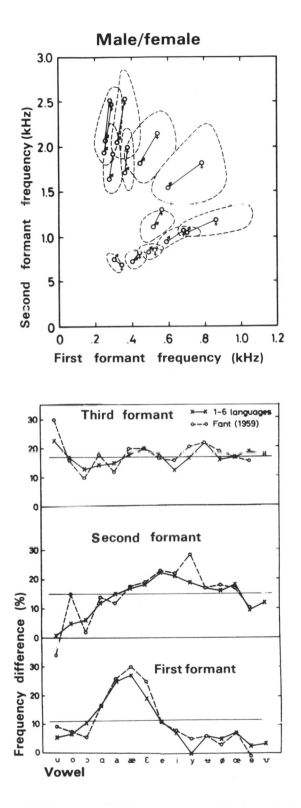

Figure 5.9. Formant frequency differences between adult male and female speakers. Upper graph: Averages for male and female speakers of the two lowest formant frequencies in the vowels indicated. The dashed contours represent the vowel "islands" shown in figure 2.12, p. 24. Lower graph: Differences for the three lowest formants expressed as percentages according to Fant (1973).

the largely unknown processes used by our sense of hearing and our brain in order to identify vowels. But it is also possible that our knowledge about the differences between the male and female vocal tracts is still not sufficiently detailed.

We correctly infer that the actual reasons for the formant frequency differences between children and adult males and females are not understood in every detail. However, it is also interesting to see to what extent the voice timbre differences between these groups of speakers can be accounted for by the formant frequency differences. Coleman (1976) has published an interesting investigation on this topic. In an experiment in which subjects tried to identify the sex of speakers by listening to the voice quality, he found that phonation frequency was a much more important factor than formant frequencies as illustrated in figure 5.10; the average of the three lowest formant frequencies showed little or no correlation with maleness and femaleness in voice timbre. The faint trace of a correlation that appears to exist between the average of the three lowest formant frequencies and the perceived maleness or femaleness was due to an equally low correlation between phonation frequency and this formant frequency average.

It may be important to these results that the three lowest formant frequencies were not separated but were converted into an average in this investigation. It is not clear whether such an average catches all of the timbral voice differences between the sexes, and it is also possible that the results would have come out differently if the fourth formant had been included in the average; the higher the formant frequency, the

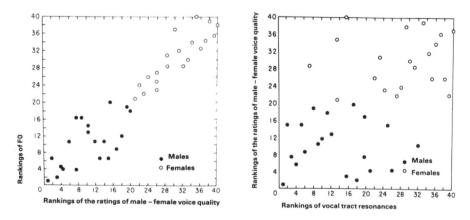

Figure 5.10. The relevance of phonation frequency and of the average of the three lowest formant frequencies to the femaleness in the voice timbre. The order between the points along the horizontal axis is the rank order between voice samples according to votes for femaleness, and the order along the vertical axis reflects the rank order according to phonation frequency. The right graph shows what happens if the average of the three lowest formant frequencies is substituted for the phonation frequency for the rank order along the vertical axis. Open and filled circles represent female and male voices. (From Coleman, 1976.)

more its frequency depends on nonarticulatory factors such as vocal tract length.

It seems clear that the perceptually most important difference in voice quality between the two sexes depends on phonation frequency rather than formant frequencies. The mean phonation frequency difference is almost one octave, which is much greater than the formant frequency difference. We realize that our brain is quite smart: it is more impressed by the great phonation frequency difference than by the small formant frequency difference when guessing the sex of a speaker.

This dominating role of phonation frequency regarding the maleness and femaleness in voice quality seems to complement experience. It is a common observation that the voice maleness disappears almost completely if a male speaker skillfully uses his falsetto register. For instance, the voice of a countertenor, who is a male singer singing alto parts, certainly sounds more female than male, although his vocal tract dimensions would offer him a male selection of formant frequencies. The voice source difference that has been observed between falsetto and modal register may very well add to the female voice timbre.

If we really want to find out the perceptual relevance of the formant frequency differences between male and female speakers, we have to eliminate the salient phonation frequency difference. This is sometimes possible using real speech, since some men speak with an unusually high phonation frequency, and some women speak with an exceptionally low phonation frequency. Thus, in real life, a difference in phonation frequency does not always exist between male and female speakers. If one compares such pairs of male and female voices, it is very difficult indeed to tell the speaker's sex by the voice quality. This supports the conclusion that the formant frequency differences between male and female voices contribute only to a very small extent to the perceived maleness or femaleness of the voice.

In singing, things appear to be a bit different. Even though many countertenors sound more similar to an alto than to a tenor, one generally can tell what the singer's sex is after having listened for a while. Moreover, a boy soprano generally sounds quite different from an adult female soprano. Finally, the voice timbre differences between a tenor and an alto remain considerable even when they sing in the same phonation frequency range.

This poses an interesting question. Do we find the same formant frequency differences between male and female singers as between the average male and female speaker? This question was investigated in a study using two tenors and two altos (Ågren and Sundberg, 1978). The singers sang the same song in the same phonation frequency range, so that the tenors sang in the high part of their range, and the altos sang in the low part of their range. The two parts of figure 5.11 show the formant frequencies in different ways. The left graph shows that the singer's two lowest formant frequencies lie outside the vowel islands that we have seen several times before, so we must infer that these islands do not encompass all the formant frequency combinations that give the vowel quality of the island. The right

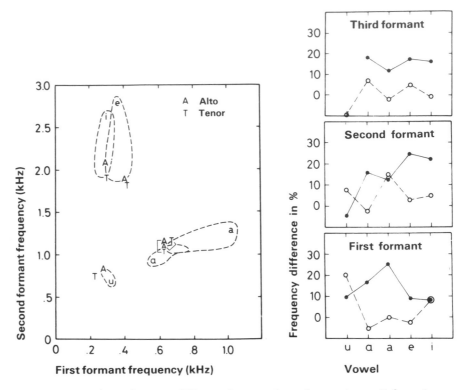

Figure 5.11. Formant frequency differences between alto and tenor singers. Left graph: Averages for the two lowest formant frequencies: the dashed contours represent the vowel "islands" shown in figure 2.12, p. 24. Right graph: Differences for the three lowest formants expressed as percentages. (From Ågren and Sundberg, 1976.)

graph indicates that these singers show no consistent, sex-dependent percentage differences for the three lowest formants. But if tenors and altos have basically similar formant frequencies and a partially similar phonation frequency range, what explains the considerable timbral differences between their voices?

One difference already mentioned is the voice source (see figure 4.11, p. 70). Another difference is in the fourth formant which was consistently higher in the altos than in the tenors, as can be seen in figure 5.12. As was just mentioned, the fourth formant is very dependent on the larynx tube dimensions. This tube is typically smaller in adult females than in adult males; the vocal folds constituting the bottom of the larynx tube are only 9 to 13 mm long in adult females but 15 to 20 mm long in adult males. If we assume that such larynx tube differences exist also between altos and tenors, it does not seem surprising that the fourth formant frequency was found to be higher in the altos than in the tenors. We will return to the lower formant frequencies in altos and tenors later. But now we will digress a little and speculate about the perceptual significance of the difference in the fourth formant.

It was mentioned in the beginning of this chapter that the ability of the

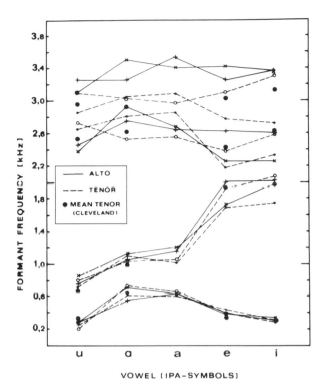

FORMANT FREQUENCY [kHz]

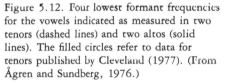

VOWEL [IPA-SYMBOLS]

Figure 5.12. Four lowest formant frequencies for the vowels indicated as measured in two tenors (dashed lines) and two altos (solid lines). The filled circles refer to data for tenors published by Cleveland (1977). (From Ågren and Sundberg, 1976.)

vocal tract to transfer sound is increased near and between two formants, if the frequency distance between these formants is decreased. Now, if altos and tenors have approximately the same frequency values for the three lowest formants, and if at the same time the fourth formant frequency is higher in altos than in tenors, it follows that the frequency distance between the third and fourth formants must be greater in altos. Consequently, the spectrum partials in the corresponding frequency region of 2.6 to 3.3 kHz must be stronger in tenors than in altos, provided that there is no typical voice source difference in this region.

The significance for voice timbre of this spectral difference between altos and tenors can be elucidated if we digress once more, this time in the direction of hearing theory. There are many timbral dimensions, that is, respects in which two tones having the same pitch and loudness may differ. A timbral dimension that seems particularly relevant to the timbre difference between tenors and altos has one extreme often referred to by words such as "soft" or "smooth." For the other extreme, "rough" or "harsh" is used.

According to Terhardt (1974), this timbral dimension depends on the amplitudes of the spectrum partials and the frequency distance between them. However, this distance should be measured on a special frequency scale, which is characteristic for our hearing system. This auditory frequency scale does not resemble any other frequency scale. For low frequencies, the scale is linear; it switches over to being logarithmic near 500 Hz.

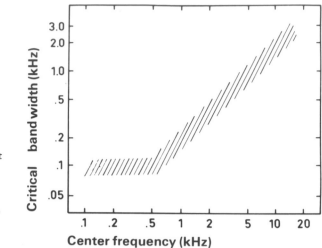

Figure 5.13. The critical band of hearing at various center frequencies. The critical bandwidth is about 100 Hz in the bass region, and above 500 Hz it is approximately 20% of the center frequency.

This means that one step, or unit, in this frequency scale of hearing corresponds to a given number of Hertz for low frequencies, but for higher frequencies it corresponds to a frequency ratio. Thus, both Hertz and semitone are inadequate as units. Instead, the unit is called a *critical band*. A critical band of hearing is thus a frequency band, the width of which varies over the frequency range we can hear. Figure 5.13 shows that the critical bandwidth is about 100 Hz in the bass region, and above 500 Hz, it is approximately 20% of the center frequency.

If two equally strong spectrum partials fall within the same critical band, it is virtually impossible for our hearing to single out either of them—to hear one of them as a sounding tone along with the other. The two tones have merged into an indissoluble unit. The condition for our ability to hear one of two equally strong spectrum partials as an individual tone is that they are separated by at least one critical band. The timbral effect of such a pair of spectrum partials is quite special. All pairs of partials that are similar in amplitude and separated by less than a critical band contribute to the roughness of the timbre. If the pair of partials is high in amplitude, the contribution is substantial.

Which are the spectrum partials that can contribute to roughness, then? If we spend a minute on this question and confine our thinking to the harmonic spectra occurring in voice sounds, we will arrive at a very simple answer. When the fundamental frequency is lower than 100 Hz, all pairs of adjacent spectrum partials are spaced by less than a critical band, so all of them may contribute to roughness. When the fundamental frequency is higher, only those pairs of partials may contribute to roughness, which are spaced by less than about 20% in frequency, or, to express it in musical intervals, a minor third. The frequency separation of the five lowest spectrum partials is greater than a minor third: if we let the partials be represented by their numbers in the harmonic series, the intervals between them are as follows:

Partials	Interval
1 and 2	Octave
2 and 3	Fifth
3 and 4	Fourth
4 and 5	Major third
5 and 6	Minor third

We note that the musical interval separating adjacent spectrum partials becomes increasingly narrow, the higher up in the spectrum we go. We also observe that all pairs of adjacent spectrum partials above the fourth partial may contribute to roughness, provided that the fundamental frequency is higher than 100 Hz.

Most of us would probably agree that male and female voice timbre differs with respect to roughness, among other things. The male voice sounds rough, sometimes even gurgling, when the fundamental frequency is sufficiently low—vocal fry is an extreme example. But if we think of the frequency range common to altos and tenors (about 250 to 500 Hz), we find that it is only pairs of partials above the fourth partial that can generate roughness.

What type of formant frequency combinations would contribute most efficiently to the roughness in the tenor's voice timbre? If we consider the case of a phonation frequency of 260 Hz (corresponding to the pitch of C4, approximately) or higher, a moment's calculation tells us that it must be the spectrum partials above 1,300 Hz. Thus, in order to increase roughness of voice timbre, two adjacent partials above 1,300 Hz need to have high and approximately equal amplitudes. The frequencies of the third and fourth formants are rather independent of the vowel, as is also the voice timbre. Consequently, the third and fourth formants are likely to be involved in creating the roughness difference between the tenor and alto voice timbre.

If the third and fourth formants approach each other in frequency, they will both gain in amplitude, and hence the amplitude of the partials near and between them will increase. If the frequency separation between these formants is equal to or less than a critical band, the formants are likely to emphasize a pair of partials which may generate roughness. In the study mentioned (Ägren and Sundberg, 1978), the mean frequency distance between the third and the fourth formants was found to be 16% in the case of the tenors, which is narrower than a critical band, and 27% in the case of the altos, which is wider than a critical band. This suggests that a pair of partials that is likely to generate roughness is enhanced in the tenor voice because of a narrow frequency separation of the third and the fourth formants. This supports the assumption that these results, although obtained from four subjects only, may be valid for many altos and tenors. It is possible that voice source differences contribute to the same effect. For instance, a low amplitude of the higher source spectrum partials will reduce the roughness of the voice timbre.

What about the voice timbre differences between women and children?

Here very little seems to be known; so let us speculate, just for the pleasure of it. Apart from phonation frequency differences, we recall that children have formant frequencies about 20% higher than those of adult females on the average (whatever an average child may be as regards age, vocal tract, and body length!). Such formant frequency differences are significant for the voice timbre, and the resulting timbral differences should help us to tell whether it is a child or a woman who speaks. In addition, there may be typical voice source differences between children and women. But even dialects would be an important factor; probably children have their own way of articulating speech sounds.

Raising all formant frequencies by 20% will not lead to any difference in roughness. Still a timbral difference apparently exists between a boy soprano and a boy alto on the one hand, and their adult female counterparts on the other; perhaps the adult female voice can be described as somewhat smoother. One possible reason for this might be that the boy who has had enough musical education to perform solo parts is so old that his larynx has grown to a larger size than that of a female singer. If so, the fourth formant frequency, being strongly dependent on the larynx tube, would be closer to the third formant in the boy singers. But, unfortunately, this is sheer speculation, and we have to wait for evidence from thorough future investigations.

Formant Frequencies in Tenor, Baritone, and Bass Singers

The tenor, baritone, and bass voice categories were studied by Cleveland (1977). He examined formant frequencies and source spectrum in some representatives from the three categories. The formant frequencies of the vowels /u:/, /o:/, /ɑ/, /e:/, and /i:/ were measured in eight male professional singers who all sang these vowels on identical pitches. The sung vowels were then presented in random order to singing teachers, who were asked to classify the voices as tenor, baritone, or bass. The results from this classification test could be used to determine sets of formant frequencies that could be assumed to be typical of each of the three categories. These sets are shown for the lowest two formant frequencies in figure 5.14. The average of the four lowest formant frequencies in the five vowels examined correlated with the classification; voices with high average formant frequencies were classified as tenors, and voices with low average formant frequencies were classified as basses. Also, as in the previously mentioned investigation of maleness and femaleness in voice timbre, fundamental frequency was a factor of considerable importance; vowels sung at a high pitch caused subjects to classify the voice as a tenor, and those sung at a low pitch were often classified as basses. This is one more example demonstrating the perceptual relevance of fundamental frequency to voice timbre classification.

Listening-test materials, in which all sound properties are varied systematically, cannot easily be obtained from singers. Apart from formant frequency differences found between the voice categories, other differences may exist that are even more important for voice classification. In order to determine the relevance of such unknown factors, Cleveland synthesized a

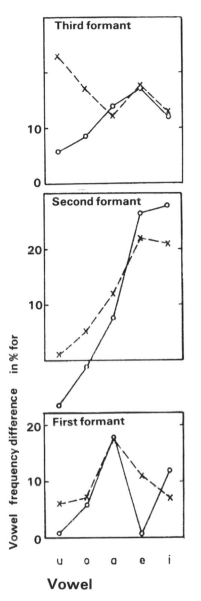

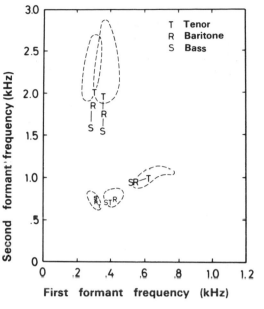

Figure 5.14. Formant frequency differences between male singers with different voice classifications.

Upper graph: Averages for the two lowest formant frequencies in tenor, baritone, and bass singers. The dashed contours represent the vowel "islands" shown in figure 2.12, p. 24.

Left graphs: Solid lines show the differences for the three lowest formants as percentages, and the dashed lines represent the corresponding differences between male and female speakers according to Fant (1975).

set of similar vowels and had it classified by the same group of singing teachers. Those formant frequency combinations were selected that could be expected to be typical for the three voice categories according to the results from the first listening experiment. The results confirmed the relevance of the formant frequencies, although pitch was still found to be an influential factor.

Regarding the singers' classification of their own voices (which can be assumed to be very reliable indeed), it turned out that the results were probably not based on voice timbre and formant frequencies but rather on phonation frequency range. Does this range, measured in terms of its center pitch, relate to other factors of relevance to this type of voice classification? Apart from a single case, this turned out to be so; the center pitch of the phonation frequency range and the average of the four lowest formant frequencies were significantly correlated: the higher the center pitch, the higher the average of the formant frequencies. Although this average appeared to be relevant to the voice classification, it merely means that there is a correlation between the range and the classification of a singer's voice. A moment's reflection will tell us that this result is not surprising: indeed, one would be suspicious if these factors did *not* correlate in professional singers. If a voice has the range of a bass and the formant frequencies typical of a tenor, it is not likely to make its owner a professional singer. In other words, a criterion for a successful career for an opera singer must be that voice timbre and range match.

Cleveland also found some formant frequencies in particular vowels to be more revealing of the voice classification than others. For instance, the second formant frequency in the vowels /ɛ:/, /e:/, and /u:/; the third in the vowel /i:/; and the fourth in the vowels /e:/ and /o:/. In these vowels, a high and a low frequency value of these particular formants were found to be indications of a tenor and a bass voice, respectively.

It is interesting that, for a given vowel, the percentage differences in formant frequency between tenors and basses are strikingly similar to those found between male and female voices, as can be seen in figure 5.14. This suggests that, once more, there is a difference in pharyngeal length that is significant to the timbral classification of the voice. Of course, the pharyngeal length depends on the vertical larynx position. This may be the explanation for the ability some baritone singers have to change their voice category to tenor; these singers manage to expand their phonation frequency range upward, probably adopting a technique that uses a slightly higher larynx position, so that the formant frequencies become more tenorlike. In any case, we should recall that we can vary our formant frequencies for a given vowel rather widely. Also, every vowel can be articulated in various ways, not only with respect to the vertical larynx position but also with respect to jaw opening, tongue shape, and so on, so that the voice timbre acquires varied coloration. In singing and in emotional speech, such coloring is probably very important, a subject we will return to later.

It was stated before that the formant frequencies of altos and tenors did not seem to differ consistently except for the fourth formant, which was found to be lower in tenors. Now we have just seen that tenors differ from basses in a way similar to that in which male and female adults differ. The very small difference between altos and tenors therefore seems natural; the formant frequencies of a tenor must already be a bit on the higher side of the male average, and thus a bit closer to the female values. However, the difference between the tenors and the altos as regards the fourth formant is probably typical and important, as it would give the tenors a somewhat rougher voice timbre than altos.

Before leaving this subject of the male formant frequencies and voice categories, it should be stressed that all voice classifications are rather heterogenous. If we ask voice experts, we will learn that there are a number of subdivisions within each of the classifications considered here, such as lyrical, dramatic, and so on. We do not know what characterizes these categories acoustically. Probably they differ with respect not only to formant frequencies, but also to voice source, particularly in the way in which the voice source changes with phonation frequency and loudness. For instance, it is tempting to guess that the formant frequencies of a Wagnerian tenor are more similar to those of a baritone than to other types of tenors.

Formant Frequencies and Vertical Larynx Position

The vertical position of the larynx, which we will call the *larynx height,* generally varies in normal speech (figure 5.5). The vowel /i:/ is mostly articulated with a higher larynx than the vowel /u:/. Further, in untrained speakers, the larynx tends to rise with increasing phonation frequency in the modal register. In the education of the singing voice, one generally strives for a comfortably low larynx position, regardless of vowel and pitch. The singing teachers try to establish an articulatory habit which is different from what the student is used to in normal speech.

As to the reason for this, one could speculate that a low larynx position is favorable for singing and perhaps also for speech that puts stress on the voice organ; it is not unusual that voice patients speak with a habitually elevated larynx position, and in such cases, a successful therapy often is to lower the frequency of phonation so that the larynx is lowered. In the preceding chapter we saw that pressed phonation is often associated with a high larynx position. Thus, there are reasons to assume the existence of a relationship between larynx height and an economical way of using the voice.

It is generally not difficult for a person with a good ear for voices to decide by listening whether a speaker's larynx position is abnormal. The general impression is that the vowel quality becomes dark when a speaker's larynx has been depressed, while the voice sounds more shrill when the larynx is elevated. In other words, there seems to be a relationship between larynx height and voice timbre. This comes as no surprise; a change in the larynx height changes the vocal tract length, and hence the formant frequencies. But how, exactly, does the larynx height affect the formant frequencies?

This question was the topic for an investigation in which this author participated (Sundberg and Nordström, 1983). Data were collected from two subjects who were both accustomed to varying their larynx height for demonstration purposes. Their formant frequencies were measured in different vowels. The first two formant frequencies consistently changed along a straight line in a vowel diagram, as can be seen in figure 5.15; the values pertaining to normal larynx height lie about midway between those for raised and depressed larynx, the vowel /u:/ forming an exception. For most vowels the lowered larynx gave a formant frequency combination outside

Varied larynx position

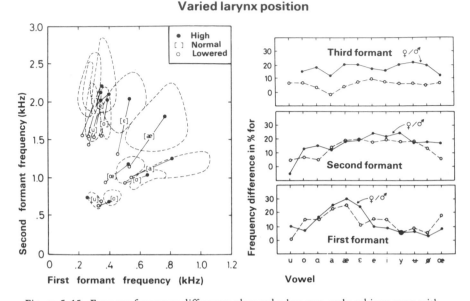

Figure 5.15. Formant frequency differences observed when two male subjects sang with deliberately varied vertical positioning of the larynx.
Left: Average formant frequencies for the vowels indicated for raised (filled circles), normal (vowel symbols), and a lowered larynx (open circles). The dashed contours are the vowel islands of figure 2.12, p. 24, showing the distribution of values observed in speech. Values pertaining to normal larynx height lie just about halfway between those for raised and depressed larynx. The data points for all vowels concentrate in a small area under conditions of lowered larynx.
Right: Formant frequency differences in percent. (After Sundberg and Nordström, 1977.)

the proper "vowel island" in the formant chart of figure 5.15 and located in a comparatively narrow area in the vicinity of the vowel /oe:/. This seems to correspond to experience; when a vowel is pronounced with a low larynx position, it acquires some kind of similarity with this vowel.

A comparison of the percentage formant frequency differences between adult males and females shows many striking parallels with the differences between raised and lowered larynx, as figure 5.15 also shows. The rise of the first formant frequency is greatest for the vowels /ae:/ and /a:/, and the increase in the second formant frequency is greatest for the vowels /e:/, /i:/, and /y:/ both in the male and female and in the high and low larynx voices. These parallels suggest that the differences in pharynx length, necessarily associated with a shift of larynx height, are decisive also for the male-female formant frequency differences.

A raising of the larynx must result not only in a shortening of the pharynx but also in a narrowing of the lower part of it; when the larynx is lowered, the pharyngeal sidewall tissues must be stretched, so that the lower pharynx is widened. When the larynx is raised, the wall tissues must pile up and fill part of the lower pharynx. In addition, the lower and the middle pharyngeal constrictor muscles may be important. These constrictor muscles originate at the cricoid and thyroid cartilages and at the hyoid bone, run upward and posteriorly, and insert in the median raphe of the back pharynx wall. By contracting, they would contribute to a raising of the larynx and thereby constrict the pharynx.

As we will see later in this chapter, we may expect a lowering of the fourth formant frequency as a result of a lowering of the larynx. In the investigation mentioned (Sundberg and Nordström, 1983) a change from high to low larynx positioning was observed to be associated with an average lowering over vowels and subjects of 17% for the fourth formant frequency. The corresponding value for the third formant frequency was a bit lower, only 11%. It is interesting that a shift in the vertical position of the larynx slightly reduces the frequency distance between the third and fourth formants.

To summarize: The formant frequency changes resulting from a shift of the larynx height are similar to some of those we have observed before in adult males and females, and tenors and basses. As women have shorter pharynxes than men, the similarity between the male/female formant frequency differences and those associated with high and low larynx voice is by no means unexpected. It also supports the assumption that tenors have shorter pharynxes than basses and that a shift of voice category from baritone to tenor involves, among other things, a habitually higher larynx position.

Formant Frequencies in Male Opera Singers

Until now we have considered the two or three lowest formant frequencies, and we have seen how they differ with particular types of voices. Next we will see that in Western opera singing, formants number four and five are also relevant to the voice timbre.

There are obviously considerable differences between the voice timbre in normal speech and the voice timbres that can be heard from singers in opera and concert houses. There, extremely high demands are made on the voices, not only for musical expression and performance in general, but also for sufficient power in the presence of a loud orchestral accompaniment. If we replace a professional singer with an untrained speaker in an opera performance, the result would probably be that the audience could not hear the speaker's voice at all, except possibly when the accompaniment was soft. Or, if the speaker's voice could be heard initially, it would soon wear out. The art of the professional singer includes the important ability to make the sound of the voice audible with a loud orchestral accompaniment.

A primary question, then, is how much louder in terms of sound pressure level the voice of a professional singer is in comparison to those of normal, untrained voices. Such a comparison is presented in figure 5.16, which combines data from two different investigations (Bloothooft, 1985; Coleman et al., 1977). Both these investigations concern the mean maximum intensity that subjects, regardless of their classification, could produce in phonation. Still, the values are not fully comparable: for trained voices, values pertain to musically acceptable tones, and the top pitches were sung

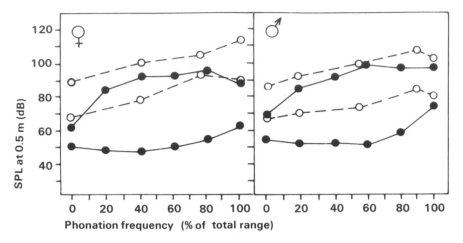

Figure 5.16. Data on the average range of sound level variation in singers and nonsingers. The singers produce higher sound levels, particularly at the extremes of the phonation frequency range; the differences are greater for females. Phonation may be much softer in speech than in soft singing. Data adapted from Bloothooft (1985) and Coleman et al. (1977).

in falsetto register in the case of male voices. In the case of the untrained voices, all kinds of sounds were accepted.

It is interesting to compare the meaning of "soft" in these two groups of subjects. As can be seen in figure 5.16, what is called "soft" among singers is between 20 and 40 dB louder than the minimum sound level produced by the untrained subjects. Probably, the lowest sound levels of the voice are hard to use for musical purposes.

If we compare these averages for singers and nonsingers in figure 5.16, we see that for both male and female voices, the singers beat the non-singers. Particularly for females, the differences are greatest at the extreme ends of the pitch range. For the top female pitch the difference amounts to no less than 20 dB. These substantial disparities, of course, partly explain how singers manage to make the sound of their voices audible even in the presence of a loud orchestra; they simply have learned how to produce sound at exceptionally high levels. Later we will see what makes up such a capacity.

In addition to these sound level differences, other factors, having to do with the spectral characteristics of the singers' sounds, help make the best opera singers' voices audible even with loud orchestral accompaniment. The explanation has to do with the definition of loudness of phonation. Mostly loudness is expressed in terms of the measured sound level in dB, as in figure 5.16. However, sound level is not a perfect measure of the loudness that we perceive, as will soon be evident. For the moment, we can conclude that not even a small difference in sound level between a professional singer's and an untrained voice necessarily implies that these voices sound equally loud.

If one listens carefully to the vowel qualities typically used by male opera singers, one finds rather great deviations from those used in normal speech. The formant frequencies of four singers were measured in various vowels and were compared with those measured in nonsingers' speech (Sundberg, 1974). Considerable differences were found, as can be seen in figure 5.17. The second and third formant frequencies in the front vowels do not reach the high values they have in speech. The fourth and the fifth formant frequencies vary much less in singing than in speech. Also, the fifth formant frequency in the sung vowels is slightly lower than the fourth formant frequency in speech. Apparently, there is an "extra" formant between those formants corresponding to the third and the fourth in the spoken vowels.

The notion of an "extra" formant is not accurate, although it appears so in the graph, because it is impossible to give rise to extra formants in the vocal tract. What is possible is to change the frequencies of already existing formants. Thus, what we call the extra formant actually exists also in spoken vowels, even though it is tuned to a higher frequency, where the voice source overtones are mostly so weak that this formant does not appear clearly in an analysis of the spectrum. For the sake of convenience, though, we will keep the term *extra formant*.

Such formant frequency differences are readily perceptible. With respect to the two lowest formant frequencies, some of us would perhaps use such terms as "darkening," "covering," or "coloring" to describe the effect. Appelman (1967) describes it as "vowel migration." Let us take some examples: the three lowest formant frequencies for the sung vowel /i:/ are more similar to those of the spoken /y:/ than to those of the spoken /i:/. Some singing teachers would even recommend that their students "color"

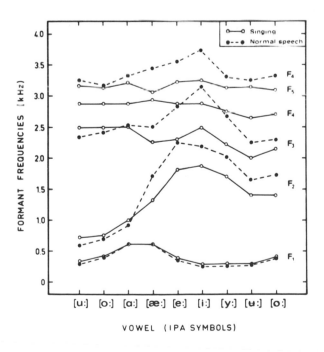

Figure 5.17. Average formant frequencies in the vowels indicated on the vertical axis as produced by nonsingers and as sung by four singers (dashed and solid lines, respectively). The second and third formant of the front vowels are lower in the sung vowels, and the fifth formant in singing is lower than the fourth formant in the spoken vowels. (After Sundberg, 1974.)

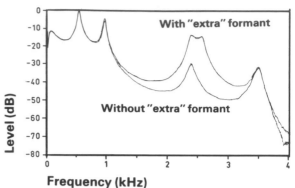

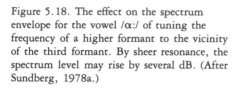

Figure 5.18. The effect on the spectrum envelope for the vowel /ɑ:/ of tuning the frequency of a higher formant to the vicinity of the third formant. By sheer resonance, the spectrum level may rise by several dB. (After Sundberg, 1978a.)

the sung /i:/ toward the /y:/ in order to obtain the effect. Similarly, the sung /a:/ is colored toward the spoken /o:/, and the sung /e:/ and /ae:/ toward the spoken /oe:/.

If an extra formant is created in the vocal tract, the sound transfer ability of the vocal tract in the vicinity of that formant is greatly improved. This effect, illustrated in figure 5.18, is an application of the principles illustrated earlier, in figure 5.2. It can be seen in figure 5.18 that this extra formant improves the ability of the vocal tract to transfer sound by no less than 20 dB, if tuned to a frequency very close to the third formant as in the case shown in the figure. Such an extra formant would lead to a spectrum envelope peak in the frequency region of this formant.

A spectrum envelope peak also occurs in real singing, as is illustrated by the two spectra in figure 5.19. They show two versions of the vowel /u:/ as sung and spoken by a male professional opera singer. In the spoken version of the vowel, there are two peaks in the frequency region 2–3 kHz, one for the third and one for the fourth. In the sung version, the two peaks have merged into one complex, which is about 20 dB higher than the two peaks in the spoken version.

This spectrum envelope peak in the neighborhood of 3 kHz is typical for all voiced sounds produced by male opera and concert singers in Western musical culture. (We will return to the case of female singers in the next section.) The peak is generally referred to as the *singer's formant,* and we will

Figure 5.19. Spectrum envelopes for the vowel /u:/ as sung and spoken by a male professional opera singer. The peak in the spectrum envelope near 3 kHz is typical of all voiced sounds in singing except in sopranos; it is called the singer's formant. (After Sundberg, 1974.)

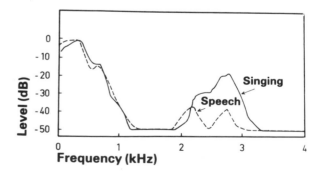

use this term for it, even though it is somewhat misleading. The singer's formant has been observed by most researchers who have studied vowel spectra of male professional singers (e.g., Bartholomew, 1934; Rzhevkin, 1956; Winckel, 1953; and Sundberg, 1974; a wealth of references can be found in Schultz-Coulon et al., 1979). Some singing teachers refer to this phenomenon as "head resonance" or "placement in the mask," according to Gibian (1972). The center frequency of the singer's formant varies with voice type (Dmitriev and Kiselev, 1979). Seidner et al. (1983) report that, depending on pitch and vowel, the center frequency of the singer's formant varies between 2.3 and 3 kHz in basses and between 3 and 3.8 kHz in tenors.

The main acoustical contribution to the generation of the singer's formant stems from a clustering of the third, fourth, and fifth formants (Sundberg, 1974). In other words, the frequency separation between these formants is smaller in the sung vowels. As a result, the sound transfer ability of the vocal tract in the frequency range of these formants will increase, and a spectrum envelope peak will arise, other things being equal. The amplitude of the transfer function peak depends on the frequency separation of the third, fourth, and fifth formants.

The amplitude of the singer's formant depends not only on the frequencies of the third, fourth, and fifth formants but also on the amplitudes of corresponding voice source partials. As we know, these amplitudes reflect the closing rate of the glottis; if the flow glottogram has a comparatively low closing rate—for instance because of an incomplete glottal closure—then the amplitude of the singer's formant will also be comparatively low. Inversely, if for some reason the closing rate is unusually high, then the amplitude of the singer's formant will be unusually high; in fact, Rothenberg (1981) has occasionally observed such unusually high closing rates in glottograms of professional singers.

In the previous chapter it was mentioned that louder tones have stronger overtones than softer tones, because the fall-off of the voice source spectrum is less steep in loud phonation than in soft (see figure 4.15, p. 75). This implies that the amplitude of the spectrum peak called the singer's formant will be higher in spectra of loud tones, as is illustrated by figure 5.20. Moreover, to the extent that the source spectra of high-pitched notes are more dominated by overtones than the source spectra of low-pitched notes, a similar reasoning applies, as has been demonstrated by measurements made by Hollien (1983). On the other hand, Bloothooft (1985) has shown that the pitch *per se* does not have any clear effect on the level of the singer's formant; the effect that it has can be ascribed to the fact that higher notes are normally sung louder than lower notes.

Another factor influencing the level of the singer's formant is the vowel, as we would expect. For male professional singers' vowels with a high second formant frequency, such as /i:/ or /e:/, the singer's formant is, on the average, about 12 dB weaker than the overall sound level. For vowels with a low second formant, such as /u:/ or /o:/, the corresponding average is about 20 dB, according to Bloothooft (1985).

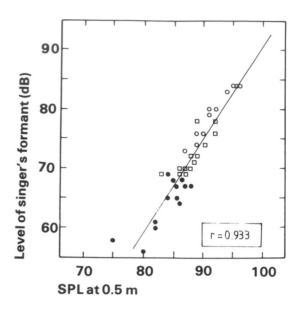

Figure 5.20. Sound level of the singer's formant in a baritone singer singing the tones of a chromatic scale on the vowel /ae:/ in soft (filled circles), middle (squares), and loud phonation (open circles). The gain in the level of the singer's formant is greater than the rise in the overall sound level which indicates that the louder the phonation, the more dominating the singer's formant. (From Cleveland and Sundberg, 1983.)

We know that formant frequencies depend on articulation. It is, then, appropriate to ask what kind of articulation gives rise to the singer's formant. As early as 1934, Bartholomew suspected that the larynx tube played an important role in the generation of the singer's formant. There were good reasons for assuming this. We saw previously that the fourth formant frequency is particularly sensitive to the shape of the larynx tube. Also, the singer's formant is present in all sounds, so it must be comparatively insensitive to vowel articulation. The larynx tube is the part of the vocal tract that varies the least with vowel articulation.

Figure 5.21 shows tracings of X-ray pictures of a male singer singing and speaking the same vowel. The larynx is seen to be lower in singing, and this seems to be a typical observation in male professional singers (Shipp and Izdebski, 1975; see also figure 5.5). Figure 5.21 also illustrates, by means of tracings of frontal X-ray pictures of the deep pharynx, the contour changes observed when the larynx is deliberately raised and lowered; the lowering of the larynx is associated with a widening of both the laryngeal ventricle and, particularly, the bottom part of the vocal tract surrounding the larynx tube, the sinus piriforms.

The acoustical effects of these articulatory changes depend on two things. One is quite simple: a lowering of the larynx lengthens the vocal tract by increasing the pharynx length. The lengthening of the pharynx is particularly important to the second formant frequency of front vowels, as was illustrated in figure 5.15. Second, as was mentioned earlier, a lowering of the larynx apparently widens the bottom part of the pharynx. For example, the fourth formant frequency becomes highly dependent on the dimensions of the larynx tube as soon as the larynx tube opening is sufficiently narrower than the pharynx.

According to measurements on models of the vocal tract, the clustering

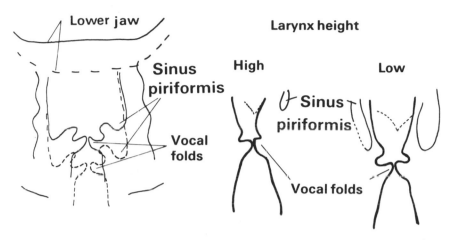

Figure 5.21. Left: Tracings of frontal X-ray pictures of a male singer singing and speaking the same vowel (solid and dashed contours). In singing, the larynx was lower and the piriform sinuses were wider. (From Sundberg, 1970.)
Right: Contours shown in frontal X-ray pictures of the deep pharynx, when a subject deliberately raised and lowered his larynx. The laryngeal ventricle and the sinus piriformes expanded considerably when the larynx was lowered. (From Sundberg, 1974.)

of the higher formant frequencies required for generating a singer's formant can be achieved. It is necessary, however, that the pharynx be lengthened and the cross-sectional area in the pharynx at the level of the larynx tube opening be more than six times the area of that opening (Sundberg, 1974; Childers et al., 1983). Particularly if the lowering of the larynx expands the laryngeal ventricle, the fourth formant frequency can be lowered from its typical value of 3.5 kHz in adult males all the way down to, say, 2.8 kHz. There are good reasons for assuming that the extra formant, which in the data shown in figure 5.17 appears in the vicinity of 3 kHz in all vowels, is identical with the formant that in the model experiments showed a strong dependence on the larynx tube. Thus we may say that the larynx tube seems to be an important tool for obtaining the clustering of the higher formant frequencies needed for generating a singer's formant.

Some singing teachers recommend that their students breathe through the nose as often as possible and that they also maintain a sensation of inhalation during singing, perhaps because a quiet inhalation through the nose is often associated with a lowering of the larynx and a dilation of the pharyngeal sidewalls (Strohl and Fouke, 1985).

This is not to say that it is impossible to generate vowels with a singer's formant without a lowering of the larynx. The individual shape of the pharynx and larynx may very well be such that there is no need for lowering the larynx in order to obtain a singer's formant. Also, there may be other articulatory and phonatory configurations that generate it. Wang (1983), investigating ten tenor singers representing Chinese opera tradition and the type of singing often used in performing medieval music, found that singing with a strong singer's formant occurred even when these singers did not lower their larynxes.

It was mentioned that the larynx tube opening often expands considerably when phonation frequency is raised. According to what we have seen, this may threaten the combination of higher formant frequencies that is required for generating the singer's formant; when the larynx tube opening is not considerably narrower than the pharynx width, the fourth formant frequency will be more influenced by other parts of the vocal tract than by the larynx tube. In order to avoid this, the singer can keep the pharynx very wide or even increase the widening with rising frequency of phonation. The latter concurs with figure 5.5: the higher the phonation frequency, the more the singers lowered the vertical position of the larynx. It is likely that some singing teachers use the term "covering" to indicate this widening of the pharynx as a function of phonation frequency.

Here we see a clear contrast between what is normal in speech and what an opera singer is supposed to do. In many normal speakers the larynx height almost mirrors phonation frequency. A professional singer has to abandon this unconscious habit and replace it by the opposite, that of lowering the larynx with rising phonation frequency. This relearning, naturally enough, takes time. The time needed may, in some cases, be greatly extended if the teacher avoids instructing in direct terms and prefers a suggestive terminology—for example, that the tone must "go forward," that the tone must "play in the nose," that the "steel" must be maintained in the tone, that the tone must be "covered," and so on. Some students may have a hard time grasping the real meaning of such terms. It may be that visual aids displaying the spectrum of the tone sung would be a means of helping the student understand exactly what sound characteristics the teacher is speaking about; a notorious difficulty in speaking about sounds is that we have no pointer to help us indicate exactly what we mean.

The presence of the singer's formant in male Western opera and concert singing seems to be a necessary requisite of acceptable phonation. Why is this so? The answer appears to be related to the acoustical environment in which such a singer has to work and which may be most demanding with respect to the voice: he often has to sing with a loud orchestral accompaniment.

The loudest partials of the orchestral sound tend to appear in the neighborhood of 450 Hz. It so happens that the loudest partials of the human speaking voice tend to appear in the same frequency region, as is illustrated in figure 5.22 showing long-term average spectra of orchestral music and normal speech over a long time interval (several minutes). These two curves in the graph are rather similar (for the moment we shall disregard the considerable difference in sound level). We also observe that in the orchestral sound, the partials falling in the frequency range of the singer's formant (just below 3 kHz in this case) are considerably weaker than the partials at 450 Hz. This means that the singer who sings with loud partials in the neighborhood of 3 kHz encounters only moderate competition from

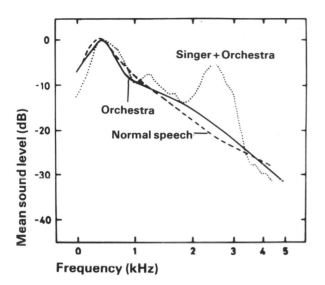

Figure 5.22. Long-term-average spectra for the sound of a symphony orchestra with and without a singer soloist (solid and dotted curves) and for normal speech (dashed curve). The "singer's formant" constitutes the major difference between the orchestra with and without the singer soloist. (From Sundberg, 1972.)

sound components of the orchestra accompaniment in that frequency region. There he can rule the roost, so to speak. Consequently, the singer's voice is easier to discern when the orchestra is loud. The effect is illustrated in a phonograph record appended to an article on this subject by the author (Sundberg, 1977b).

There is probably yet another advantage to the singer's formant. The phenomenon is related to the sound radiation characteristics produced by the singer. The lower partials of the voice sounds scatter almost equally well in all directions, so that the radiation can be described as nearly omnidirectional. The higher partials, on the other hand, radiate more forward than backward and toward the sides of the singer: the higher the frequency of the partial, the more pronounced the effect. If the singer were to concentrate most of his sound energy around 450 Hz, as in normal speech, a considerable percentage of the sound energy produced would disappear behind and above. The higher partials in the frequency region of the singer's formant are not lost to the same extent, because they radiate more directly to the audience, provided that the singer is facing toward it (Winckel, 1953; Marshal and Meyer, 1985).

The singer's formant thus seems to facilitate our hearing of the singer's voice when the orchestral accompaniment is loud. We recall that a singer's formant can be generated by a clustering of the higher formants and that one way of achieving such a clustering is by lowering the larynx. It does not require any great muscular effort to lower the larynx, so it seems important from the point of view of vocal economy to learn how to sing with a singer's formant. The singer's formant improves the audibility of the voice without extra cost in vocal effort.

It is interesting that the sound characteristic of an orchestra appears to be an important reason that singers learn to sing with a singer's formant. We would not expect to meet the same technique in singing accompanied by other types of sounds; the vowels of a person singing with lute or guitar accompaniment no doubt sound more like those in normal speech than like those of opera singers. Likewise, we would not expect to meet the opera singer's technique in rock concerts, where sound amplification systems handle the balance between voice and accompanying instruments.

In these cases, the singing techniques appear to reflect the acoustical working environment of the singer plus the importance of hearing his voice in the environment. In most choral singing, the opposite rule is applied; it should not be possible to hear the voice of a particular choir member in the ensemble sound. An opera singer's voice can (and, depending on the music, may unfortunately) cut through the sound of a choir quite efficiently. For this reason the ideal choir voice should differ from that of an ideal solo voice. In the next chapter we will see how they differ.

If we return to figure 5.16, we may now understand it better. The acoustical strength as given by the sound level in dB does not fully tell us whether we can hear the singer's voice through a loud orchestral accompaniment. The spectrum of the vowel must also be taken into account, because it can be of decisive importance.

Formant Frequencies of Female Opera Singers

A major difference between female singers and nonsingers is in the maximum sound level, as figure 5.16 also showed. With respect to the level of the singer's formant, Bloothooft (1985) found that the difference between singers and nonsingers is much greater in females than in males; however, he pointed out that most of this difference depends on the substantially greater difference in sound level in the case of females. Thus, in reality, the singer's formant has a lower amplitude in female voices, particularly in sopranos, than in male voices (Hollien, 1983; Bloothooft, 1985).

What are the vocal effects used by female singers to produce such loud sounds that they can be heard through the accompaniment without putting too much stress on the voice? The answer to this question will be found in the following summary of two investigations (Sundberg, 1975; Johansson et al. 1983).

Let us start by raising another question. In chapter 2 we found that every vowel in normal speech has a formant frequency combination of its own. In a female speaker, the first formant frequency in the vowels /u:/ and /i:/ is found near 350 and 300 Hz, respectively, as was illustrated in figure 5.9. An alto and a soprano are supposed to be capable of singing with phonation frequencies as high as about 700 and 1,000 Hz (near pitches F5 and C6) or still higher. This means that the lowest partial in the spectrum occurs at these frequencies. Is this really compatible with a first formant which appears at the frequencies just mentioned, or, in other words, one octave or more below the frequency of the fundamental? Do female singers really waste good vocal tract resonance at a frequency where there is no sound to which to give resonance?

It is not easy to find the answers to this last question, because formant frequencies are hard to determine when fundamental frequency is higher than about half of the frequency of the first formant. However, just by synthesizing what we probably know already we may qualitatively guess that the answer must be no. If one studies the articulation of a professional female singer, one may observe at least three typical deviations from what happens in normal female speech: (1) The singing voice sounds very much louder than the speaking voice; (2) It is often difficult to hear what vowel is intended, particularly at high pitches; and (3) The jaw opening appears to be more dependent upon the phonation frequency than on the vowel, particularly at high pitches; whether a soprano sings the vowels /u:/, /i:/, or some other vowel having a narrow jaw opening under normal conditions, the jaw opening is typically much wider in her highest notes than in her low notes. Figure 5.23 offers typical examples of this.

It seems that vocal economy is the motivation behind the difference in vowel articulation in speech and singing. We know that the jaw opening is particularly decisive to the frequency of the first formant. Thus, we would expect that by widening the jaw opening, the soprano tends to increase the frequency of the first formant in synchrony with phonation frequency.

Figure 5.24 confirms this expectation. It shows data collected by the author in a highly unusual experiment with a professional soprano. She sang various vowels at various pitches, first normally, while holding a vibrator (a so-called artificial larynx) against her neck. When the vibrator was started by the experimenter, the soprano stopped singing but continued

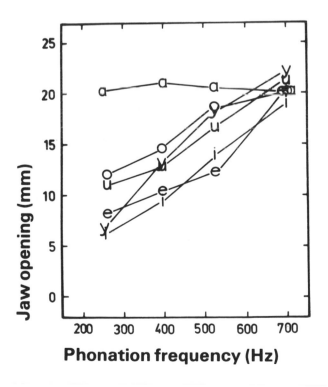

Figure 5.23. The width of the jaw opening of the indicated vowels observed in a professional soprano who sang various vowels at different pitches. The trend is that the jaw opening increases with rising pitch except for the vowel /ɑ:/, which has a wide jaw opening anyway. (After Sundberg, 1975.)

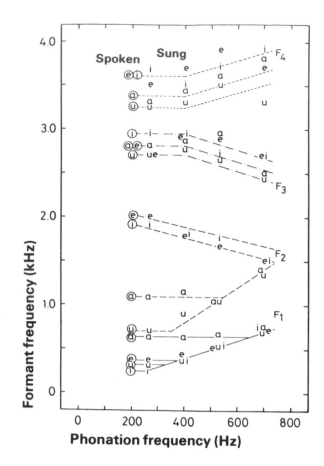

Figure 5.24. The four lowest formant frequencies (F_1, F_2, F_3, F_4) in the vowels indicated used by a professional soprano singing at various pitches. The circled values pertain to the subject's speech. The lines illustrate the trends; the first formant is not allowed to be lower than the phonation frequency; the second formant of back vowels /u:/ and /ɑ:/ rises and that of front vowels /e:/ and /i:/ drops with rising phonation frequency. (After Sundberg, 1978c.)

articulating the vowels silently. In this way, the formant frequencies could be estimated in spite of the extremely high fundamental frequencies. The resulting data were corroborated by combining them with a standard voice source in a vowel synthesizer. Later on, they were also supported by results from an X-ray investigation of a different soprano, where acoustical models of the various vocal tract shapes produced by the singer were derived from the X-ray pictures and analyzed with respect to their formant frequencies (Johansson et al., 1983).

The results shown in figure 5.24 illustrate the principle behind the vowel modifications; as soon as the ordinary value of the first formant frequency is *lower* than the phonation frequency, the first formant is changed and tuned to a frequency near the phonation frequency. Even though there is probably no exact agreement between the frequency of phonation and that of the first formant, they are quite similar at high pitches. Thus, by adjusting the jaw opening in accordance with phonation frequency, the singers apparently tune the first formant frequency to a value close to frequency of phonation. If the latter is changed, the jaw opening will be changed accordingly.

The gain from this simple principle of adjusting the jaw opening in accordance with phonation frequency can be considerable; the singer might gain

30 dB in extreme cases. (For those who enjoy the excitement of large numbers, it is probably nicer to abandon the logarithmic dB unit and say that the vowel is radiated with a thousandfold increase in energy!) It is self-evident that the vowel sounds become easier to hear under such conditions.

The gain arises as soon as the frequency of the first formant joins the frequency of phonation, or, in other words, as soon as phonation frequency is driven higher than the normal value of the first formant. This strategy would account for most of the differences between the maximum sound level reached by female nonsingers and professional singers shown in figure 5.16; the untrained voice would hardly be as skilled as the professional singer's in utilizing the formants for maximizing the radiated output.

It does not require much muscular energy to increase the jaw opening, even if we do not stand in an upright position. In order to raise intensity of phonation, subglottic pressure needs to be raised by contraction of the muscles of exhalation; in addition, contraction of certain laryngeal muscles is also required. We realize that the pitch-dependent tuning of formant frequencies gives the singers' vowels a high loudness at a low price in terms of muscular energy. Thus we find the principle of vocal economy not only in the case of male but also female professional singing.

Note that phonation frequency of the soprano is often above 500 Hz. This is higher than the frequency range where the orchestral accompaniment tends to have its loudest partials, according to figure 5.22. For this reason, singers should have better chances of being heard above this frequency, which corresponds approximately to the pitch of B4. For altos, who often sing at lower phonation frequencies, the situation is worse. It seems that they use the help of a singer's formant; according to Seidner et al. (1983) and Bloothooft (1985), the singer's formant is more prominent in altos than in sopranos. What articulatory tricks they use for producing their singer's formant is not known, unfortunately.

It was recently shown that the tuning of the first formant to a frequency slightly above the phonation frequency has quite particular effects on phonation. Schutte and Miller (1985) measured the airflow variations just above the glottis in some sopranos. They found that the flow actually reversed during a short portion of the glottal vibration cycle; air was actually streaming *down toward the lungs* during a portion of the open phase, while the sopranos were singing! The explanation for this truly unexpected finding is to be found in the fact that sound is reflected in the vocal tract as shown by Rothenberg (1985) and Fant and Qi-guang (1985). These reflections may be so strong that they override the airstream from the lungs. This situation should give the singer a quite special sensation of her phonation. Presumably, it would feel as if the air were being used for a particularly efficient phonation. Such a sensation, arising only when the first formant is slightly higher than the phonation frequency, should be helpful when the singer is learning this formant strategy.

Naturally, these drastic changes in vowel articulation entail consequences not only for the loudness of the vowel sound but also for the other formant frequencies. This also is illustrated in figure 5.24; the second formant frequency drops in the front vowels /i:/ and /e:/ with rising phonation frequency. In the back vowels /u:/, /o:/, and /ɑ:/, the second formant is tuned to a frequency in the vicinity of the second partial, in other words, to twice the phonation frequency. The third and fourth formant frequencies start to drop and rise, respectively, as soon as the phonation frequency increases above about 440 Hz.

Looking once more at figure 5.24, we note that, at the top pitch, the formant frequencies of the various vowels studied have become pretty similar. At least the first and second formants are approximately the same for all the vowels represented in the graph. This suggests that the underlying articulations may also not be very different. The X-ray investigation of a professional soprano and an alto by Johansson et al. (1983) confirmed this. The tongue shape for the vowels /u:/, /ɑ:/, and /i:/ was found to be almost the same at 960 Hz phonation frequency, as can be seen in figure 5.25.

It was mentioned that the jaw opening is a handy tool for tuning the first formant frequency, and here we have seen that it is used this way in female singing. However, there are also other articulatory factors influencing the frequency of the first formant. One is the vocal tract length, which can be shortened both by raising the larynx and by retracting the mouth corners. Some sopranos can be seen to retract their mouth corners in a pitch-dependent way, and some female professional singers also use a pitch-dependent vertical positioning of the larynx, as illustrated in figure 5.26. It is assumed by many singing teachers that this last strategy is harmful to the voice (see, for instance, Ruth, 1963). However, it is also true that the larynx height behavior shown in figure 5.26 can be combined with a long and successful career as a singer (see also Wang, 1983).

But what about the vowel quality under these conditions of truly abnormal vowel articulation and formant frequency values? A study of the

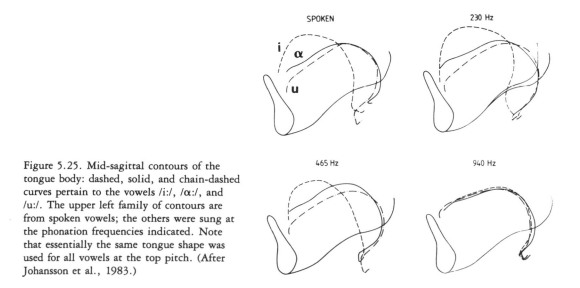

Figure 5.25. Mid-sagittal contours of the tongue body: dashed, solid, and chain-dashed curves pertain to the vowels /i:/, /ɑ:/, and /u:/. The upper left family of contours are from spoken vowels; the others were sung at the phonation frequencies indicated. Note that essentially the same tongue shape was used for all vowels at the top pitch. (After Johansson et al., 1983.)

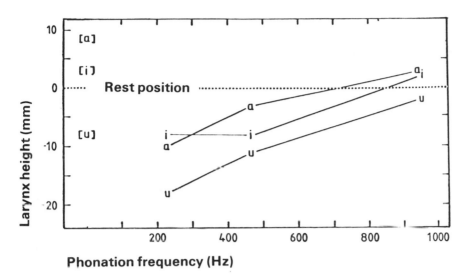

Figure 5.26. Vertical larynx position observed in a professional female singer. The bracketed symbols refer to speech; the unbracketed to singing. (After Johansson et al., 1983.)

identification of vowels sung at very high pitches (Sundberg, 1978b) demonstrated that vowel quality would suffer greatly if the formant frequencies used in normal speech would be used in high-pitched singing. Very high phonation frequencies lead to a dilemma: normal vowel qualities cannot be produced, whatever formant frequencies are chosen. This point will be treated in more detail in chapter 8. Probably, the main thing is that the female singer does not lose very much vowel intelligibility by applying the principle of pitch-dependent formant frequencies, and, more importantly, she gains greatly in loudness, which is indeed a vital thing for a professional singer.

Finally, a word on which voice categories would profit from a pitch-dependent jaw opening. If we look again at figure 2.12, (p. 24), we can see the answer: every time phonation frequency goes higher than the normal value of the first formant frequency, a gain in loudness will result from an increase in the first formant frequency. For some vowels, such as /i:/, /y:/, and /u:/, this will occur in the vicinity of pitches as low as E4. The vowels /ɑ:/ and /a:/ have higher first formant frequencies, so they will not require reconsideration of the first formant frequency until pitches as high as C5 and F5 are reached. A question appears: Is this the reason for the abundance of the vowels /ɑ:/ and /a:/ in voice pedagogy?

To summarize: The pitch-dependent jaw opening may serve as a purpose for basses in some vowels sung at their very highest pitches, for tenors in several vowels in the upper part of their phonation frequency range, and for altos and sopranos in most sung vowels except at very low pitches. As yet, however, formal measurements have been made only with respect to a very few female singers, so there is need for more data.

Voice Category and Vocal Tract Length

We have seen that there are considerable formant frequency differences between various types of voices that are due to differences in the vocal tract dimensions. The relationship between vocal tract length and certain spectral characteristics that would reflect formant frequencies has been studied explicitly. Dmitriev and Kiselev (1979) used twenty professional singers and examined the acoustic characteristics of their singing, apparently in terms of long-time-average spectra showing the distribution of average sound energy as a function of frequency.

A long-time-average spectrum of the human voice normally exhibits at least one more or less pronounced peak. It appears around 500 Hz and is related to the first formant frequency; the exact frequency location of this peak seems to depend on the average value of the first formant frequency in the particular subject's voice. In singers of both sexes, a second peak also appears, in the vicinity of 2 or 3 kHz; it corresponds to the singer's formant. In the case of sopranos, this peak is much less pronounced, as mentioned. In any case, the exact frequency location of this peak depends on the average frequencies of the higher formants in the particular subject's voice.

Dmitriev and Kiselev determined the center frequency of these two spectrum peaks. They also measured the vocal tract length by means of lateral X-ray pictures of the subjects. The investigation gave a positive result, as can be seen in figure 5.27. The center frequencies of both these spectrum peaks increase with the range of the voice; the peaks appear at the lowest frequencies for the basses and at the highest frequencies for the high sopranos. But this is not all: the vocal tract length also varies systematically with the range of the voice, so that high sopranos show the shortest vocal tracts, and basses show the longest. Even though there are no data on alto voices, it is clear that there is a definite relationship between vocal tract length and the center frequencies of the two main long-time-average spectrum peaks of singers' voices.

The mezzo-soprano category does not adhere to the general trend shown in the graphs. The center frequency of the lower spectrum peak of mezzo-soprano is as low as that of baritone voices. Still, the mezzo's vocal tract length is about 5.5 cm shorter than those of baritones. With respect to vocal tract length, mezzo-sopranos are similar to sopranos. But the center frequency of the first peak in the soprano voices is about 200 Hz higher than that of the mezzo-sopranos. What does this mean?

We know already that the lower peak of a long-time-average spectrum is related to the average frequency of the first formant, which is very sensitive to articulation, particularly the width of the jaw opening. If we keep this in mind while contemplating the case of the soprano and the mezzo-soprano, we might arrive at the following speculation. The primary difference between these two voice categories is the difference in phonation frequency range, which depends upon the dimensions of the vocal folds. Perhaps, mezzo-sopranos "color" their voice timbres by lowering the first formant in

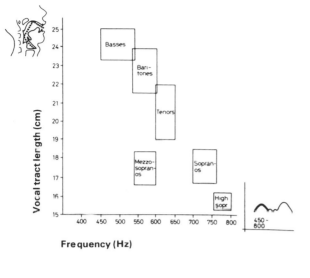

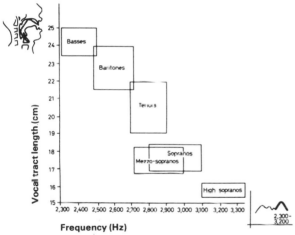

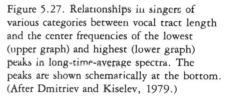

Figure 5.27. Relationships in singers of various categories between vocal tract length and the center frequencies of the lowest (upper graph) and highest (lower graph) peaks in long-time-average spectra. The peaks are shown schematically at the bottom. (After Dmitriev and Kiselev, 1979.)

most vowels so much that they arrive at the same average as the baritones. In this way a voice timbre difference is created between the sopranos and mezzo-sopranos even though there is no difference in the vocal tract length.

While this explanation is plausible, it is nothing more than merely that. Dmitriev and Kiselev do not say exactly how they got their data and averages. Also, they studied Russian singers, whose singing voice timbre appears to differ from that cultivated further west. Some complementary studies seem needed.

Some Pedagogical Points of View

We have just seen that male and female opera and concert singers behave very differently in the articulation of vowels. While the male singer basically keeps his formant frequencies throughout his phonation frequency range (except for the top notes on certain vowels sung by tenors and baritones), articulation must vary with phonation frequency in most notes sung by female singers. This is because their phonation frequency is often higher than the normal value of the first formant frequency, as we have seen above. Larynx lowering, or at least a wide pharynx, is important to male voices because it is needed for the generation and maintenance of the singer's formant. Such an articulation tends to lower the first formant frequency of some vowels, and therefore it ought to be a drawback for a female singer at higher pitches. Against this background, it seems highly remarkable that skilled singing teachers are capable of teaching students of both sexes how to sing; they are actually teaching two entirely different techniques of vowel articulation.

The reason that good singing teachers manage regardless of their own sex and the sex of the student may be that the teachers tend to pay more attention to voice timbre than to the underlying articulation. An efficient voice teacher may try to develop a "free" tone in the student, which probably means a tone relieved of those characteristics that a listener would associate with a person in vocal distress. Then, the student has to find, in a more or less intuitive way, the type of phonation and articulation which satisfies the teacher.

A danger with a more specific type of instruction, utilizing terms such as tongue, jaw, subglottic pressure, and so on, is that it might cause students to focus attention on these features, which are truly unmusical—actually *means* rather than *goals*. On the other hand, some students find it difficult to interpret the instructions of a teacher using an impressionistic terminology, and much time is then wasted. It is even possible that students having such difficulties are considered ungifted. In any event, the ultimate goal in educating singers must be to give them an obedient instrument through which they can realize musical ideas, without any audible technical limitations. The teacher's terminology should never prevent the student from reaching this goal.

The relevance of a vertical larynx position in the case of male singing seems to underlie a number of suggestive expressions frequently used in vocal pedagogy. Instructions such as "take your breath as in a yawn" or "take your breath as if you were smelling the odor of a rose" are likely to lead to inhalation associated with an activation of the diaphragm and a lowering of the larynx. A similar example of the same thing is "Sing as if you were crying," a condition that often seems to involve a lowering of the larynx and a widening of the pharynx.

It is important to realize that a lowering of the larynx may be favorable for other reasons than the purely acoustical ones we have described. The lowering of the larynx is performed by an extrinsic laryngeal muscle, namely the sternothyroid muscle. The elevation of the larynx is handled by muscles which are also involved in the articulation, and the entire larynx is suspended in the hyoid bone which in turn is suspended in structures involved in articulation, such as the tongue. For example, the middle constrictor muscle originates in the hyoid bone and inserts in the median raphe of the pharynx. The superior part of it runs almost vertically and is probably active in elevating the larynx. If so, the pharyngeal width must decrease when the larynx is raised which will prevent a normal articulation of all vowels requiring a wide pharynx, such as /i:/ and /e:/. Thus, an elevated larynx is likely to modify the formant frequencies of some vowels, but also, and perhaps still more important, it may reduce the *articulatory variability* available to the singer. If the larynx is not raised, but on the contrary lowered, all muscles leading upward from the hyoid bone would be relaxed, so that articulatory changes of the pharynx are not disturbed.

There is probably an interrelationship between larynx height and phonation, too. For instance, the voice source may work more steadily as long as the larynx is not raised. On the other hand, a lowering of the larynx is often associated with glottal abduction, if we may infer this from the typically breathy sound quality of a voice in yawning. This means that it is not enough to lower one's larynx in order to acquire a singer's formant.

Moreover, several voice patients speak with a habitually raised larynx, and a typical recommendation to such patients is, as mentioned, to lower the frequency of phonation. In most untrained speakers, the physiological effect of lowering phonation frequency is a lowering of the larynx. As a lowering of phonation frequency is successfully used in order to improve voice function, it seems that a lowering of the larynx is likely to lead to a relaxation of the musculature of phonation.

According to experiments with synthesized singing (Sundberg and Askenfelt, 1983), the auditory impression of an elevation of the larynx is promoted by a voice source having a weak fundamental, which is typically affiliated with "pressed" phonation, as we know. This suggests that a raised larynx is typically associated with a general muscle tension in the voice organ, while a lowered larynx can be combined with "flow phonation" (abduction) and a general relaxation of the voice organ. On the other hand, as demonstrated by the X-ray investigation of the soprano, it is perfectly possible to sing beautifully with an elevated larynx.

How do female singers learn how to tune their first formant frequency to the phonation frequency? Many singing teachers teach their students to "relax the jaw." Perhaps their aim is to establish a mobile and sensitive jaw opening that can always be quickly adjusted in synchrony with phonation frequency. It is also thought-provoking that the vowel /a:/ is so commonly used in voice training. This vowel has a high first formant frequency. The need for adjusting the jaw opening in accordance with the phonation frequency is therefore avoided up to the vicinity of rather high pitches (cf. figures 2.12, 5.23, and 5.24).

6

Choral Voice

Choral singing is probably the most widespread type of singing. Therefore, the particular voice usage under such conditions is an important subject to research. Yet, almost all research on the singing voice concerns operatic singing. For this reason this chapter is a short one; there are not many facts to report about choral singing. But it would have been much shorter if Sten Ternström and the author had not recently had the opportunity to carry out some investigations in this field (Ternström et al., 1983; Ternström and Sundberg, 1984, 1986, and forthcoming).

Some scientists have studied choral singing from the point of view of phonation frequency adjustment and particularly what facilitates it. A couple of studies have been devoted to the timbral similarities and dissimilarities between choral and solo singing, particularly regarding the singer's formant.

How Similar Are the Phonation Frequencies?

To what degree do choral singers sing in tune? The answer to this question naturally depends on the skill of the ensemble and of the choir director. In the most horrible choirs, there would be as many versions of phonation frequency as there are choral singers, but the unity must increase as skill improves. Unfortunately, those who have measured the extent of agreement among choral singers as to phonation frequency have used widely differing methods, so the results cannot easily be compared. Henceforth we will use the term *degree of unison* for this characteristic of choral singing.

Sacerdote (1957) was the first scientist to study the degree of unison. He measured it in four soprano singers, but he did not describe the degree of sophistication of these singers. He compared their distribution of phonation frequencies with that obtained when noise was passed through a narrow bandpass filter. He found that the singers produced a distribution similar to that obtained when the bandwidth of such a filter was 1.3 semitones.

Lottermoser and Meyer (1960) applied a different method. They analyzed phonograph records of choral music using a 1 Hz wide filter. The distribution of phonation frequencies used by the singers appeared as a narrow peak in the spectrogram. The researchers measured the width of this peak which was defined as the separation between the two frequencies where the amplitude had decreased to 70% of the peak amplitude; engineers use the term *bandwidth* for this measure. The average of this bandwidth was $+/-$ 25 cents in the four choirs studied. The greatest bandwidth was $+/-50$ cents, while the narrowest was $+/-$ 10 cents.

Ternström and the author measured the degree of unison in the bass section of a good amateur choir that sang the cadence shown in figure 6.1. After rehearsing, the choir sang the cadence four times. Six of the basses had contact microphones fastened to their throats, and these signals were recorded on a multichannel tape recorder. In this way each of the singers' phonation frequencies could be determined and compared. There was no training effect; the agreement was not better in the fourth rendering than in the first one. Therefore, the data from all renderings were pooled, and the averages were determined for each of the nine chords. The standard deviation of phonation frequency was used to estimate the degree of unison. The results are plotted in the same figure 6.1. The various chords all gave similar values, implying that they were all about equally difficult to tune. The standard deviations varied between 10 and 16 cents, with an average over all the chords of 13 cents. This means that two-thirds of the phonation frequency values of these bass singers lie within a 26-cents-wide frequency band. In other words, deviations greater than 13 cents were rather unusual.

As mentioned, it is hard to compare these results. It seems, however, that the degree of unison that Sacerdote found is smaller than that in the other two studies. The reason for this might be that the singers in Sacerdote's investigation used vibrato. The results from the other two studies seem in better agreement. Apart from the skill of the choir, the vibrato is the factor that would most likely influence the result; as we have seen before the vibrato eliminates beats, which could serve as a cue for the individual choral singer's intonation, at least in small ensembles.

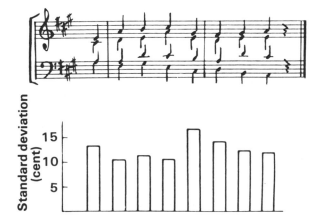

Figure 6.1. The standard deviation, or the average deviation from the mean, in phonation frequency for six choral singers who sang the bass part of the cadence shown above. (From Ternström and Sundberg, forthcoming.)

TABLE 6.1 *Average interval sizes in chords sung by four choirs (according to Lottermoser and Meyer, 1960).*

Interval width (semitone)	Size in pure intonation (cent)	Mean size in four choirs (cent)	Mean deviation from pure (cent)
3	316	275	−27
4	386	421	+25
5	498	501	+3
7	702	697	−5
8	814	795	−21
9	884	905	+21
12	1200	1200	0

Accuracy of Interval Intonation

The material gathered by Lottermoser and Meyer allowed them to also measure how various intervals were tuned in the choirs. Averages for some consonant intervals in the four choirs are given in the table 6.1.

We can see that the perfect intervals, that is the fourth, the fifth, and the octave, were all very nearly pure. In the case of the major and minor third and sixth, there was a trend to narrowly tune minor intervals and widely tune the major intervals, or, in other words, to somewhat increase the pitch contrast between these intervals. This seems generally typical of tuning in music practice (Sundberg, 1982).

In the Ternström and Sundberg investigation it was difficult to measure the mean interval sizes; it would have been necessary to determine the phonation frequency of a great number of tones. Instead, researchers investigated the influence of various properties of the sound reaching the choral singers' ears on their intonation of an interval. Choral singers heard a synthetic reference tone in earphones and were asked to sing a fifth or a major third above this reference tone.

A basic hypothesis was that certain spectrum partials might be more relevant than others in such situations. We realize that certain partials share the same frequency values in two spectra that form a consonant interval, provided, however, that both spectra are harmonic. This condition is fulfilled in the case of sung vowels, as we know.

Let us take an example. A fifth results if the two tones have a fundamental frequency ratio that can be expressed as 3/2, for instance, 300 Hz and 200 Hz. We also know that the frequencies of the partials form a multiplication table. The overtones of a 300-Hz tone have the frequencies of 600, 900, 1200, 1500, 1800 Hz, etc., and those of a 200-Hz tone occur at 400, 600, 800, 1000, 1200, 1400, 1600, 1800 Hz, etc. We observe that every third partial of the 200-Hz tone has the same frequency as every second partial in the 300-Hz tone, if the frequency ratio is 3/2. The same applies to all intervals; if the frequency ratio can be expressed as a ratio between small integer numbers, as is the case with the harmonic intervals, the lowest common partial will appear as one of the lower spectrum partials. These partials are called *common partials*. It may be assumed that the presence of these common partials facilitates a perfect intonation. Therefore, the relevance of common partials was investigated.

In the reference tones, common partials were either present or totally missing. There were also two other acoustic characteristics that were varied in the reference tones. One of these was vibrato, so that the reference tones either had or lacked vibrato, the obvious reason being that the presence of vibrato eliminates beats between partials having nearly identical frequencies. Finally, the reference tones either had or lacked high partials.

Eighteen male choral singers participated as subjects. As a measure of the facility of intonation, the mean deviation from the group mean was used; if all subjects chose very similar phonation frequencies, the interval must be easy to tune.

The results showed that all three factors were relevant to ease of intonation. Whether a particular factor had any effect depended on the presence or absence of other factors in the reference tone. This was not an unexpected finding; if it is easy to tune a fifth with a reference possessing certain acoustic characteristics, adding more characteristics does not necessarily make intonation still easier. Anyway, the results supported the conclusion that low common partials, lack of vibrato, and high partials may all facilitate the tuning of harmonic intervals.

In a later experiment, we could show that not only the presence of common partials but also their sound levels influenced the ease of intonation. It is possible to chose the vowel and the fundamental frequency in such a way that the frequency of the first or second formant is almost identical with the lowest common partial, the sound level of which is thereby considerably increased. Consider a fourth between the frequencies of 300 and 400 Hz. The lowest common partial appears at 1200 Hz. This partial can be enhanced by the second formant in /a:/. We tried this in practice. We recorded a choral bass section singing selected combinations of phonation frequency and vowel. These vowel sounds were then presented as reference tones to choral singers, who were asked to sing certain harmonic intervals with them. Again, the results showed that the singers agreed more closely in phonation frequency when the common partial was enhanced by a formant.

The above seems to imply the possibility of facilitating the intonation of chords that are difficult to tune, if one adapts the text during rehearsal so that a formant is used to enhance a common partial (if there is one). The trick is first to find out the phonation frequencies of the tones constituting the chord, for which table 6.2 is helpful.

TABLE 6.2. *Phonation frequencies in Hz for the tones of the equally tempered scale.*[1]

C	C#	D	D#	E	F	F#	G	G#	A	A#	B	C
261.6	277.2	293.7	311.1	329.6	349.2	370.0	392.0	413.3	440.0	466.2	493.9	523.3

[1]If one wants to find out the frequency one octave up or down, the numbers should be doubled or halved, respectively.

By writing down the multiplication tables for the chord notes' fundamental frequencies, one can see which partials should coincide in frequency. Then, by using a formant chart like the one shown in figure 2.12, p. 24, one can guess which vowel has either the first or the second formant closest to the lowest common partial. If one listens carefully, one can usually hear when a formant is coinciding with a partial: that partial then becomes so loud that one can discern it as a clear pitch in the vowel timbre.

The sounds that the choral singers hear their colleagues produce possess more characteristics relevant to the facility of chord tuning than those already mentioned. One obvious factor is how *loud* this sound is; Ternström and the author carried out an experiment in order to find out its significance. Four choral singers participated in this experiment, and their task was simple: they heard a reference tone and were asked to sing that tone for as long as it sounded, which was signaled also by means of a small lamp. The reference, which represented the sound of a section of colleagues, was either an /ɑː/ or a /uː/, and its loudness varied within an almost 40 dB wide dynamic range. However, the singers were always asked to sing at a constant level, and they could monitor the level of their tones on a dB meter. When the reference was presented at maximum loudness, the singers could not hear their own voices. When the reference was presented at the lowest levels, the subjects could not hear it while they were singing.

Again, the average deviation from the ensemble mean was used, and it is shown in figure 6.2. This average deviation was small within a reference tone range of approximately 25 dB. This shows that the level of the sound

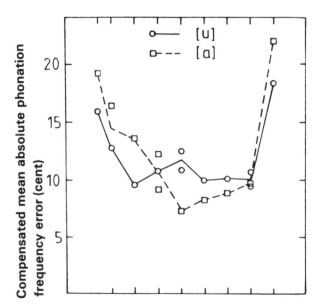

Figure 6.2. The average deviation from the ensemble mean for a group of choral singers who sang a tone with constant sound level and with the same pitch as a simultaneous reference tone presented at different sound levels. The average deviation was great when the reference tone was so loud that the singers could not hear their own voices and also when it was so soft that the singers' own tone masked the reference. (From Ternström and Sundberg, forthcoming.)

Level difference (5dB/div.)

that the choral singers hear from the rest of the choir may vary within quite a wide range without causing intonation problems. However, when the reference tone was very loud and the singers could not hear their own voices, the situation became chaotic; the curve rises quite steeply for the loudest reference. When the reference tone was very soft, a more moderate increase in the difficulties was observed.

However, this conclusion is not really accurate. As figure 6.3 shows, the subjects' phonation frequencies varied considerably when the reference tone was a /u:/. The singers responded with a tone that was about 25 cents sharp and 45 cents flat for the softest and loudest reference tones, respectively. (This effect was compensated for in figure 6.2.) In other words, by increasing the reference tone level by about 40 dB, the mean phonation frequency of the response dropped by no less than 70 cents, or slightly less than a semitone step! No corresponding effect could be observed when the reference tone was an /ɑ:/, as seen in the same figure.

This effect is well known from sinewave signals, the perceived pitch of which depends on the level. Mostly the effect disappears when the signal

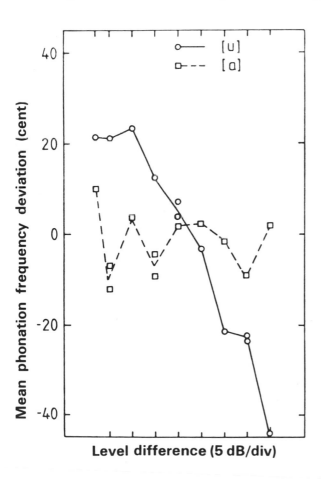

Figure 6.3. The average phonation frequency error for a group of choral singers who sang a tone with constant sound level and with the same pitch as a simultaneous reference presented at different sound levels. When the reference tone was the vowel /ɑ:/, the error was not influenced appreciably by the sound level of the reference, but when the vowel was /u:/ the singers were about 20 cents sharp or 40 cents flat, depending on the sound level of the reference. (From Ternström and Sundberg, forthcoming.)

contains a sufficient number of overtones. We may assume that there were not enough overtones in the reference tone in the case of the vowel /u:/, which, on the other hand, sounded quite natural in the experiment. From chapter 4 we know that this vowel has comparatively soft overtones because of the low frequencies of the first and second formants.

This implies that it is important that choral singers hear each other at a reasonable loudness as compared with the level at which they hear their own voices. One may suspect that difficulties are likely to occur in a choir where the singers sing at very different levels, because of great differences in individual singing technique. We may dare one more guess: If there are intonation problems in a chord sung on the vowel /u:/, the problems might disappear if, during the first rehearsals, the vowel were changed to /ɑ:/ or to another vowel with louder overtones.

Here we may mention that the sound the singers hear from the rest of the choir varies around the 80 dB sound pressure level, according to measurements made in two choirs. However, considerably higher values also occur; in a soprano section, a 115 dB sound pressure level occurred several times. Such loud sounds would not be detrimental to hearing, because the sensitivity of the hearing organ is decreased as soon as one starts to phonate; a muscle in the middle ear reflexively contracts so that the level reaching the inner ear is reduced.

We have now seen how different spectrum characteristics influence the ability of a choral singer to sing in unison with others. Perhaps a factor of still greater relevance to choir singing is *how* the singers hear their own voices as well as the room reverberation. This aspect has been studied by Marshall and Meyer (1985). They asked a quartet of singers to sing in an anechoic room in which various kinds of room reverberation were simulated and presented over loudspeakers that surrounded the singers.

The reverberating sound in a room contains two main parts. One is the individual *early reflections* that arrive within 50 or 100 msec. These reflexes are generated by sound-reflecting surfaces in the neighborhood of the sound source. As the number of reflections increases with time, the reflections are gradually smeared and constitute the second part, which is a continuous sound of decreasing level. This sound is called the *reverberation sound*.

Marshall and Meyer found that the singers liked those types of reverberation in which they found it easiest to sing together, as we might expect. Strong early reflexes were appreciated, provided that they arrived within a time span of 40 msec. This corresponds to a distance between the singer and a sound-reflecting surface of up to 7 meters. The stronger these reflexes were, the more they were appreciated. If the reflexes arrived later, that is, if the closest sound reflector was more than 7 meters away from the singers, the reverberation sound was more important than the early reflexes. It did not matter very much if the duration of the reverberation sound was 1, 1.5, or 3 sec. This explains why the positioning of a choir in a room is an important factor in choral singing.

Solo Versus Choral Singing

Choral directors and singing teachers sometimes heatedly discuss whether or not future solo singers should sing in choirs: is choral singing advantageous for learning solo singing? Choir directors tend to argue that the ability of making music is promoted by choral singing and that, after all, the voice is used for singing in both cases. Voice teachers often maintain that the voice use is different and that solo singing, as opposed to choral singing, requires individual musical initiative.

Lively discussions tend to emerge when the base of objective knowledge is fragile; the less one knows, the stronger one feels. The facts needed in order to resolve the argument in this case are, at least in part, those related to the differences in voice use between choral and solo singing. Do singers develop the same type of voice timbre in both situations?

Goodwin (1980) compared how sopranos used their voices when they sang to create a choral blend and when they sang as soloists. Spectral analysis revealed not only that the singers sang more loudly but also that the overtones were louder when they performed as soloists. As we know, the levels of the higher overtones increase more than those of the lower overtones when loudness of phonation is increased. Therefore, it is possible that the stronger overtones merely reflected the higher sound level in this experiment.

Rossing et al. (1985 and 1986) studied the same question in two investigations, one concerning male singers and the other female singers. Attempts were made to separate the contributions from voice source and articulation.

The subjects were singers who were experienced both as choral singers and as soloists. In other words, it could be assumed that they were skilled in using their voices in both ways (in case there were more than one way). In order to offer realistic conditions to the subjects, a selection for choir was recorded with the microphones mounted in the ears of an artificial head which was placed in the choir as if it belonged to a member of the choir. This recording was replayed over headphones mixed with the frontal sound of the subject. In this way a rather realistic auditory image was created, and the task of the singers was to join the choir they heard. For the solo situation, the piano accompaniment of a song was recorded in the corresponding way.

In the case of the male subjects, pairs of tones sung at the same pitch, on the same vowel, and with the same loudness in both experimental settings were compared. The results revealed certain differences that seemed typical, as shown in figure 6.4. In the solo situation, each singer had a louder singer's formant and slightly softer overtones below about 500 Hz. Also, the singers adapted the loudness more closely to that of the earphone reference in the case of choral singing; as soloists they were often much louder than the accompaniment, as we might expect.

In the case of the female subjects, it was important to base the conclusions on a greater selection of tones equal in loudness, pitch, and vowel. A

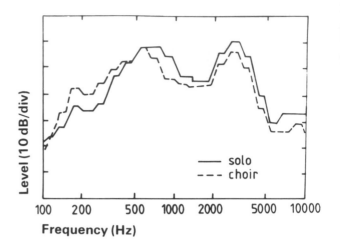

Figure 6.4. Average spectrum envelopes for a male singer who sang a phrase as a solo singer and as a choral singer. In the latter case his lowest partials are somewhat stronger and his singer's formant is slightly weaker. (From Rossing et al., 1986.)

piece for soprano solo and choir was selected in which the soprano part of the choir repeated the phrases sung by the soloist, and long-term-average spectra were used to evaluate the result. Figure 6.5 shows typical results. Notice that subjects had louder high overtones in the 2–4 kHz range when they sang as soloists.

In order to find out whether these results were typical, two more subjects with a good international reputation as opera singers were asked to perform the solo part of the same piece under the same conditions as the other subjects. It turned out that these singers sang with still louder high frequency overtones in the 2–4 kHz range than the other subjects. This suggests that a high level of these high overtones is essential not only to male singers, as we have seen before, but also to female singers. (Whether it is appropriate to speak about a singer's formant in the case of sopranos is hard to decide until the mechanism underlying this phenomenon has been

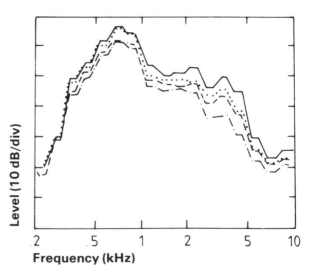

Figure 6.5. Average spectrum envelopes for a female singer who sang the same phrase at two different sound levels as a solo singer and as a choral singer. Solid and dashed curves refer to loud and soft solo singing, and dotted and chain-dashed curves pertain to loud and soft choral singing. Choral singing gives slightly weaker high partials. (From Rossing et al., 1985.)

determined. One could argue that the term "singer's formant" should be used for a spectrum peak that is generated not simply by raising loudness of phonation but by a clustering of the higher formants.)

In any event it seems that voice use in choral and solo singing differs in certain respects that are probably important for the success of a solo singer. It seems fair to assume that students of solo singing who have no problems with their voice timbres could gladly join a choir and, in this way, enrich their musical experience. If, on the other hand, the student has problems in developing an acceptable voice timbre and if he or she also has a hard time learning two slightly differing types of voice use at the same time, it seems wiser to concentrate on one thing at a time. In any event it would be advantageous to know that the same type of voice timbre is not sought in choral and in solo singing.

It is important to stress that this is merely *one* of several differences between solo and choir singing. Another difference is probably the above-mentioned need for individual musical initiative that would be much more important in solo singing than in choral singing. A third difference might be that choral singers strive to tune their voice timbre in order to mesh with the timbre of the rest of the choir, while a solo singer would try to develop his or her own individual timbre.

The Intrinsic Pitch of Vowels

One more experiment that the author carried out together with Ternström is relevant to choral singing (Ternström et al., 1983). The starting point was the typical experience of choral directors that intonation tends to go flat or high depending on the vowel. It is as if the vowel had a pitch trend in itself. This is far from impossible. We know that vowel articulation involves adjustments in jaw opening and tongue shape. Thus, a change of articulation might easily disturb the adjustment of the laryngeal cartilages that determine phonation frequency.

In this experiment, choral singers sustained long tones, and in the middle of each tone they were asked to shift the vowel according to a given scheme. The phonation frequency was measured, and all changes that occurred at the moment of vowel shift were analyzed. During part of the experiments the subjects could not hear their own voices because the auditory feedback was eliminated by noise in earphones.

Figure 6.6 shows the result for all pairs of vowels that were included in the experiment. In many cases no clear trend was observed. The vowel /i:/, however, was mostly associated with a high pitch; when the subjects switched from /i:/ to either /ɛ:/, /e:/, or /a:/, phonation frequency tended to drop. Some other vowels seemed associated with a low pitch, so that when the vowel was changed from /o:/ or /ɸ:/ to /y:/ pitch rose in most cases.

These effects would be relevant not only to choral but also to solo singing, and obviously they cannot be accepted under any circumstances. Perhaps solo singers learn how to avoid them by reducing the influence exerted by the articulatory system on the pitch regulating system. Also,

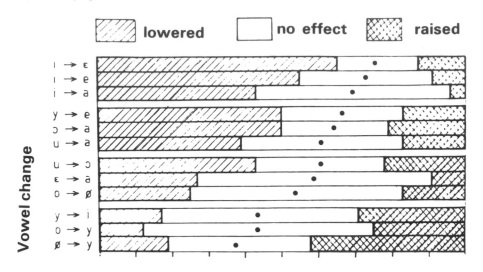

Occurrence of phonation frequency shifts (10%/div.)

Figure 6.6. Average shift in phonation frequency observed when choral singers attempted to maintain a constant pitch while changing the vowel. When the vowel was shifted from /i:/ to either /ɛ:/, /e:/, or /a:/, phonation frequency tended to drop, while it tended to rise when the vowel was changed from /o:/ or /ɸ:/ to /y:/.

choral and solo singing conditions differ in an important way: solo singers generally have a stable reference in terms of an instrumental accompaniment, so they can always check their tuning by listening to the accompaniment. In a choir the reference is provided by the fellow singers who all fight against the same tendencies. Therefore, these tendencies are more likely to manifest themselves in terms of intonation problems in choral singing.

Some Remaining Questions

The reader has probably already observed that most of the questions regarding choral singing were not mentioned in this chapter. This is not surprising, because of the scarcity of choral research in the past, as mentioned. Here we can only mention some of the questions that seem possible not only to pose but also to answer.

Many aspects of intonation have been studied already. However we do not seem to understand very well how melodic and harmonic demands on tuning are weighted in cases where they conflict. Consider, for example, the chord progression dominant-tonic in traditional harmony. Generally, the third of the dominant chord moves one semitone upward to the root of the tonic in such cases. A pure major third is narrow, so for this reason we would expect the third in the dominant chord to be low. On the other hand, in music practice there is a trend to make minor intervals narrow and major intervals wide, as we saw before. One way to satisfy this desire is to tune the root of the tonic a bit flat. However, this does not seem to represent a plausible solution. Another possibility is to raise the third in the dominant chord and, according to both the testimony of musicians and some measurements, this is the solution generally used even though it implies a deviation from a pure tuning of the dominant chord. In this example, then, the melodic principle that minor melodic intervals should be a bit narrow overrides the harmonic principle that the major third should be narrow. But are the melodic demands always considered more important than the harmonic ones? In order to find the answer one should study intonation in choral practice as well as in other genres of musical practice.

We have seen that the various voice categories differ with respect to formant frequencies. For instance, we saw in chapter 5 that the center frequency of the singer's formant is low in basses and high in tenors. What happens to these formant frequency differences in a good choir? Do the members compromise so that all choir members agree on approximately the same formant frequencies, or do all section colleagues arrive at such an agreement, or is this an unimportant factor? In any event the formant frequency distribution within a choir must be relevant to the choral timbre. Perhaps there are differences in this regard between choirs and perhaps also between the choral traditions in various countries.

The formant frequencies do not represent the only method of varying the voice timbre. The voice source can also be changed. In particular we have seen that the level of its fundamental can be shifted. Is this variability something that is used in choral singing? We just observed that male solo singers develop more energy at the singer's formant and less energy in the low frequency region than choral singers. Are there corresponding differences between the voice categories in a choir? Do tenors sing with less low-frequency energy and more high-frequency energy than basses? The author's intuitive feeling, developed from his experience of choral singing, was that one always had to make one's voice timbre "lighter" when singing the higher bass part in a piece with a split bass voice. Possibly this coloring of the voice was achieved by singing with a less dominant fundamental in the voice source.

Another factor of great relevance to the choral sound is the reverberation characteristics of the room. Typically, intonation problems may appear or vanish when the choir moves from one room to another. The acoustics of the room influence the level at which the singers hear the rest of the choir. Here we have seen that this level may have an effect on the individual singer's intonation. Does intonation also depend on how loud one hears one's own voice? Is tuning easier if the overtones are efficiently reflected back to one's ears, as in a bathroom?

Evidently, choral singing offers a large field for scientific research, full of questions that can both be formulated and answered. Let us hope that it will attract the attention of a greater number of researchers in the future than in the past!

Speech, Song, and Emotions

The emotional state of a speaker has a considerable effect on the way in which the voice is used. One sentence can be pronounced in a vast number of ways revealing, among other things, the speaker's state of emotion. The differences can be found in the voice pitch contour, in the duration of the various syllables, and in other aspects of speech. Many listeners are very skilled in detecting the emotional state of a speaker just by listening to the voice. The importance of the emotional state for voice use may even cause problems. Among phoniatricians, it is a general clinical observation that stress typically influences a speaker's voice use, sometimes to the extent that a voice problem develops.

In regard to singing, the gross contour of the voice pitch, which we may view as a sort of *macrointonation,* is decided by the composer. What can the singer add in order to convey the emotional atmosphere implied in the text? It is possible to add to the performance of the song some characteristic details of the code used in speech for signaling emotions, though without violating the compositional framework, the macrointonation. We may assume the singer can solve this problem by working in the domain of *microintonation,* that is, the small details of the phonation frequency contour. It seems, then, that the way emotions are manifested acoustically in speech and singing deserves our interest.

Different investigators have applied different strategies in attempts to find an answer to the question of how emotions are conveyed acoustically. Most of them have analyzed the sound, but some have examined production aspects, and one author has studied the interrelationships between gestures and sound. Three reviews on the subject should be mentioned: Crystal (1969), Kramer (1963), and Scherer (1979). These treat the combination of emotions and voice in a broad sense, studying, for instance, such aspects as personality judgments based on voice and the influence of stress on voice. Scherer's review article summarizes his own extensive investigations in this field.

Oddly enough, several contributions to this topic of voice and emotions were indirectly generated by astronautics; when people were shot away to

Portions of this chapter appeared in *Music, Mind, and Brain,* edited by Manfred Clynes, published by the Plenum Press, 1982. Permission to quote courtesy of the Plenum Press.

be left alone in space for several days, it became important to use all possible means to survey their emotional state. But this chapter, however, goes neither into aspects of stress nor personality. Instead, we will concentrate on the question of how specific emotions influence vocal behavior.

Emotional Speech

Where in the sound of the voice do we find information about the emotional state of the speaker? As mentioned, one parameter is the pattern of phonation frequency which can be varied within wide limits without encroaching on the information afforded by the linguistic contents of the sentence. The breathing pattern can also be influenced by emotions, so effects on subglottic pressure can be expected. If this pressure is raised, loudness and, to some extent, phonation frequency will increase. Moreover, faster breathing should reduce the phrase length in speech. Drying of the mouth is a symptom of certain emotions, as are disturbances of the motor functions, such as tremor ("shaking with anger," "trembling with fear"). These factors ought to have some effect on the glottal voice source. Thus, there are good reasons to expect that a number of voice parameters are influenced by the speaker's emotional state.

Lieberman and Michaels (1962) investigated the relevance of various voice source parameters. In a series of listening tests, they deprived emotional speech produced by male speakers of a systematically increased number of acoustic parameters. Thus they reduced the listeners' ability to correctly identify the emotion underlying different utterances from 85% (for nonmanipulated speech) all the way down to 14% for speech retaining nothing but the original amplitude modulation. A great step in this decrease, from 85% to 47%, resulted from the elimination of the supraglottal or articulatory contributions to the speech signal. Similarly, phonation frequency movements were found important; a drop from 47% to 25% in the percentage of correct responses resulted when these movements were eliminated. Lieberman and Michaels also found that the various emotional modes did not affect all the acoustic parameters to the same extent. For instance, fear seemed to rely more heavily on amplitude information than other emotions.

Sedlacek and Sychra (1963) had twenty-three actors read one sentence so as to express eight emotional states: neutral, love, joy, solemnity, comedy, irony, sorrow, and fear. Listening tests with different groups of observers revealed that a correct identification of these modes did not depend on the individual's ability to understand the language spoken in the test phrases. Nor did the cultural background of the observers seem relevant; students from Asia, Africa, and Latin America gave practically the same answers as a group of Czech students, who were the only subjects familiar with the language spoken in the test sentences. The authors examined phonation frequency, amplitude, and spectra in those sentences which showed the highest scores in the listening tests. Mean phonation frequency was found to be raised in joy, lowered in sorrow, and intermediate in neutral mode.

Phonation frequency movements seemed important as well. Thus, one single phonation frequency peak, followed by a slowly falling movement, appeared typical for sad modes while the occurrence of two peaks during the utterance seemed associated with more active modes.

Trojan, in a series of articles (for instance, 1952), revealed formal evidence, mainly in terms of pupil dimensions, supporting the assumption of two distinct phonatory dimensions associated with the expression of emotions. One dimension has the extremes of sparing-voice ("Schonstimme") and power-voice ("Kraftstimme"), which he claimed corresponded to the two poles of the "automatic rhythm." The other dimension is the pharyngeal width which, according to Trojan, is used to express pleasure and disgust. Referring to these hypotheses, Trojan and Winckel (1957) studied the acoustical consequences of these phonatory and articulatory dimensions. Phonation in sparing-voice and power-voice modes differed with respect to amplitude, as we might expect, while the articulatory adjustments of the pharyngeal width affected the formant frequencies, as the spectra published in their article show.

Later, Williams and Stevens (1972) considered the voice effects of four emotional states: sorrow, anger, fear, and neutral. Actors performed a short, spoken play in which different states of emotion were displayed. On the phonation frequency curve, a neutral state of emotion was found to be associated with slow changes with no sharp contrasts (figure 7.1). The phonation frequency used for anger was normally higher than that for a neutral state. Further, a few syllables showed high peaks in the phonation frequency contour. Apart from such peaks, the curve was even and continuous. Sorrow presented a completely different pattern, with low phonation frequency and little variation. The frequency fell slowly, almost without interruption, until the end of the sentence. Fear was manifested in several ways, among them, fast increases and decreases and sharp contrasts. Statistically, the average phonation frequency was lowest for sadness, higher for the neutral state and for fear, and highest for anger, as can be seen in figure 7.2. The variation was smallest for sorrow and greatest for fear.

The same sentence ("For God's sake!") was pronounced in the shortest time with a neutral state of emotion and in the longest for sorrow. This was due not to longer vowel sounds but mainly to longer consonants. The average number of syllables per second was 4.3 for a neutral state, 4.2 for anger, 3.8 for fear, and 1.9 for sorrow. For sorrow, a lack of stability was also observed in the voice source: the individual voice pulses were not similar with respect to the overtone contents. Anger also seemed to have higher values for the first formant, probably caused by an exaggerated mouth opening.

Long-term-average spectra of speech contain information about the amount of overtones of the voice source. The results shown in figure 7.3 indicate that the overtones above 1 kHz were most powerful in anger and weakest in sorrow. One can assume that anger is associated with a higher subglottic pressure and, possibly, a high activity of the adduction muscles. If so, the glottis will close more rapidly in the vibratory cycle, and the

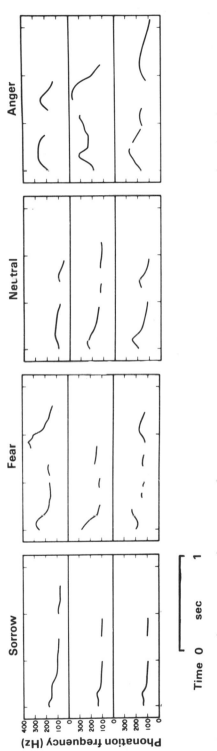

Figure 7.1. Phonation frequency curves for the voices of three actors who pronounce the same sentence in the various modes indicated. Phonation frequency descends slowly in sorrow and exhibits rather wild jumps in the more excited emotional modes. (From Williams and Stevens, 1972.)

Figure 7.2. Median and range of the phonation frequency (points and bars, respectively) for three actors speaking in various emotional modes: S = sorrow, N = neutral, F = fear, and A = anger. Phonation frequency was lowest in sorrow and highest in anger. (From Williams and Stevens, 1972.)

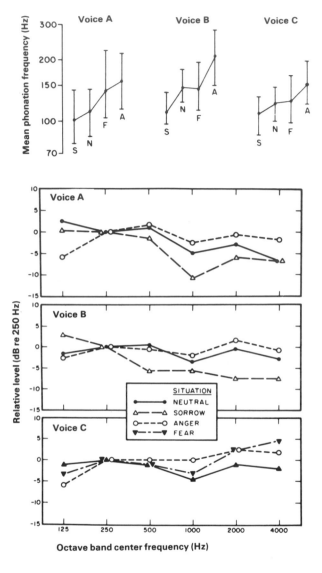

Figure 7.3. Average spectra of actors speaking in the different modes indicated. Sorrow and neutral show the lowest amplitudes for high overtones. (From Williams and Stevens, 1972.)

source spectrum overtones will become stronger. In sorrow, a lowered activity in all muscles may be the reason for the opposite effect.

A unique piece of evidence has been preserved and can be studied: the recording of Chicago radio newscaster Herbert Morrison (WLS) who described the arrival of the airship *Hindenburg* and its subsequent explosion at Lakehurst, New Jersey, on 6 May 1937. A time spectrogram of his voice before and after the explosion is shown in figure 7.4. Some typical effects can be observed: before the catastrophe, phonation frequency shows smooth upward and downward changes. After the catastrophe, it is higher and varies very slowly but within a larger range. It shows, furthermore, sudden small irregularities, apparently some type of tremor which suggests that the newsman momentarily lost control over his phonation frequency.

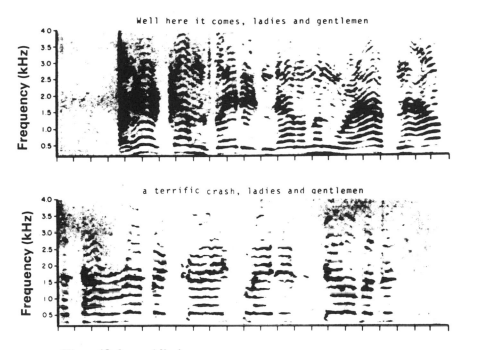

Time (0.1 sec/div.)

Figure 7.4. Time spectrogram of the voice of a radio announcer speaking before (top) and after (bottom) the crash of the Hindenburg. The voice characteristics change drastically when the speaker suddenly witnesses the death of several passengers. (From Williams and Stevens, 1972.)

In summary, the following profiles for the various states of emotion can be presented for speech, according to Williams and Stevens:

Anger: The phonation frequency is almost half an octave above the normal level in neutral speech, and the range is greatly expanded. Some syllables are forcefully emphasized by increases in intensity and sudden increases in phonation frequency, sometimes in combination with a high first formant frequency. The articulation is almost excessively distinct.

Fear: Phonation frequency is lower as compared with anger, and it contains sudden peaks and irregularities. The articulation is more precise than in a neutral situation.

Sorrow: Little variability is observed in phonation frequency. The articulation is slow, and vowels, consonants, and pauses are long; irregularities, such as traces of hoarseness, can be found in the voice. Phonation frequency falls almost monotonously toward the end of the phrase and sometimes shows traces of tremor.

Neutral: The speaking rate is generally faster than for the above states of emotion. The consonants were often pronounced imprecisely, but the vowels show a well-defined pattern with few examples of those irregularities that evidence lack of voice control.

Singing with Emotional Expression

Kotlyar and Morozov (1976) carried out a study of emotional singing in which they had eleven professional singers sing specific phrases from different songs or arias several times. The singers' task was to create different moods: happiness, sorrow, fear, anger, and neutral. With a formal test procedure they ascertained that the singers did in fact succeed with this task and then examined a number of different acoustic aspects of the song. The results can be seen in figure 7.5.

The tempo, determined as the average syllable duration, was fastest for fear and slowest for sorrow. Fear was characterized by the longest pauses between the syllables. A neutral state of emotion showed the shortest pauses. Anger had the loudest voice amplitude and fear the softest. Sorrow was characterized by the slowest tone onsets, anger and fear by the fastest.

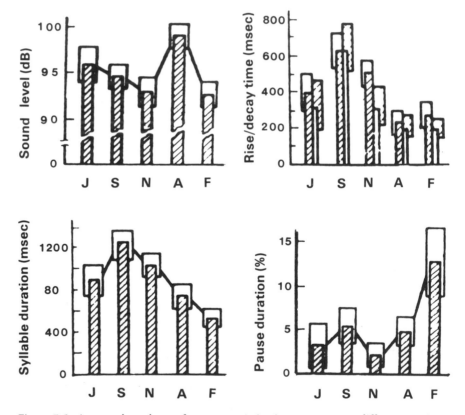

Figure 7.5. Average dependence of some acoustical voice parameters on different emotional modes as expressed in singing by professional singers. The modes are indicated as follows: J = joy, S = sorrow, N = neutral, A = anger, F = fear. In the graph at the upper right, the hatched columns show the voice-onset time, and the white columns show the corresponding value for the decay. Everything seems to move slowly in sorrow. The rectangles represent the scatter of the underlying data. (From Kotlyar and Morozov, 1976.)

In this way, each mood investigated showed a typical pattern of acoustic characteristics.

The authors also tried to find out how much of the entire story they had been able to identify; they presented to observers an electronically generated signal whose time-dependent characteristics (pitch, loudness, onset, etc.) varied in accordance with what they had found to be significant in the studied moods. These tone signals consisted of a simple sound with variable loudness and pitch and lacked vowel and consonant characteristics. The question was whether it was possible for listeners to determine what mood the signal represented.

The observers succeeded pretty well with these unusual stimuli, although joy presented severe difficulties for the subjects; the tone never sounded really happy. A possible interpretation is that although the temporal variations they studied are typical of the various moods, other signal characteristics may also be relevant, especially in the case of joy. In other words, it is perhaps not only by duration of syllables and pauses, by voice amplitude, and by rise and decay time of the tones that we express happiness in singing. Still, these parameters are involved in the patterns typical of sorrow, fear, anger, and a neutral state.

Emotional Phonation

Fonagy has, alone or in collaboration with others, carried out a series of interesting and stimulating investigations regarding the ways in which the state of emotion affects speech. We shall examine those studies having a direct relation to the way a speaker's mood is unveiled in speech.

Fonagy and Magdics (1963) compared the fundamental frequency of speech with various composers' melodic lines related to ten different states of emotion and attitudes: joy, tenderness, longing, coquetry, surprise, fear, plaintiveness, mockery, anger, and sarcasm. Thus, the investigation compared phonation frequency patterns with what we initially called the macrointonation.

Fonagy (1962) published measurements of glottal behavior during emotional speech. Two methods of measurement were used, a throat mirror and X-ray tomography. Three speakers repeatedly articulated the vowel /i:/, thereby trying to represent different emotions and attitudes. Fonagy described the types of voicing in the following way: (1) soft and voiced; (2) soft and unvoiced, as in a tender whisper; (3) hard and unvoiced, as in a spiteful whisper; (4) hard and hateful voiced, with pressed phonation, a creaky voice; (5) contemptuous growling. The vocal folds were found to be hidden by advanced ventricular bands during tense phonation with glottal fry; during unvoiced phonation, they did not close. The lateral positioning of the ventricular bands was different during tender and spiteful whispers. The laryngeal ventricle was wide and enlarged during soft, weak, voiced phonations, somewhat smaller during tender whispering, and rather small when whispering spitefully. The vocal folds were thick and looked swollen during contemptuous growling. Fonagy thus found good support for the conclusion that the emotional state or attitude of a speaker has considerable effects on the laryngeal adjustment. He interprets all these emotion dependent glottal profiles as "preconscious expressive gestures."

Emotional Articulation

It does not seem farfetched to assume that emotions and attitudes have articulatory effects. This topic was studied by Fonagy (1976) in an investigation that concerned the patterns of the tongue and the mouth opening in utterances pronounced with different emotional backgrounds. Clear effects were revealed: a vowel could be produced in a manner so far removed from normal that it partly assumed the articulatory characteristics of a different vowel. Anger was found to be associated with violent movements between extreme articulatory positions, while tenderness was characterized by slow, more supple movements. In the pronunciation of a menacing expression, the tongue first assumed a tense, extreme articulatory position, in order, as it were, to "shoot like an arrow" toward the next articulatory position.

Disappointment was characterized by a progressive relaxation of the tongue and the soft palate and decreasing speed of articulatory movement. Fonagy thinks there is a parallel in this behavior with the emotional paradigm of disappointment: expectation-suspense-disappointment-resignation. Furthermore, he finds similarities between articulatory movements associated with other states of emotion and their meanings. Every attitude is also expressed by its own articulation reflecting the mental contents of the attitude. Fonagy wants to interpret this as a materialization of the state of emotion, a reinterpretation into a movement that differs from the movement that accompanies a neutral state. According to Fonagy, a correct interpretation of the state of emotion behind an expression demands, therefore, knowledge of the manner of pronunciation for a neutral state of emotion. Thus, it is the deviations from the (expected) neutral, that carry the information concerning the state of emotion of a speaker.

In another investigation, Fonagy and Berard (1972) examined how an actress pronouncing a very common phrase ("Il est huit heures," or "It is eight o'clock.") used both glottal and articulatory equivalents of facial gestures. Fonagy has also investigated the extent to which a listener can infer the facial expression just from listening to the voice, as one may do during a telephone conversation (Fonagy, 1967).

Emotional Body Movement and Sound

We have seen that Fonagy convincingly assumes a close correlation between body movements observable with the naked eye and hidden body movements. Examples of normally invisible body movements can be found in the laryngeal cartilages, most of which are involved in the regulation of voice pitch. If it is true that a particular pattern of expressive body movements is typical of a specific emotional mode, then we would expect a corresponding pattern of, for example, voice pitch in speech produced in this same emotional mode. In other words, it is likely that expressive body movements are translated into acoustic terms in voice production.

According to Clynes (1969), phonatory and articulatory gestures are manifestations of what he calls a common expressive "sentic form" that underlies both the perception and the production of expression in different modalities. Clynes (1980) asked subjects to press on a button-like transducer in such a way as to express one of seven emotional modes: anger, hate, grief, love, sex, joy, and reverence. The vertical and horizontal components of the resulting dynamic pressures were recorded. The vertical component was converted into dynamic acoustic parameters, namely the pitch changes and the amplitude envelope of a sinusoidal signal. Clynes then presented these acoustic signals to observers and asked them in a forced-choice test to identify the signal as the expression of an emotional mode. The result showed that this could be done with a rather high accuracy. He received about 80% correct responses, only slightly lower than when the subjects watched the finger movements (without sound) by means of a videotape recording. It seems that these results can be readily understood if the voice function exemplifies the way the body movements may be coded into acoustic signals.

Discussion

In contrast to most of the studies mentioned earlier, which offer acoustic descriptions, Fonagy's papers concern articulatory and phonatory observations. He and Clynes both attempt to put these observations into a general psychological framework. Fonagy's results support the assumption that there is a relationship between the way in which the voice organs are used and the emotional content of the utterance. The tongue, which shoots "like an arrow" between extreme articulatory positions in a menacing utterance, can be seen as a symbol of the threat, and its slow movements during tender phonation seem to fit well with the idea of tenderness.

A possible reason for this symbolic behavior in phonation and articulation may be that each emotion and attitude has its own typical pattern of movement which exerts an influence over the behavior of the entire body, including the voice organs. For instance, most muscle activity would typically be minimized in sadness and depression; people are not really disposed to express themselves by means of wild gestures in sadness, tending rather to minimize movements to mere hints. Such a low level of muscular activity also seems characteristic for the speech tempo. The flat course of the phonation frequency curve suggests a low activity in the cricothyroid and other muscles. The low number of overtones in the voice source seems to indicate a low activity in the expiratory muscles, resulting in a low subglottic pressure. In fact, all muscles seem rather passive in a sad person's speech.

The opposite seems to apply to the voice of an angry person. The level of phonation frequency is high, strong peaks appear in the course of the phonation frequency curve, the voice source is rich in overtones, speech tempo is rather fast, and presumably the voice intensity is high. This indicates a vigorous and rapidly changing activity in many of the muscles of the speech organs. One can easily imagine the related visible violent gestures of an angry person.

Thus, for both sadness and anger, one can see a connection between the voice and the gestures. What else could be expected? Those gestures are what we can observe with our eyes while the gestures in the speech organ are invisible; on the other hand, we can hear their acoustic consequences.

There seems to be a relationship between the words we use to describe a certain manner of phonation and the characteristics of that phonation. A *tense* phonation is characterized by high subglottal pressure combined with high adduction activity. High *tension* is placed on both the expiratory muscles and certain phonation muscles. Presumably, it is this type of conformity which enables us to imagine correctly what a person means in describing a way of phonation that is characterized by physiological signs actually hidden to both speaker and listener.

We have seen several examples of the influence that the emotional state of a speaker exerts on the ways the voice organ is being used. This seems to explain why the emotional relationship between teacher and pupil has a decisive influence on the result of the voice training. If the atmosphere in the studio is not relaxed, the kind of phonation learned in that studio is not very likely to be relaxed either.

A Rhapsody on Perception

When we listen to voices, few of us think of formant frequencies, voice source fundamental, phonation frequency, intensity in dB, and so on. Rather, we process these acoustical data in a sophisticated way, so that we hear voice properties such as pitch, loudness, voice timbre, aggression, tenderness, insinuation, and whatnot. Until now, we have primarily dealt with voice as described in objective, physical terms. In this chapter we will try to bridge the gap between some of these objective terms and certain perceptual terms, to the extent that something definite is known. The reader should not expect to find a systematic, continuous text in this chapter, but rather a variety of information presented in quasi-random order, like a rhapsody.

It seems revealing of the way in which we perceive voice sounds that our processing of the acoustic voice signals, which is mostly unconscious, often results in a description in production terms; as we listen, we tend to imagine how the voice organ producing the sound is being used. We seem to identify with the speaker or singer in this sense. Moses (1954) coined the term "creative hearing" for this way of perceiving voices. In reality it would be both practical and efficient to describe the sound of a voice as, for instance, "tense" or "relaxed." Behind this fact lies our solid but still mainly intuitive knowledge about voice function. Probably in our imagination we project the voice timbre we hear from our own voice organ, and we analyze how phonation would feel under these imagined conditions. Then we describe the timbre via this imagined phonation. This must be why one's own voice might feel strained after having silently listened to an apparently strained phonation. To a great extent, the work and success of the teaching of voice and singing must rely on this same introspective talent. Indeed, Fonagy (1967) managed to demonstrate in an experiment, our ability to "hear" the shape of the lip opening!

To Hear and Sense One's Own Voice

Many of us have had the experience of listening to hi-fi recordings in which everybody—except oneself—sounds exactly as in reality. This perception is a good demonstration that one hears one's own voice rather differently than that of other speakers. There are two main reasons for this.

One reason is that sounds travelling from the lip opening reach the ears with very different degrees of success, depending on the frequency of the sound; the higher the frequency, the more the radiation is concentrated along the longitudinal axis of the mouth. Therefore, what reaches a speaker's own ears with negligible amplitude reduction are the low frequency components of the spectrum. The phenomenon is illustrated in figure 8.1. The curves show the differences between spectra recorded at the speaker's ear and in front of the speaker's mouth (Sundberg and Gauffin, 1974). Had the two spectra been identical—in other words, had all spectrum partials scattered equally well in all directions from the lip opening—the difference would have been zero at all frequencies. This is not the case, as we can see. The difference is small only in the bass region. This means that only the low frequencies are efficiently radiated backward to the ears. (In fact, low frequencies scatter equally well in all directions.) The figure also demonstrates that the higher frequencies do not radiate as efficiently backward as they do sagittally from the speaker. These differences are typical of wave propagation; low frequencies corresponding to long waves can bend around obstacles, while high frequencies with shorter waves cannot.

These experiments concerned the sound propagation around the head of the speaker, which differs from the sound propagation as measured at a distance from the speaker. For instance, at a greater distance from the speaker, the radiation of sound is much less frequency-dependent; so the radiation differences between spectrum partials in other frequency ranges are much smaller than what is shown in figure 8.1 (Flanagan, 1965; Marshall and Meyer, 1985).

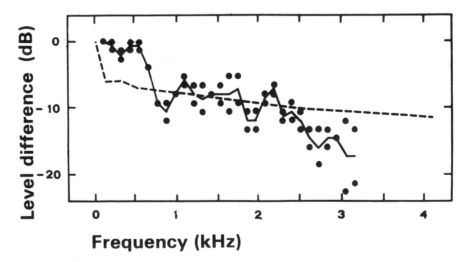

Figure 8.1. Differences between two spectra, one recorded at the speaker's ear and the other in front of the speaker's mouth. The amplitudes are similar up to about 500 Hz, but then the amplitudes of the overtones at the ears are about 10 dB weaker than those radiated frontally. The dashed curve represents the average over several vowels, according to von Békésy (1960). (After Sundberg and Gauffin, 1974.)

The above mentioned measurements comparing spectra at the ear and in front of the mouth were made in an anechoic room, where the sound hitting the floor, the ceiling, and the walls is almost completely absorbed. The experiment shows that speakers will not hear very much of their higher overtones unless they are close to a sound reflector. If there is no efficient sound reflector near us when we speak, the voice timbre we perceive of our own voice sounds more "bassy" than it sounds to people sitting in front of us. The degree of this "bassiness" depends on how poor the high frequency sound reflection is in the room. If large surfaces are covered with porous materials in the room, this reflection will be very poor. An extreme example is a dressing room or closet where the hanging clothes make the sound of one's own voice very dull indeed. The opposite is true for the bathroom, where the hard tile walls reflect sounds of all frequencies very efficiently. In such rooms one hears the high frequency components abnormally loud.

There is one more reason that a voice sounds different to speakers and listeners. The sound from our voice organs propagates not only in air but also within the tissues of the speaker's body. The sound level in the vocal tract is extremely high during phonation, no less than 10 times, or 20 dB, higher than the threshold of pain. If we could shrink so that we could crawl into the mouth of a speaker, our ears would ache when the person phonated; our hearing might even be damaged by such loudness. And even if this is a playful way of putting it, it *is* true that sounds of such high amplitudes will travel through the walls of the vocal tract into the structures of the head just as the sound of noisy neighbors tends to travel through the walls of a house. The sound from the vocal tract will therefore reach the hearing organ with a quite considerable amplitude. This means that part of the sound one perceives of one's own voice has traveled directly from the vocal tract to the hearing organs by so-called bone (as opposed to air) conduction. The bone-conducted sound differs from the air-conducted sound in one important respect; at high frequencies, bone-conduction is less efficient than air-conduction, so that the received spectrum of a bone-conducted sound falls off toward higher frequencies at a 6 dB/octave faster rate than airborne sounds. Higher spectrum partials are less dominant in bone-conducted sound than in air-conducted sound because the sound spectrum is boosted by 6 dB/octave when it is radiated from the lip opening.

We must conclude that a voice can never sound the same to a listener as to its owner. This suggests a complication for voice training. Let us assume that the student, hearing a singer with an ideal voice timbre, wants to acquire this timbre. If the student phonates in such a way that the timbre in his or her own ears is identical with that ideal sound, then the sound of the student's voice is *not* identical with the ideal sound in a listener's ears!

There are at least two ways out of this dilemma. One is to learn the translation between what one hears in one's own ears and the voice timbre that the listeners perceive. Another way, as we shall see in a moment, is to find complementary feedback signals in order to control phonation.

We can see that the auditory feedback is not a very reliable source of information for the singer as to the voice use; it depends on the room acoustics, and it probably always differs from the sound perceived by the listeners. It seems that professional singers gradually become more and more independent of the deceitful auditory image of their own voices and increasingly rely on other types of feedback. When singing in anechoic chambers, where the auditory feedback lacks the components normally provided by the sound reflection from the walls, the ceiling, and the floor, highly experienced professional singers are generally much less disturbed than other subjects.

However, it would not be a good idea for singers to forget about auditory feedback. For instance, in the preplanning and aftercontrol of jumps in pitch, or in other words, of melodic leaps, auditory feedback is apparently crucial. Also, singers may be able to develop a very reliable "timbral translator" so that they can tell what the sound is in front of them, given the sound in their own ears.

Body Vibrations

It has been mentioned that the singer can use types of feedback other than the auditory for the purpose of controlling phonation. What other kinds of signals are there, then? Vibrations in the head and chest may be one kind of signal. Such vibrations also have the advantage of being independent of the acoustics of the room.

When we phonate, we can often feel vibrations in various parts of the body, such as the nose, the skull, the lips, the throat, and the chest. Kirikae et al. (1964) measured such vibrations caused by phonation. They observed that the wider the jaw opening, the smaller the amplitude of the vibrations measured on top of the skull, as is illustrated in figure 8.2. As we saw in the previous chapter, the first formant frequency is particularly sensitive to the jaw opening. Therefore we conclude that the frequency of the first formant must be important to the amplitude of phonatory skull vibrations.

In their investigation, Kirikae et al. studied the vibrations caused by phonation not only on top of the skull but at no less than forty different

Figure 8.2. Skull vibration amplitude observed at various jaw openings. The greater amplitudes for smaller jaw openings suggest that a low first formant frequency yields large vibration amplitudes. (After Kirikae et al., 1964.)

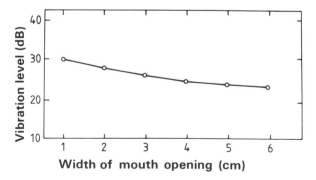

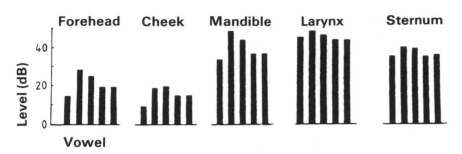

Figure 8.3. Vibration amplitudes measured at various places on the body during production of various vowels. In each group, the columns represent the following vowels from left to right: /a:, i:, u:, e:, o:/. The vowel dependence is greater in the locations above the larynx. (After Kirikae et al., 1964.)

locations on the body surface. Some results are shown in figure 8.3. It can be seen that the amplitude of these vibrations is rather small on the forehead and on the cheek. Moreover, it is strongly vowel-dependent in all locations above the larynx, while on the larynx and on the sternum, all vowels generate similar vibration amplitudes. This is not surprising, since the vowel differentiation is achieved in the vocal tract.

Later Pawlowski and co-workers used holography for visualizing the vibratory patterns of the face and neck of singers (Pawluczyk et al., 1982; Pawlowski et al., 1983). This method shows the distribution of vibration amplitude on the skin in the same way as a topographic map shows altitude. The results showed that the vibration amplitude is high on the larynx and on the lips. It was found to decrease with rising phonation frequency, and it varied depending on the vowel and the singer.

To summarize: It is clear that vibrations on the skull reflect not only phonation but also articulation, since the amplitudes of the skull vibrations are vowel dependent. In other words, they do not relate in a simple way to phonation.

The author investigated phonatory vibrations in the chest wall (Sundberg, 1983). The amplitude measured in terms of the displacement of the chest wall was found to decrease with rising frequency, as illustrated in figure 8.4. The threshold of vibration sensation, corresponding to the amplitude of a barely noticeable vibration, is V-shaped, when plotted as a function of frequency in a logarithmic scale. The greatest sensitivity is reached in the vicinity of 180 Hz. Above this frequency region, the threshold rises; or, to put it otherwise, our sensitivity decreases. In the same figure we also see that the amplitude of phonation-caused chest wall vibrations decreases with rising phonation frequency; actually, the general slope of these chest wall vibration curves is similar to that of the threshold of vibration sensation below 180 Hz. Above this frequency the phonatory vibrations keep decreasing while the threshold starts rising with increasing frequency. Therefore, it is not possible to sense the chest wall vibrations at phonation frequencies higher than, say, 300 Hz, which is close to the pitch of D4. Thus, chest wall vibrations would be of little help to sopranos,

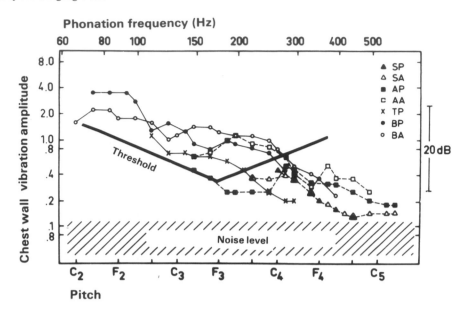

Figure 8.4. Vibration (peak-to-peak displacement) amplitudes in μm recorded on the sternum of seven singer subjects. The first letter in the subject symbols refers to voice category (S = soprano, A = alto, T = tenor, B = bass) and the second to their status (P = professional, A = amateur). The heavy solid line represents an estimate of the weakest sternum vibration amplitude that the subjects could perceive. Phonatory sternum vibrations cannot be perceived at high phonation frequencies. (After Sundberg, 1979b.)

except in the bottom part of their phonation frequency range. Incidentally, this range is often referred to as chest register.

What exactly is it that brings the chest wall to vibration? The author's investigation revealed that it is the amplitude of the lowest source spectrum component—in other words, the voice source fundamental—that was mirrored in such vibrations. The stronger this fundamental, the stronger the chest wall vibrations. In chapter 4, dealing with the voice source, we saw that the amplitude of this partial is an indication of where phonation is located along that phonatory dimension which ranges from the extreme of pressed phonation to the other extreme of breathy phonation, flow phonation being the least pressed but still nonleaking phonation. This means that a male singer (but probably rarely a female because of her higher phonation frequency range) can sense a change in the chest wall vibrations when he changes the mode of phonation along this dimension. If the sensation of vibration disappears while phonation frequency is well below 300 Hz, the singer probably changed his phonation in the direction of pressed phonation. Strong vibration sensations are likely to be sensed only as long as phonation is not too close to the pressed extreme and the phonation frequency is below the pitch of D4.

It is often assumed that body vibrations contribute to the sound. However, it seems that the vibration amplitude of the chest wall is not high enough to contribute significantly to the sound radiated from the singer;

the sound from the lip opening is so loud that it will override the faint contributions from the chest wall.

It should be stressed that vibration sensation in the chest wall is far from constituting a sufficient condition for an acceptable type of phonation. For example, even a clearly breathy phonation results in a source spectrum with a very strong fundamental, thus generating strong chest wall vibrations. Obviously, a constantly breathy phonation is not what voice pedagogues would consider ideal, because it would hardly lead a singer to more jobs on opera stages and in concert halls. Thus, a singer must also use other criteria in monitoring his phonation.

The amplitudes of the higher partials of the voice source spectrum, or, in other words, the closing rate of the flow glottogram, may give rise to sensations in the frontal part of the face. At least, this is suggested by the very widespread opinion among voice teachers and singers that the tone must be placed "in the mask." We saw before that the vibrations in the head are very vowel-dependent, and that they apparently report the quality of phonation in a rather involved way. On the other hand, it might be possible that such sensations "in the mask" stem from changes in the blood supply caused by the vigorous vibrations generated by phonation. However, here we stray outside the border of knowledge: this remains pure speculation.

Vibrato

Physical Attributes

Before describing the vibrato in physical terms, it is important to stress that different types of vibrato exist, and they probably differ from a physical point of view. Here we will concentrate on the vibrato occurring in Western operatic singing.

Almost all professional opera singers develop vibrato without thinking about it and without trying actively to acquire it (Bjorklund, 1961). Thus, vibrato develops more or less by itself as voice training proceeds successfully. Before entering into some perceptual aspects of vibrato, a few words should be spent on its physical characteristics and its possible origins.

Physically, the vibrato corresponds to a periodic, rather sinusoidal, modulation of the phonation frequency (Schultz-Coulon and Battmer, 1981). The regularity of this modulation is considered a sign of the singer's vocal skill: the more regular the vibrato, the more skilled the singer. Moreover, in well-trained singers the regularity is generally not influenced appreciably even if the auditory feedback is masked by noise (Schultz-Coulon, 1978). As the vibrato corresponds to a regular undulation of phonation frequency, it is characterized by two parameters: the *rate* and the *extent* of the undulations. The vibrato rate specifies the number of undulations per second. The extent describes how far phonation frequency rises and falls during a vibrato cycle.

The rate of the frequency modulation is generally considered to be constant within a singer; that is, the singer is usually unable to change it. In fact, however, it is difficult, though not impossible, to change one's vibrato rate by training; some singers are even able to deliberately change their vibrato rate. Generally a vibrato rate of less than 5.5 undulations per second sounds unacceptably slow, and vibrato rates exceeding 7.5 undulations per second tend to sound nervous. However, it seems that the rate may be affected by the emotional involvement of the singer (Shipp et al., 1980).

The amplitude of the vibrato undulations varies with loudness of phonation, according to Winckel (1953). Generally, the extent is $\pm$ 1 or 2 semitones (we recall that a semitone step along an equally tempered scale corresponds to a frequency difference of almost 6%). Vibrato rates smaller than $\pm$ 0.5 semitones are more typical of wind instruments than of singers, and vibrato rates exceeding $\pm$ 2 semitones tend to sound bad. Particularly when combined with a slow rate, they are typical of people who are—regrettably—still singing in spite of their advanced age.

The vibrato is similar to two other types of phonation frequency modulation in singing, namely, tremolo and trillo. According to Schultz-Coulon and Battmer (1981), the tremolo is characterized by less regular and more rapid modulation; the rate is 7 undulations per second or more. The trillo typically has a modulation amplitude generally exceeding $\pm$ 2 semitones.

The result of the modulation of the phonation frequency is that the frequencies of all the overtones vary regularly and in synchrony with the phonation frequency modulation. All these variations in the frequencies of the spectrum partials are accompanied by variations in the overall amplitude. For two reasons, this is not surprising. First, the overall amplitude of a vowel sound is normally identical with the amplitude of the strongest spectrum partial, which, as we know, is usually the partial lying closest to the first formant. Second, as is also well known to us, the amplitude of every spectrum partial is determined by its distance from the formant frequencies (for the moment we disregard the importance of the source); if a partial approaches a formant, the amplitude of that partial will increase, other things being equal.

We may safely infer that the vibrato will cause the overall amplitude to vary; when the fundamental frequency increases in the vibrato cycle, the frequency of the strongest partial may either bring that partial closer to the first formant, so that the amplitude of that partial and hence the overall sound level will increase, or it may bring the partial further away from the first formant. Both these cases are illustrated in figure 8.5. In one case the fundamental frequency and the overall amplitude will undulate in phase (both increase and decrease in synchrony), and in the opposite case they will vary in opposite phase, so that an increase in one is associated with a decrease in the other. Whichever case applies depends on whether the strongest partial is slightly lower or slightly higher than the first formant frequency.

A third case may also occur: the frequency of the strongest partial undulates symmetrically around the frequency of the first formant. Then the amplitude vibrato will actually be twice as fast as the frequency vibrato. In any case, the phase relationship between amplitude and frequency vibrato depends on the frequency relationship between the first formant and the strongest spectrum partial.

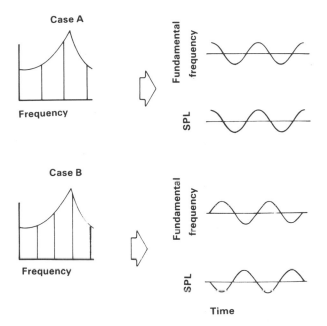

Figure 8.5. Illustration of the relationship between fundamental frequency and overall sound pressure level (SPL) in a vibrato tone. The SPL depends mainly on the strongest spectrum partial, which normally is the partial lying closest to the first formant. If this partial approaches a nearby formant when the frequency rises, amplitude and frequency will vary in phase, and vice versa.

The perceptual significance of the amplitude vibrato is often overestimated. The main perceptual effect of the vibrato depends on the frequency modulation. The author's experience from informal listening tests with synthesized vowel sounds is that it is hard to focus one's attention on the amplitude fluctuations. Indeed, the importance of the frequency undulations is so great that the auditory image of a perfectly normal vibrato persists, even when the amplitude vibrato is twice as fast as the frequency vibrato. Also, if the amplitude vibrato is very small—which happens when the strongest partial is far away from the first formant—the impression is almost the same as when the strongest partial is quite close to the first formant and the amplitude vibrato is consequently great. All this supports the general impression that the amplitude part of the vibrato is unimportant to perception.

Physiologic Attributes

What mechanism generates the vibrato? Again, we lack definitive answers and clear facts. However, variations in synchrony with the vibrato have been observed in two systems, both of which affect phonation frequency; they are the laryngeal musculature (mainly the cricothyroid muscles) and the breathing system.

Regarding the laryngeal musculature, some data have been collected by means of EMG measurements on singers (Vennard et al., 1970). The EMG electrodes were inserted into the cricothyroid, the vocalis, and the lateral cricoarytenoid muscles. As we recall, the cricothyroid muscles stretch the vocal folds; the vocalis muscles tense them; and the lateral cricoarytenoid muscles adduct them (see figures 2.7, 2.8, and 2.9, p. 15, 17, and 18). Figure 8.6 shows a typical case. In some cases a clear covariation between

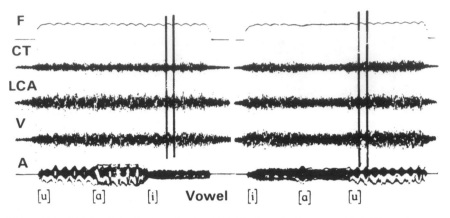

Figure 8.6. EMG activity in the cricothyroid (CT), lateral cricoarytenoid (LCA), and vocalis (V) muscles during a professional singer's singing of the note C4 on the vowels indicated below the sound pressure recording (A) at the bottom. The top curve shows phonation frequency (F). All these muscles tend to start contracting at the instant of the minima in the phonation frequency curve. (After Vennard et al., 1967.)

phonation frequency and the EMG activity in all three muscles can be seen, particularly the vocalis.

The synchrony between phonation frequency and EMG activity is particularly interesting to examine. At the moment when phonation frequency passes its minimum in the vibrato cycle, the vocalis muscle in particular shows a maximum EMG activity, suggesting a maximum contraction, and vice versa. This is not surprising, at least for the cricothyroid and the vocalis, because in modal register both these muscles are active in increasing phonation frequency. These results have been corroborated by Shipp et al. (1982). In his investigation of the EMG activity in the cricothyroid muscles during a singer's production of vibrato tones, Shipp consistently found that the EMG activity culminated in synchrony with the valleys of the fundamental frequency fluctuations.

The vibrato pulsations in these laryngeal muscles are often accompanied by similar pulsations in other muscles more remote from the larynx, such as the mylohyoid muscle (Mason, 1965). It seems that tremor-like pulsations of muscle contraction such as those affiliated with vibrato often scatter to adjacent structures and muscles. It can be observed in an X-ray film of singers made by Ondrackova (1969) and in some more recent fiberoptic movie films (e.g., Selkin, 1982) that many structures in the voice organ, such as the velum, the tongue, and the side walls of the pharynx, are sometimes engaged in a rhythmic pulsation synchronous with the vibrato. In some singers, females in particular, one can sometimes observe with the naked eye that the tongue and the lower jaw are shaking with the vibrato. Such satellite shaking of articulatory structures is sometimes regarded as a sign of poor singing technique. Still, according to the author's experience informally gained in front of the TV, this effect can sometimes be observed in female singers who undisputably belong to the international top rank.

The pulsating EMG activities shown in figure 8.6 also concerned an adducting muscle: the lateral cricoarytenoid. A pulsating adducting force must result in a pulsation of glottal resistance; if adduction is increased, glottal resistance must rise. An increased glottal resistance leads to a reduced amplitude of the voice source fundamental. For this reason we might expect that vibrato is associated with an undulation in voice source characteristics, such as the amplitude of the fundamental. Unfortunately, a parallel investigation of the voice source and of the activity in the main laryngeal muscles has not yet been carried out.

Having said this about the glottal resistance, our interest must turn to the subglottic system: how does the subglottal pressure behave during vibrato phonation? Here, some data published by Rubin et al. (1967) are informative. In most cases, such as those illustrated in figure 8.7, undulations can be observed in both the subglottic pressure and in the airflow. Sometimes they are in phase, so that an increase in one occurs simultaneously with an increase in the other, but sometimes the opposite case applies. Such undulations in subglottic pressure can result from the vibrato; but it is also possible that they actually are responsible for generating the vibrato, because, as we know, fluctuations in subglottic pressure generate fluctuations in phonation frequency, other things being equal. It appears necessary to examine the phase relations between airflow and subglottic pressure.

When the pressure and flow undulations are in phase, the subglottic pressure variations may be the cause of the airflow variations; a heightened subglottic pressure will cause the airflow to increase, other things being equal. In this case we would expect no pulsating activity in the adductor muscles. However, when pressure and flow vary in counterphase, a pulsating

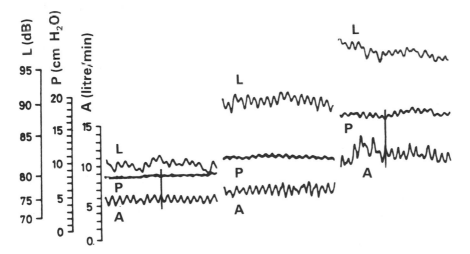

Figure 8.7. Three different examples of synchronous recordings of overall sound level (L), subglottic pressure (P), and airflow (A). Flow and pressure are sometimes in phase and sometimes in counterphase. (From Rubin et al., 1967.)

activity in the adductor (and/or abductor) muscles must be postulated; if the adductor muscles contract, glottal resistance must rise, airflow will decrease, and subglottic pressure will increase. However, both variations in phase and in counterphase seem to occur (see figure 8.7); therefore, we can draw no conclusions on these matters.

However, it seems unlikely that subglottic pressure variations alone are responsible for generating the vibrato. In experiments with a complete model of the voice organ, Scully and Allwood (1983) generated a vibrato by subglottic pressure variations, and the result was published in the sound illustrations. It sounds strikingly similar to a very special type of vibrato, which is used in certain pop singing but certainly not in operatic singing. One characteristic of this type of vibrato is that its rate can be varied substantially, and this does not seem possible in the case of the operatic vibrato.

It is seldom easy to infer the movement of structures resulting from a contraction of a specific muscle, as evidenced, for instance, by EMG measurements. The reason is the complexity of our muscular system. For instance, while the activity in one particular muscle may show an almost perfect correlation with the movements in a particular structure and thus appears to be its cause, this activity may be merely a reaction to the contraction of a different muscle which is the real agent behind the motion. In other words, it may be difficult to realize what is the hen and what is the egg. If one muscle group causes subglottic pressure to fall, other muscles would try to restore the pressure resulting in synchronous undulations in a great number of muscles. It is also possible that the primary agent behind the vibrato is the entire pitch regulating system as a whole.

What might shed some light on the question of the mechanism that generates the vibrato is a synchronous registration of phonation frequency, subglottal pressure, airflow, and EMG signals from muscles in the larynx and in the breathing apparatus. Unfortunately, data on phonation frequency are missing in the Rubin et al. (1967) investigation, and there are no data on subglottic pressure in the Vennard et al. (1970) study. As long as we lack such a thorough study, nothing definite can be said about the origin of the vibrato.

In order to increase our confusion a bit more as to what generates the vibrato, two things can be mentioned. First, there is a resonance in the breathing system occurring at about 6 Hz, which is almost identical with the normal vibrato rate. The relevance of this to the vibrato has not yet been assessed.

A second source of confusion is an investigation by Deutsch and Clarkson (1959), showing that the rate of the vibrato is influenced by the auditory feedback. They delayed the auditory feedback, so that the subjects could hear their own voices with a small delay. The average vibrato rate was found to slow down considerably with increasing delay, as illustrated in figure 8.8. The authors returned to the same question in a subsequent study (Clarkson and Deutsch, 1966). Here they first had nonsinger subjects sing vibrato tones. Then they temporarily reduced the subjects' ability to

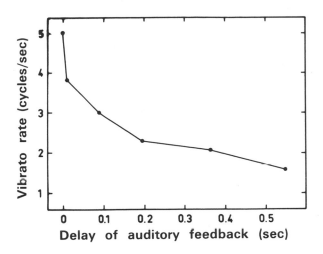

Figure 8.8. Effect of a delayed auditory feedback on vibrato rate in nonsingers. Vibrato becomes very slow when the feedback is substantially delayed. (Data taken from Deutsch and Clarkson, 1959.)

detect pitch differences and asked them to perform the same task again. A comparison of the subjects' performances revealed that the vibrato extent was significantly reduced when the subjects could not hear pitch differences normally. The authors argue that these results reflect the role of the auditory feedback in controlling phonation frequency; the hearing system perceives the changes in phonation frequency induced by the vibrato, and these changes cause the brain to order the pitch regulating system to compensate. If this is true, the delay inherent in the auditory feedback system can be regarded as a plausible origin of the vibrato.

Some of the vibrato rates reported by Deutsch and Clarkson are very low indeed, the lowest being 1.5 undulations per second. This is very far below the normal variation range of the vibrato. Therefore Shipp et al. (1984) repeated the experiment, using singers as subjects. A slightly different result was found; as illustrated in figure 8.9, these singers' normal vibrato was basically undisturbed by the delay of the auditory

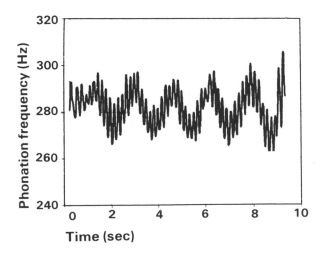

Figure 8.9. Phonation frequency recording from a singer singing with a 300 msec delayed auditory feedback according to Shipp et al. (1984). The singer retains his vibrato rate, but a slowly cycling "searching" movement is superimposed on his phonation frequency.

feedback, about 300 msec in this case. In addition, a slow undulation superimposed on the vibrato undulations was also observed; the rate of these slow undulations was similar to the vibrato rates reported by Deutsch and Clarkson. This slow undulation seemed to result from the singer's hunting for the target pitch; so in this hunting, auditory feedback was evidently involved, just as Deutsch and Clarkson suggested. The difference in the results would depend on a difference in the subjects' acquaintance with singing. However, it seems that auditory feedback does not generate the vibrato in singers.

Large and Iwata (1971) had singer subjects sing the same tones with and without vibrato. The sound pressure level of the vowel was kept the same. The results demonstrated that vibrato tones consume more air than vibrato-free tones, as shown in figure 8.10. We recall that airflow is determined by the glottal resistance which, in turn, depends on the degree of adduction activity. The results therefore suggest that glottal resistance, and hence adduction activity, was higher in the case of the nonvibrato tones.

Vibrato and Pitch

The vibrato corresponds to a periodic undulation of the fundamental frequency, as we have seen. We know that the fundamental frequency normally determines which pitch we perceive. If this fundamental frequency is not steady but moves continuously, what pitch do we hear? This is one question regarding the perceived pitch of vibrato tones. But there is also another. One could suspect that the pitch we hear from a vibrato note is not as accurately and precisely perceived as the pitch we hear from vibrato-free notes. If this is the case, the singer has a good reason for using the

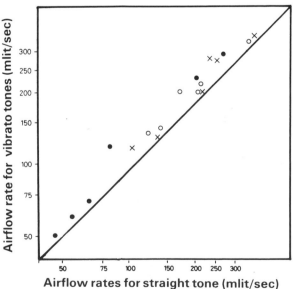

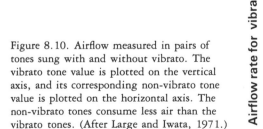

Figure 8.10. Airflow measured in pairs of tones sung with and without vibrato. The vibrato tone value is plotted on the vertical axis, and its corresponding non-vibrato tone value is plotted on the horizontal axis. The non-vibrato tones consume less air than the vibrato tones. (After Large and Iwata, 1971.)

vibrato: the demands for accuracy with respect to phonation frequency would be reduced as soon as there is a vibrato.

In one investigation the author had musically trained subjects adjust the fundamental frequency of a vibrato-free tone so that its pitch agreed with the pitch of a preceding vibrato tone (Sundberg, 1978a). In order to gain complete control over the stimuli, synthetic sung tones were used throughout. The results showed that the subjects tuned the frequency of the response tone so that it agreed, within a few cents, with the linear average of the vibrato note's undulating fundamental frequency, as is illustrated in figure 8.11. Essentially the same result was found by Shonle and Horan (1980) and Iwamiya et al. (1983). In addition they found that it is actually not the linear but the logarithmic average that corresponds to the pitch we hear.

In the author's investigation, the entire experiment was repeated twice; the subjects first matched the pitch of vibrato tones, and then the same subjects matched the pitch of vibrato-free tones. In this way it was possible to find out to what extent the accuracy of the pitch perceived was affected by the vibrato. The subjects' matchings of the pitch of the same stimulus tones were almost entirely consistent regardless of the presence of the vibrato. Apparently, the vibrato did not reduce the certainty with which the subjects perceived the pitch.

What role does the vibrato play in music practice, then? To interpret the above results correctly it is important to realize that this experiment was monophonic, so to speak; first the subjects heard the stimulus tone, and *thereafter* (not simultaneously) the vibrato-free response tone to which the subject had to tune was presented. The conclusion in the last paragraph therefore applies only when we listen to the pitch of a single tone sounding alone.

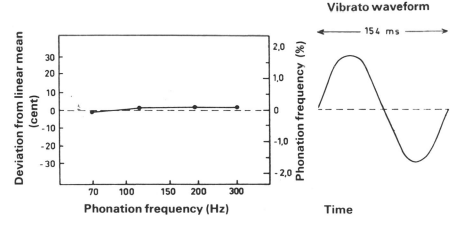

Figure 8.11. Pitch matchings of vibrato tones in which subjects tuned the frequency of a non-vibrato response tone so that its pitch was exactly the same as that of a preceding vibrato tone. The subjects' responses agreed within a few cents with the linear average of the vibrato note's undulating fundamental frequency. (After Sundberg, 1978a.)

In our Western music culture, this has become a rare case as several tones ordinarily sound at the same time. In such cases a lack of accuracy in the tuning of phonation frequencies is revealed to us not only in terms of perceived pitch but also, in the case of consonant intervals, in terms of *beats*. Examples of such consonant intervals are octaves, fifths, fourths, and major and minor thirds and sixths. As we saw in the chapter on choral singing, instruments with harmonic spectra, such as the singing voice, generate beats as soon as their fundamental frequency ratios deviate slightly from certain ideal values: 1:2, 2:3, 3:4, 4:5, 5:6, 3:5, and 5:8, respectively. The farther away from the ideal the interval is, the more rapid the beats become, and eventually they give rise to roughness.

However, if one or both of the notes that produce the consonant interval have vibrato, no beats will occur. This means that in a polyphonic situation, where more than one voice is sounding, the revealing beats can be avoided even when the consonant interval is not perfectly tuned, provided that one of the tones is sung or played with vibrato. Certainly this is a very good acoustical argument for using vibrato in singing as well as in music in general. The musician's freedom is increased regarding the choice of fundamental frequency so that it can be used artistically, for expressive purposes.

Yet another point of view should also be mentioned. We have seen that the vibrato is depicted in the EMG signals of the laryngeal muscles. From this we may infer that the absence and presence of the vibrato informs listeners about certain muscular conditions in the singer's larynx. Findings by Sundberg and Askenfelt (1983) suggest that the vibrato is often missing when the singer runs into phonatory problems (note that the vibrato may be absent for artistic reasons as well). From the study of Large and Iwata (1971), it could be concluded that probably a greater adduction force was applied when the singers avoided the vibrato. We may then guess that in vibrato singing phonation is somewhat closer to the "flow phonation" extreme than in nonvibrato singing (see chapter 4, "The Voice Source"). The following idea presents itself: Perhaps the singer is signaling to the audience that there is no phonatory trouble (for instance, phonation is far from pressed) when the vibrato appears in a high or otherwise difficult note. In other words, the vibrato might be used in order to inform the listeners that the singer is solving a difficult vocal task without a struggle. It is certainly a basic condition for creating an aesthetically and artistically satisfactory result that difficult tasks are performed without apparent difficulty.

Vibrato and Vowel Intelligibility

As we know, the fundamental is not the only spectrum partial that undulates in frequency because of the vibrato. The voice source spectrum comprises a series of practically harmonic partials, so that partial number *n* has the frequency of *n* times the fundamental frequency *in every instant,* because the frequency of each partial changes in synchrony with the frequency of the fundamental. The amplitude of a spectrum partial is determined by its number (it will be recalled that the higher the number, the weaker the amplitude in the voice source spectrum) plus the frequency distance between the partial and the formants. When a partial approaches a nearby formant because of the vibrato, it will gain in amplitude and vice versa. If a loud partial increases its amplitude considerably when the fundamental frequency is rising in the vibrato cycle, then this must mean that there is a formant just above the frequency of that partial. In other words, if the frequency and amplitude fluctuations of a partial are in phase, the frequency of the nearest formant is higher than that of the undulating partial, as was illustrated in figure 8.5. And, conversely, if a loud partial decreases in amplitude as the fundamental frequency is rising in the vibrato cycle— that is, if they vary in counterphase—there must be a formant just below the frequency of that partial. From these facts we may infer that there is more information about the frequencies of the formants in a vibrato tone than in a nonvibrato tone.

As a rule it is rather easy to see where the formant frequencies are by looking at the spectrum: they are represented by envelope peaks, as illustrated in the left part of figure 8.12. But when phonation frequency is abnormally high, as in female singing, difficulties occur. If there are four or five partials and about the same number of formants, then it is hardly possible to guess where the formant frequencies are, as can be seen in the right part of the same figure. However, the guessing may become easier if there is a vibrato. Figure 8.13 illustrates why this may be hypothesized. As the harmonic partials glide up and down in frequency, their amplitude changes depend on, and hence offer some information about where the formant frequencies are.

The author investigated this question by means of an experiment with synthetic vowels (Sundberg, 1978b). Phonation frequency was varied between 300 and 1,000 Hz. The formant frequencies were those used by a female professional soprano when she sang the vowels at the pitch of C4, corresponding to a phonation frequency of approximately 260 Hz. The vowels were presented with and without vibrato to a group of phonetically

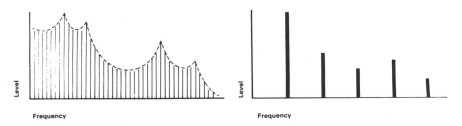

Figure 8.12. Illustration of the difficulties of determining the formant frequencies of a high-pitched vowel. When phonation frequency is low, as in normal speech, the formant frequencies can be easily identified from the spectrum, as shown in the left case. When phonation frequency is high, as in female singing, difficulties arise, as shown in the right case. It is almost impossible to see that the formant frequencies are actually the same in these two spectra.

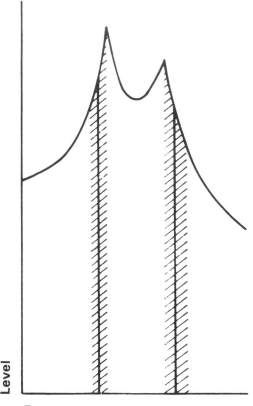

Level

Frequency

Figure 8.13. Illustration of the idea that a vibrato would help vowel identification in high-pitched vowels. The higher partials sweep along the spectrum envelope and so give more information on the ideal envelope and hence on the formant frequencies. (From Sundberg, 1978b.)

trained listeners. Their task was to identify the vowel they heard. The results are shown in figure 8.14, where the axes represent phonation frequency and the measure of agreement in the listeners' interpretations. It can be seen in the figure that the presence of the vibrato does not make a very great difference. The disagreement between the listeners' interpretations is essentially the same in both cases. The conclusion must be that the vibrato does not help the listener to guess which vowel is being sung.

Data from a similar experiment made by Stumpf (1926) with real sung vowels are shown in the same figure 8.14. It is interesting that the identification of a vowel is facilitated if the formant frequencies are those which a professional soprano singer actually chooses. Still, we know from the chapter on articulation that such formant frequency values may depart by more than one octave from the normal formant frequency values in extreme cases. We arrive at an interesting conclusion: when a singer adjusts her formant frequencies in accordance with the phonation frequency in the upper part of her range, she actually loses *less* in vowel intelligibility than she would lose if she kept the formant frequency values used at lower phonation frequencies. This seems like a very happy coincidence. Her

Effect on agreement of interpretation

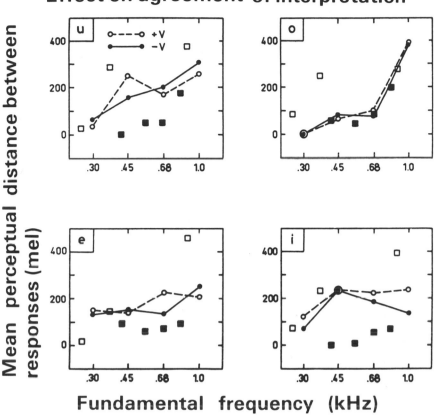

Figure 8.14. Illustration of the importance of vibrato to vowel identification. The graphs show the similarity between listeners' guesses when they listened to vibrato vowels (open circles) and non-vibrato vowels (filled circles) synthesized at various pitches with the formant frequencies of the vowels given in the upper left corner of each graph. The squares show corresponding data for natural vowels presented by Stumpf (1926). (From Sundberg, 1978b.)

pitch-dependent choice of formant frequencies not only makes her vowels much louder, it also enhances vowel intelligibility.

This is not, however, the entire story on vibrato and vowel intelligibility. In a sound example published on a gramophone recording, Chowning (1980) demonstrated that the intelligibility of synthetic high-pitched vowels was dramatically increased as soon as the partials, first presented as a successively appearing series of sine tones, started to move in synchrony. Indeed, before the vibrato is added, the partials are not heard as a voice sound at all; the sounds seem merely electronic. Using synthetic vowels, McAdams (1984) presented other examples in which the vibrato did indeed facilitate vowel identification.

Finally, it should be pointed out here that vowel identification at very high pitches is improved dramatically if the vowel is presented in a consonant-vowel context. Thus, it is much easier to identify vowels sung at very high pitches in reality than these results suggest. We will return to this topic in the next section.

Vowel Identification at Super Pitches

In high notes sung by sopranos, the vibrato does not seem to add much as far as vowel intelligibility is concerned. The formant frequencies used under these conditions appear completely strange compared with normal speech. Still, they do actually seem to improve the chances of guessing correctly which vowel the singer intends. On the other hand, most of us have probably experienced how easy it is to misinterpret a vowel sung in a high soprano range, particularly if it is presented without neighboring consonants. Furthermore, it is far from rare that similar mistakes are made with respect to notes sung by a male singer in the top part of his range.

A formal investigation of the intelligibility of sung syllables was carried out by Morozov (1965). A group of listeners was asked to identify syllables sung by professional male or female singers. Figure 8.15 shows the results. The identification is simple and sure for the lower part of both male and female singers' ranges. Above the pitch of G4 (a phonation frequency close to 390 Hz), difficulties start to appear in male voices. Interestingly, notes sung at this same pitch by female singers do not present such severe difficulties. The difference between the sexes might stem from the fact that male singers would start to modify the vowel articulation in the vicinity of this pitch; their first formant would start to join the fundamental in some vowels in this range. Note that the shape of the curve is quite different for male and female singers. The curve for the female singers slopes more steeply and reaches deeper, all the way down to 10% correct identification at the pitch of B5. This must be a consequence of the fact that there are very few partials in the spectrum, so that there is a very meager signal on which the listener might base a guess.

Figure 8.15 shows in terms of hard data what most of us probably knew

Figure 8.15. Intelligibility of syllables sung at various phonation frequencies. In the female case the difficulties are considerable above the pitch of C5. (After Morozov, 1965.)

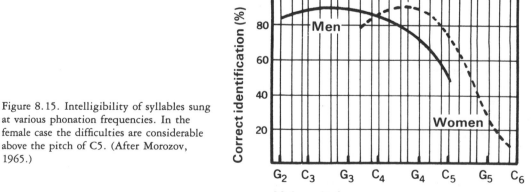

already. Above the pitch of F5, syllable identification is more or less a guesswork. However, in the case of sustained, isolated vowels, neighboring consonants have a positive effect on the intelligibility, as has been shown by Nelson and Tiffany (1968). Later Smith and Scott (1980), using real vowels deliberately sung in various ways, found that intelligibility also depended heavily on the way in which the vowels were being sung. Thus, some variability exists between singers using different singing techniques. In other words, some singers can be expected to be considerably easier to understand at high pitches than others. But still, when one listens to the fruits of a composer's endeavor, the reality depicted in figure 8.15 pops into one's mind, and one wonders if someone perhaps should have shown that figure to the composer.

In or Out of Tune

We have seen that the vibrato does not seem to help a singer to conceal phonation frequency mistakes except in the sense that the vibrato eliminates the beats in consonant intervals that are slightly mistuned in relation to the accompaniment. Thus, if there is no accompaniment, our musical ear asks for correct phonation frequency values or at least meaningful deviations from them. Investigations have revealed that the ear is extremely rigid in this respect. Phonation frequency errors exceeding 3 cents are detected by the most skilled musical ears, and musically trained listeners hear errors of 5 cents corresponding to about 0.3% of the frequency. This implies that the singer's phonation frequency average must match the ideal value within 1 Hz, if the pitch is A4 (phonation frequency = 440 Hz). How is it possible to train phonation frequency control so that this is possible?

Even more rigid demands must be met if the singer sings without vibrato together with other vibrato-free accompaniment notes. In this case, the limits are not set by the difference limen for frequency, but by the ability to detect beats, as mentioned before. Beats may be generated not only by the fundamental but also by an overtone in the spectrum of a sung note with a frequency similar to that of a partial in the accompaniment.

Let us digest this with the aid of an example. Two singers sing a major third with phonation frequencies of 200 Hz and 250 Hz. Let us first assume that both singers use vibrato. In that case they have to be in tune with an accuracy of about 5 cents or 0.6 Hz, approximately. If they sing nonvibrato tones, beats will be generated by any pair of strong partials that have almost identical frequencies. The tenth partial of the 200 Hz tone is at 2,000 Hz; and for a 250 Hz phonation frequency, the eighth partial is at the same frequency—2,000 Hz. This partial is likely to assume a considerable amplitude if the vowel is /i:/ or /e:/. If the singer's phonation frequency is 200.5 Hz, or 4 cents out of tune, this implies that the tenth partial is at 2,005 Hz, thus producing 5 beats per second with the eighth partial of the 250 Hz tone. This is likely to be audible. In order to be inaudible, the error must be reduced to, perhaps, 0.1 Hz. Singing without vibrato must be a very tricky thing indeed!

These high demands, of course, imply equally high demands on the regulation of subglottic pressure. In chapter 3 we saw that this pressure varies continuously in singing, depending on the loudness of phonation, among other things. We also saw that it has an effect on phonation frequency. If the singer, by mistake, produces a subglottic pressure that is mistuned by, say, 1 cm H_2O, a noticeable pitch error will result.

But these are all merely theoretical considerations on pitch accuracy. So what about reality? Lindgren and Sundberg (1972) studied those tones judged to be out of tune by musically experienced subjects listening to a spliced tape that contained real singing with and without accompaniment. The subjects marked all notes they felt to be out of tune in the music score. The results showed, among other things, that notes were felt to be out of tune less often than could be expected given the magnitudes of the errors in phonation frequency. However, as soon as the phonation frequency average was more than about 20 cents wrong as compared with the value in the equally tempered scale, and particularly if it was flat, the pitch was usually judged as out of tune.

However, sometimes phonation frequencies more than 20 cents off were accepted without complaint. This often occurred either (1) in unstressed positions in the meter, (2) in places where the music evoked a tragic mood, or (3) when the error was positive, so that the frequency was sharp. Also, the listeners tended to accept cases where phonation frequency slowly approached and finally reached its (correct) target value. Apparently the demands regarding intonation are not all that rigid after all, in solo singing with vibrato.

In this connection it is interesting to study what happens in vibrato-free ensemble singing. An eminent example of such a vocal tradition is barbershop singing. It is performed by four male singers; the melody is sung by the second part from the top, and the top part is sung in falsetto register. The harmonic component in barbershop music is prominent, so no wonder accurate intonation is considered particularly important. In an investigation, the intervals were measured between the tones in various chords as sung by a skilled barbershop quartet (Hagerman and Sundberg 1980). The results are shown in figure 8.16.

The accuracy of intonation was found to be very high indeed; the interval averages showed mean errors below 3 cents! Regarding the sizes of the intervals, the figure shows that this quartet uses values quite close to the pure or harmonic versions of the intervals. It will be recalled that it is only these pure intervals that do not generate beats.

The value pertaining to the intonation of one of the small thirds is particularly interesting. It was constituted by the fifth and the seventh in a dominant seventh chord. The average of this third is as small as 276 cents, which is 24 cents narrower than the equally tempered minor third and 50 cents (one half of a semitone) narrower than the pure third. How does this agree with the demands for pure, beat-free intonation?

Actually, it is in fair agreement. If we want to tune a dominant seventh chord as beat-free as possible, we should tune the minor third between the

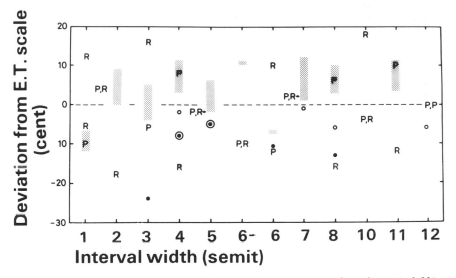

Figure 8.16. Average sizes of various intervals given in semitones (6- = diminished fifth, 6 = augmented fourth) derived from tonic chords (open circles) and from modulation chords (filled circles) as sung by a highly skilled barbershop quartet. P and R show the Pythagorean and natural/pure versions of the intervals. The hatched areas show values that have been observed in instrumental playing. (After Sundberg, 1982a.)

fifth and the seventh in the chord so that it equals the interval between the fifth and the seventh partials of a harmonic spectrum. This interval is 267 cents, or 33 cents narrower than the equally tempered minor third. The barbershop singers seemed to follow this recipe, if we overlook an error of 9 cents (24 instead of 33 cents). This error equals less than 0.5% of the phonation frequency, or 1.8 Hz at the pitch of G4 (approximately 390 Hz). The conclusion is that ensemble singing without vibrato raises high demands on phonation frequency acuity, but these demands can be met by trained singers.

The conclusion then appears that nonvibrato singing puts much higher demands on pitch acuity than does vibrato singing; we just saw that musically experienced listeners found the tone to be out of tune only when the average fundamental frequency was more than 20 cents off the correct value as defined by the equally tempered scale. On the other hand, we also saw that the barbershop singers deviated by no less than 24 cents from the equally tempered scale value in order to come close enough to a pure interval. Against this background, we must doubt that the equally tempered scale can be accepted as the ideal version for judging whether a tone is sung in tune.

Returning to the above experiment on the vibrato tones, our conclusion was that the demands regarding intonation are apparently not extremely rigid in solo singing with vibrato. We now see that this conclusion may be false. It is quite possible that the demands on pitch acuity are high in vibrato singing too. In the Lindgren and Sundberg investigation, the only available reference was the equally tempered scale. We now have seen that these equally tempered scale values cannot be equated with ideal values. Moreover, in music practice, deviations from theoretically correct fundamental frequency values are made deliberately in order to convey musical expression (Makeig and Balzano, 1982). What a musically experienced listener considers to be out of tune would be that which deviates *in an unexplicable way* from the pitch expected by the listener.

Let us now consider another point of view: why do people sing out of tune? Lacking formal investigations on this topic, we can only enjoy the pleasure of speculating. Several circumstances seem likely causes of out-of-tune singing. Phonation frequency changes reflect muscular activities in the singer just as a melody played on the piano reflects muscular activities in the pianist. Thus a pitch change is the result of a change in the muscular activity in the larynx and in the breathing apparatus of the singer.

In practice there is often little time available to correct mistakes, at least when the apparently slow pathway of auditory feedback is considered; in phonation frequency records of singers performing melodic leaps, one sometimes can observe a second pitch change, typically occurring some 200 or 300 msec after the main pitch change. This leads us to postulate that the pitch change should lead to the correct target at once. The singer, before starting the muscular maneuver, must "know" exactly what muscles to contract, at what moment, and to what extent; the goal must be accurately known before the departure. Perhaps a more musical way to express this is that singers must "hear" the next target pitch in their imagination before starting to change the pitch. Also, we can appreciate the importance of building up a "muscular memory," which is probably realized by means of experience or training.

In cases where the pitch change strategy works perfectly, the singer must have acquired a full set of correctly-imagined pitch intervals. Thus, as soon as the singer hears the first pitch of the piece, the pitches of all scale tones in that tonality are set up in the singer's imagination. Some persons may have little ability to imagine pitches in this way, and the consequence would then be intonation problems; such singers may arrive at intended, but incorrect, pitch targets.

This cannot be the only reason for singing out of tune. There are several highly musical persons—conductors, violinists, pianists—who cannot sing in tune, no matter how hard they try. In such cases it does not seem convincing to assume that they lack the ability to correctly imagine the scale tones. A better explanation is that their brains give the correct orders to the correct muscles, but still the audible result deviates from the intended result, because some irrelevant laryngeal muscle is under constant contraction as soon as this person tries to sing. Such disturbing additional muscle contraction then destroys the result. A similar case would be a singer who fails to sing in tune because of a cold; when the vocal folds are swollen, they respond with the wrong phonation frequency, even though the neural instructions to all of the muscles involved are correct.

To summarize: One cause of singing out of tune would be that the singer does not really know in advance how the pitch of the next tone sounds; this kind of singer does not imagine the next pitch before starting to change the pitch. Another reason would be an imprecise imagination; the singer imagines the wrong pitch and arrives at it. A third reason might be lack of training; the singer miscalculates the muscular activities needed in order to change the pitch to the imagined next target.

Voice Disorders

It sometimes happens that speaking or singing hurts the voice. There is no theory available explaining why this is so. It may be that the voice organ was not meant to produce sound, but to protect the lungs, so that it is damaged when used to make sounds too frequently. In any event, some information on voice disorders will be discussed here.

Before continuing, the author should state that, compared to phoniatricians (voice doctors) and laryngologists, he possesses only moderate knowledge regarding aspects other than the acoustic signal characteristics associated with various voice disorders, though he has been greatly helped in writing this chapter by his friends, phoniatricians Björn Fritzell and Peter Kitzing. On the other hand, the author strongly felt a need for a chapter on voice disorders in a book such as this, which is likely to be read by singers, actors, voice teachers, and others depending on a perfect voice function; many people entering a voice career know far too little about how to treat their voices, and because of this lack of knowledge, they risk running into voice troubles. It is hoped that this chapter will be able to help readers avoid unnecessary voice troubles. Its main purpose is to show not only how voice troubles manifest themselves acoustically, but also what may cause them and how they can be avoided.

As sound generation in the voice organ happens in two steps, namely, phonation and articulation, it would seem logical to treat the voice disorders that may develop in these two steps separately. However, most voice disorders are phonatory, and we will concentrate on these.

There are two types of phonatory disorders. One type depends on changes in the laryngeal tissues such as swelling, the formation of nodules, and so on. The voice disorders emanating from such changes are called *organic*. There are also disorders not associated with any visible changes in laryngeal tissues but which arise because of inappropriate use of the voice. These disorders are called *functional*. There are no clear boundaries between organic and functional disorders, since it often happens that misuse of the voice leads to tissue changes. Still, this classification is useful for practical purposes.

Origin

There is great variety among the origins of *organic voice disorders*. The most common cause is *acute laryngitis*. Sometimes it occurs in connection with a cold, and the risk of developing laryngitis seems to increase if one strains the voice during or immediately after a cold. Laryngitis causes a reddening and a slight swelling of the vocal folds. It can exist in a chronic form, in which the symptoms become more or less permanent. In such cases an infection in the upper airways and/or smoking and alcohol consumption are usually in the background, often in combination with a habitually exaggerated activity in the phonatory muscles. Chronic laryngitis makes the voice coarse, pressed, and hissing, and it may even develop into cancer.

Women in their forties, who use their voices extensively by profession or habit, sometimes develop a chronic edema on the mucosa of the vocal folds. This edema is called *Reinke-edema*. The voice timbre becomes coarse, and phonation frequency gets abnormally low. The vocal folds become swollen.

Vocal fold *polyps* consist of growths on the vocal folds. Often the cause is a straining of the voice during an infection of the airways, sometimes laryngitis. The voice sounds breathy. A *contact ulcer* may develop on the edges of the vocal folds in the region of the arytenoid cartilages. The cause is believed to be exaggerated adduction activity during phonation. Other types of organic changes include benign and malignant *tumors*.

The treatment of these organic disorders generally includes resting the voice (through silence), voice therapy, and, in the case of tumors, often also surgery.

A slightly different type of organic voice disorder is *recurrent laryngeal nerve paralysis*. The recurrent laryngeal nerve is responsible for controlling all laryngeal muscles except the cricothyroid muscles. If this recurrent nerve is damaged, for instance, by a virus infection or during surgery, the corresponding vocal fold becomes paralyzed, so that neither adduction nor abduction can be efficiently performed. Then, the vocal folds fail to make contact, and the voice sounds extremely breathy and dull. Often the damaged nerve regenerates, so that normal voice function is restored. In other cases a quite normal sounding voice function can be gained if teflon is injected into the paralyzed fold, so that the fold reaches almost halfway into the former glottal chink.

The *functional voice disorders* have their origin in inappropriate voice use, and they sometimes become organic. Many school children between eight and twelve years of age have a more or less permanently *hoarse voice,* particularly boys. The reason is generally too much shouting, sometimes with an infection in the upper airways as the starting factor. Apart from the hoarse, pressed, and hissing voice sound, the symptoms often also include small nodules on the vocal folds as well as an incomplete glottal closure in the arytenoid region. Resting the voice generally improves its status, while straining it tends to aggravate the symptoms.

When the larynx grows during puberty, the *mutational voice change* occurs. The growth is much greater in boys than in girls, so the voice break is much more noticeable in the boys. In connection with this voice change, voice disorders sometimes appear. A boy may encounter trouble trying (or wanting) to find and use the new phonation frequency range offered him by the increased laryngeal dimensions. Sometimes the vocal folds fail to close the middle part of the glottis, and this symptom is assumed to be caused by an insufficient activation of the vocalis muscles.

Phonastenia is the term used to describe tiredness of the voice, or phonatory fatigue. The patient experiences a sense of tiredness in the throat, sometimes in combination with sensations of pain, burning, or a lump in the throat, as well as increased secretion and need for repeatedly clearing the throat. The problems increase when the voice is used and decrease when the voice is allowed to rest. The origin of phonastenia is inappropriate voice use.

If we try to view these voice troubles from the point of view of phonation, we might discern traces of a common physiological cause. It seems that the vocal folds are exposed to excessive stress when the vibrations happen too forcefully or for overlong periods. Then, the vocal folds react in various ways.

The reaction of human tissues to work or friction is by no means unfamiliar to us. The skin on our palms, for instance, will react if it is exposed to exaggerated stress for too long by activities such as rowing or splitting wood. We might expect the vocal folds to react in some analogous way if they collide with each other too much or too violently. Phonation under conditions of high adduction activity, high subglottic pressure, and high activity in the cricothyroid and vocalis muscles (high pitch) may involve unnecessarily exaggerated stress of the vocal folds. Many singing teachers agree that coloratura singing with one adduction-abduction gesture for each note (the "Ahahahahahahamen" type of coloratura) is unhealthy, because of the frequent and vigorous vocal fold collisions associated with the frequent adductions.

Closely related to this reaction of the vocal folds to the mechanical impacts associated with the vocal fold vibration during phonation is a failing lubrication of the phonatory apparatus. The vocal folds need maximally moist air in order to work without problems. If they are allowed to dry, the function is easily disturbed. The calm nasal inhalation often advocated in singing pedagogy is optimal for humidifying the air, because, as was mentioned in the chapter on breathing, the nose, with its large mucosa-covered areas, is an excellent air-conditioning device.

The larynx tube walls are also covered with mucosa. We may safely assume that a low velocity of the air passing the glottis is beneficial during inspiration, because if this velocity is too high, the airstream would dry the laryngeal mucosa. During inhalation the air velocity in the glottis depends on two factors: (1) how forcefully one takes the breath and (2) the size of the glottis area. If the vocal folds are not fully abducted during inhalation, the velocity of the airstream through the glottis is increased, and this would raise the risk of drying the vocal folds.

It is particularly important for singers and actors to observe that the mucosa tends to dry in connection with and often immediately after a cold. Moreover, etheric vapors in the exhaled air, which result from alcohol consumption, for example, are also generally considered to contribute to drying the mucosa. It is possible that tobacco smoking also has this effect, even though many experts believe that the disadvantage is mainly a chemical one that acts directly on the vocal fold tissues.

Singers and other people relying heavily on their voices should note one more extremely important thing. The endurance of the phonatory apparatus varies considerably between individuals. Some people cannot manage to perform as long as others, no matter how economically they use their voices; it is not necessarily a sign of a difference in the quality of the vocal technique if singer A cannot sing as much as singer B.

The endurance of one's voice depends on certain factors. For instance, the need for gentle treatment of the voice generally increases substantially during and immediately after a cold. Typically the young singer who spends his or her first semester in the conservatory comes to see the phoniatrician for an unexpected voice disorder that began when the patient started to sing after a cold that was almost completely cured. The singer's preconservatory experience is that such use of the voice is harmless: it never caused any voice problem before. It is important to realize that the more one uses one's voice, the more careful one needs to be. When in good shape, the voice can be used several hours a day, but in combination with a cold or other types of vocal risk periods, almost any duration may be too much.

A similar reasoning would apply to what is vocally healthy in a general sense. It seems that anything is vocally unhealthy when it is done too much. And, to some extent, the reverse might apply too: anything is harmless to the voice provided that it is not done too often. However, what is too much and what is not depends on the nature of the singing tasks. Singing a very high and loud note may be harmless in reasonable quantities but certainly harmful if done too often, no matter how excellent the vocal technique may be. And what is a harmless quantity under normal conditions may be twice too much after a cold, after drinking alcohol, after cigarette smoking, and so on. It is a rarely realized fact that an indispensable side of a singer's career is to learn not only how but also how much to sing under what conditions.

Of course, this is not to imply that vocal technique has no significant effect on how much the voice can be used. On the contrary, technique would be the most important factor. With a sufficiently poor technique, almost any voice use may be too much. It always pays off for a singer to improve the vocal technique.

To summarize: The more the voice is used, the more wisely and economically it must be used; the risk of developing a voice disorder using one's normal voice technique increases during and immediately after a cold. Alcohol consumption, tobacco smoking, and dry air generally put an increased strain on the phonatory apparatus and raise the demands on economical and appropriate voice use.

Vocal Fold Vibration During Phonatory Disorders

It is self-evident that the normal vibrations of the vocal folds are affected or even eliminated by organic changes, such as tumors and nodules in the vocal fold tissues. For instance, a nodule may prevent the glottis from closing, in which case phonation is bound to be breathy. Generally it is not difficult to detect such changes by means of an inspection with a laryngeal mirror. On the other hand there are several phonatory disorders that are not associated with any visible changes of the vocal folds. For instance, there may be an asymmetry between the folds regarding mass or tension, so that the two folds cannot vibrate in the same way. Various voice changes have been studied by Dunker and Schlosshauer (1961), and next we will review some of their results.

Dunker and Schlosshauer used high speed photography of normal, abnormal, and supranormal voices. They analyzed parallelism and symmetry in the movements of the vocal folds, and also they examined the similarity of the vocal fold movements from different cycles of vibration.

Figure 9.1 shows an example of a supranormal voice belonging to a professional singer. The curves superimposed in the left graph compare two cycles taken from the same tone and refer to the width of the anterior/posterior midpoint of the glottis. We can see that the similarity is almost perfect; the pattern observed in period number 54 is almost identical with that observed in period number 65. The curves compared in the right part of the figure illustrate how parallel the movement of the vocal folds is; the anterior, middle, and posterior part of the glottis all describe practically the same curve. Thus, the front, middle, and back portions of the glottis open in almost perfect synchrony, and the same pattern of vibration is repeated with a high degree of accuracy in the supranormal voice. In other words, the glottis tends to assume a rectangular rather than an elliptical shape throughout the vibratory cycle.

Let us then inspect the corresponding data for disturbed voices. Such data

Figure 9.1. Patterns of vocal fold movements in a professional singer. The curves to the left show the width of the anterior/posterior midpoint of the glottis in cycles number 54 and 65 from a vowel. The curves in the right graph represent the movement of points in the anterior (A), middle (M), and posterior (P) part of the glottis during one cycle. In this supranormal voice, the vocal folds move nearly parallel to one another and repeat the same pattern of movement almost exactly. (After Dunker and Schlosshauer, 1961.)

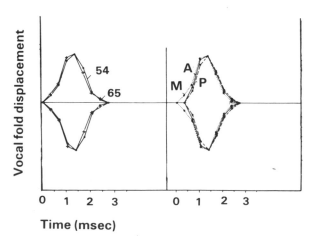

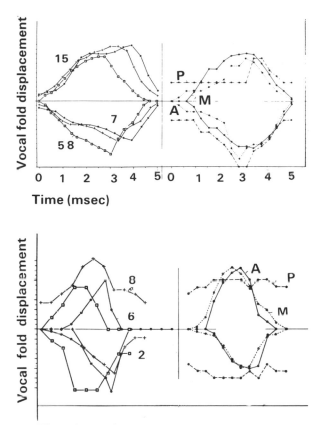

Figure 9.2. Patterns of vocal fold movements in a patient with an indisposed voice, arranged as in figure 9.1. In this voice the posterior part of the glottis is constantly open, and the pattern of movement varies between different glottal pulses. (After Dunker and Schlosshauer, 1961.)

Figure 9.3. Patterns of vocal fold movements in a patient with a voice described as "hoarse and vibrating dysphonic," arranged as in figure 9.1. In this voice, the vocal folds apparently move quite independently of each other, and there is no clear similarity in the movement pattern in different glottal pulses. The posterior part of the glottis does not seem to vibrate at all. (After Dunker and Schlosshauer, 1961.)

are presented in figures 9.2 and 9.3. In both cases what happens in one cycle is not particularly similar to what happens in the following cycle; the vocal folds do not move in the same way from cycle to cycle. Moreover, there is no great similarity between the movements of the various parts of the vocal folds.

Also, these vocal folds never close the posterior part of the glottis; the glottis is partially leaking. The similarity between different periods is small in figure 9.2, and in figure 9.3 it is really hard to detect any similarity at all; the vocal folds move chaotically, apparently completely independent of each other.

Figure 9.4 compares the vocal fold movements during onset of voicing for a normal voice and one that was "indisposed." In the normal case we can see that the vocal folds start to vibrate several cycles before they really make contact and seal the glottis. The minimum glottis area decreases for each cycle, but a full closure has not been achieved even in the eleventh cycle. The corresponding data for the indisposed voice look more erratic. The third cycle closes the glottis, but the fifth does not. Closure again occurs in the seventh cycle. Thus, the cycles are not similar; some close the glottis, while others fail to do so.

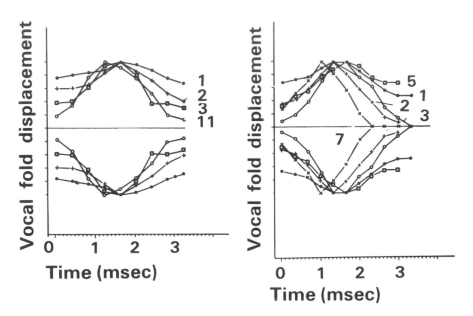

Figure 9.4. Patterns of vocal fold movements in a normal voice (left) and in a patient with a disturbed ("indisposed") voice (right). The curves are arranged as in the left part of figure 9.1. In the normal voice, the vocal folds close the glottis more and more for every cycle. In this disturbed voice, period number 5 fails to close the glottis while previous and later periods succeed. (After Dunker and Schlosshauer, 1961.)

Here it should be mentioned that the normal voice in the Dunker and Schlosshauer investigation probably did not belong to a singer. A high-speed movie film made at Bell Telephone Laboratories in the 1950s shows that the vocal folds make full contact at the first or second movement in what is referred to as a well-controlled attack. Such tone onsets would be frequently used by singers. They are characterized by a synchrony in the starting of the transglottal airflow and the adduction; the airstream is started when the adduction is almost completed. In the tone onset shown in figure 9.4 the airstream is started earlier, so that the voice sound is preceded by aspiration noise (a short /h/-sound).

Figure 9.5 illustrates three cases where there is a good periodicity of the vocal fold vibrations: the same vibratory pattern is repeated from cycle to cycle. On the other hand, there is a strong asymmetry between the movements of the two folds. In other words, the maximum excursion of the left vocal fold does not coincide with the maximum excursion of the right vocal fold. This is shown in the left and middle graphs. In the right graph one vocal fold tends to display two maximum displacements during one cycle, while the other fold merely has one.

To summarize: In a vowel sound, the vocal fold vibrations in normal and disturbed voices differ both with respect to the similarity between different cycles and in regard to the degree of parallelism with which the folds move.

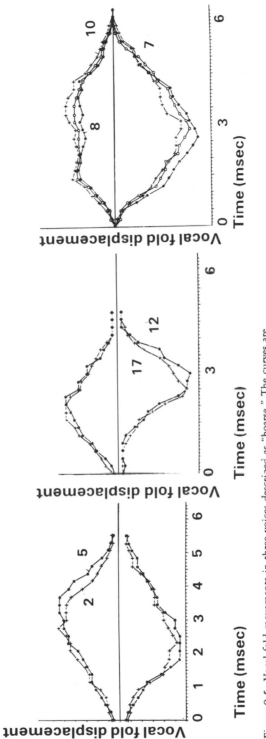

Figure 9.5. Vocal fold movements in three voices described as "hoarse." The curves are arranged as in the left part of figure 9.1. The left and right vocal fold move according to different patterns. In the right graph, one cord tends to flap twice while the opposite cord makes one excursion. (After Dunker and Schlosshauer, 1961.)

Voice Source in Phonatory Disorders

Obviously irregularities in the vocal fold vibrations such as those shown in the preceding figures must have consequences in the sound produced by the voice source. Generally, irregularities in the vocal fold vibrations result in irregularities in phonation frequency. The overtone content of the voice source depends on how fast the glottis cuts off the transglottal airflow in the closing phase, as was shown in chapter 4. We realize that if the vocal folds do not repeat exactly the same pattern from cycle to cycle, the closing of the glottis will probably be executed at different speeds in various cycles. Hence the overtone content will vary from cycle to cycle.

Cycle-to-cycle variations of the overtone content of the voice pulses are typical in voice disorders and can be inspected in spectrograms of the "Sonagram" or "Voiceprint" type. As we saw before, such spectrograms show frequency on the vertical axis and time on the horizontal axis, and the blackening represents intensity. Each voice pulse is depicted as a vertical line, the thickness (or blackness) of which culminates at the formant frequencies. As the voice pulses appear close to each other in time, they form a dense pattern of vertical lines in the spectrogram, and the formants appear as dark shadows, as can be seen in the two examples shown in figure 9.6.

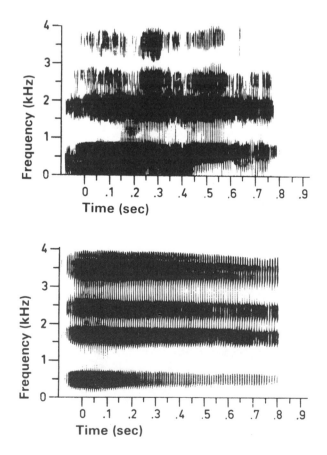

Figure 9.6. Time spectrograms of a breathy (above) and normal (below) voice. In the breathy voice, the overtone content differs between the individual glottal pulses, so that the pattern becomes irregular, particularly at higher frequencies.

If the overtone content of the voice pulses varies from cycle to cycle, the pattern of the vertical lines corresponding to these pulses will of course be irregular. Figure 9.6 compares spectrograms of a normal and a breathy voice. The difference regarding the variations in the amplitude of the overtones can be clearly observed. The opportunity to study this aspect of phonation from simple spectrograms is valuable; the alternative method just discussed, that is high-speed filming, is cumbersome to use.

Direct information on the average overtone content of the voice source can be gained from a different kind of analysis, namely long-term-average spectrography. This very simple method can be used for obtaining a spectrum of fluent speech or singing averaged over many seconds. It turns out that after some ten or twenty seconds of normal speech a very stable spectrum average is obtained. Thus, it does not matter what the speaker says; the influence from the time-varying contributions converges to a stable mean. The center frequencies of the peaks in such spectra depend on the individual speakers' average formant frequencies. Information on the voice source can be gained by comparing the sound levels within various frequency bands of a patient's long-term-average spectra, recorded before and after therapy, for example.

Figure 9.7 shows a typical difference between a normal voice and a voice suffering from recurrent laryngeal nerve paralysis. Note the considerable level difference, which ranges from about 300 Hz up to 5 kHz. As the vocal folds fail to close the glottis when one of the vocal folds is paralyzed, the closing is very slow in the glottal cycle; hence the overtones are very weak, leaving the fundamental to dominate the voice source spectrum entirely. The figure shows that the fundamental has produced a high peak

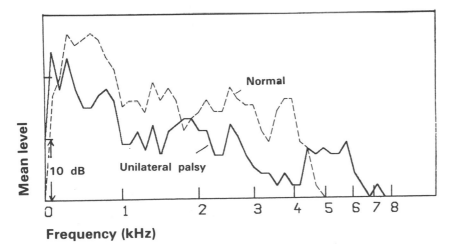

Figure 9.7. Long-term-average spectra of the voiced sounds in speech as produced by a normal voice (dashed) and a voice suffering from unilateral vocal fold paralysis (solid). As the paralyzed fold prevents closing of the glottis, the spectrum of the voice source is dominated by its fundamental. The noise generated by the glottal leakage appears in the high frequency part of the spectrum.

in the pathological voice, which is much higher than in the spectrum of the normal voice.

We recall that a low amplitude of the voice source fundamental is typical of pressed phonation, and a loud fundamental is obtained in flow phonation as well as in breathy phonation. From figure 9.7 we can infer that breathy phonation and flow phonation differ with regard to the overtone content and that this difference will be revealed by a long-term-average spectrum.

In a breathy voice source, noise is being generated by the turbulent airflow. At high frequencies, this noise reaches a considerable amplitude compared to the harmonic spectrum partials. A breathy phonation is not the only way to generate such noise sounds. Most voiceless consonants also contain noise components of sizable amplitude at high frequencies. Only if all voiceless consonants are eliminated from the signal analyzed by a long-term-average spectrum will the level in the frequency range above 5 kHz be informative with regard to a leaking glottis. Figure 9.8 shows a typical example of this.

To Warm Up

Most people who depend on perfect voice function warm up their voices before using them for heavier work. What happens and why it is important is not well understood, but still some speculations can be presented.

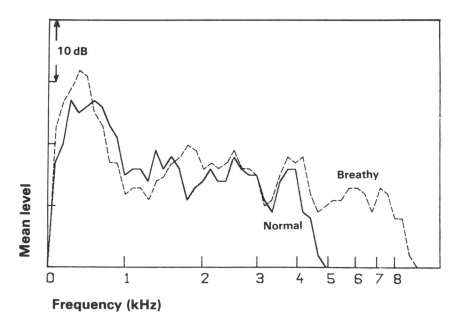

Figure 9.8. Long-term-average spectra of the voiced sounds in speech as produced by a normal voice (solid) and a breathy voice (dashed). The noise generated by the glottal leakage appears in the high frequency part of the spectrum.

Many singers need to warm up; if they do not do it, their voices will not function as readily as otherwise. Warming up in a hurry or in a wrong way also tends to result in poorer voice function than normal. It seems that the poorly warmed-up voice is less durable than the appropriately warmed-up voice.

The procedure used for warming up varies between individuals. Many prefer to sing softly at very low phonation frequencies and to make many long pauses between the first voice exercises of the day. Others sing loudly at high phonation frequencies and then rest. Many interleave the exercises with eating apples, oranges, or whatever. The methods are numerous, and each individual has to find out what best fits her or him.

What happens to the vocal folds during the warm-up? The vocal folds contain muscle tissues as a major component. As is the case with other muscles, the vocal folds depend on efficient blood circulation in order to retain good function and viscosity. It seems likely that good circulation is stimulated by an appropriate warm-up procedure. Other people who depend on perfect muscle function, like ballet dancers and athletes, tend to warm up their muscles in advance. This warming-up is realized by movements or massage. It is difficult to give massage directly to one's vocal folds, but perhaps the same effect is reached if we can use them for a gentle phonation instead. Let us hope that research will soon start to pay attention to this important but very poorly understood issue!

Treatment and Outlook

It was mentioned above that surgery is one strategy for curing certain voice disorders. It seems that doctors prefer to use this solution in cases of nonfunctional disorders. This policy is easy to understand. If the trouble is the consequence of a poor vocal technique, the voice problems are likely to return sooner or later after the surgery, unless something is done to improve the patient's vocal habits.

Medication is another important method of treatment. It is important for professional voice users to realize that many drugs have effects on the voice that can cause them problems. This applies not only to drugs taken for voice problems but also to other drugs—among them certain sleeping pills and contraceptive pills—which may also affect phonation or the control of phonation in some individuals. Therefore, singers and other people whose professions depend significantly on their voices should mention this circumstance to their doctors so that it can be taken into account in prescribing. For more information on this topic, the reader is referred to Proctor's *Breathing, Speech, and Song* (1980).

Therapy is perhaps the most important method for treating voice problems. The dispute among singing teachers and other voice experts as to what is the best method or therapy and what is the best vocal technique has gone on over the centuries, and probably there is little hope that the issue will be resolved in the near future; indeed, the question itself seems inappropriately formulated. It is not very likely that there is only one method of using the voice that is superior to all others. The individual morphology, sex, repertoire, fashion, and other factors must be of significance.

This is not to say that all methods are equally efficient and appropriate. Indeed, some methods seem either impractical or detrimental or both. It sometimes occurs that the number of patients seeing a laryngologist for voice troubles suddenly increases, simply because of the method of a new voice teacher who just moved into town and started giving lessons. In looking for a good voice teacher, it would be wise to find out how the teacher has succeeded in the past. No two students are ever identical, of course. But it generally turns out that some teachers are much more successful with students than others. The author believes that the personal relationship between teacher and pupil is a factor of generally underestimated importance, because of the substantial influence of emotional atmosphere on vocal behavior.

It is hard to judge what is a good method or technique. We may hope that objective measurements on voice characteristics will help, though; objective and relevant measures have turned out to be indispensable in the assessment of various methods in other fields, such as pharmacology and medicine.

Before leaving the issue of method it should be pointed out that method does not always refer to a pedagogical style but rather to its goal, or, in other words, *the ideal voice use.* When the word method is used with this meaning, it is obvious that there are better or worse methods. Still it seems a bit doubtful whether or not one single method exists that is optimal from a physiological point of view. In any event it remains to be proved. More doubtful still is that one method or voice use exists that fits all repertoires equally well. It would be a hard task to get a rock-and-roll audience to agree with an opera audience as to which voice use is musically the best.

After all, there are evidently quality variations among voice teachers and hence there are quality variations also among methods. The question of which method is better and which is worse is not easy, and the nature and the voice habits of the student should certainly be taken into account. The author thinks that a good method is one that is in close agreement with physiology. In the long run it must be easier for the majority of students to understand instructions that agree closely with what is actually happening within their bodies. A student might eventually find some meaning in an instruction such as "Feel the tone in your left elbow," but it is likely that understanding such instructions tends to take more time than learning from more concrete and realistic instructions.

Bibliography

Some abbreviations used in the list of references:

FP   *Folia Phoniatrica*
JASA   *Journal of the Acoustical Society of America*
JSHR   *Journal of Speech and Hearing Research*
KTH   *Kungliga Tekniska Högskolan* (Royal Institute of Technology)
MIT   *Massachusetts Institute of Technology*
Z   *Zeitschrift*

Ågren, K., and J. Sundberg. 1978. An acoustic comparison of alto and tenor voices. *J Research in Singing* 1: 26–32.

Appelman, D. R. 1967. *The science of vocal pedagogy.* Bloomington: Indiana University Press.

Baer, T. 1979. Reflex activation and laryngeal muscles by sudden induced subglottal pressure changes. *JASA* 65: 1271–75.

Baldwin, E. A., A. Cournand, and D. Richards. 1948. Pulmonary insufficiency. *Medicine* 27: 243–78.

Bartholomew, W. T. 1934. A physical definition of "good voice quality" in the male voice. *JASA* 6: 25–33.

von Békésy, G. 1960. *Experiments in hearing.* New York: McGraw-Hill.

Bennett, G. 1981. Singing synthesis in electronic music. In *Research Aspects of Singing* (pp. 34–50). Stockholm: Royal Swedish Acad. of Music.

van den Berg, J.-W. 1962. Modern research in experimental phoniatrics. *FP* 14: 81–149.

————. 1968. Register problems. In *Ann. New York Acad. Sciences* 151, article 1, ed. M. Krauss, M. Hammer, and A. Bouhuys, 129–34.

Björklund, A. 1961. Analysis of soprano voices. *JASA* 33: 575–82.

Bloothooft, G. 1985. Spectrum and timbre of sung vowels. Ph.D. diss., Vrije Universiteit te Amsterdam.

Bouhuys, A., J. Mead, D. F. Proctor, and K. N. Stevens. 1968. Pressure-flow events during singing. *Ann. New York Acad. Sciences* 155, article 1, ed. M. Krauss, M. Hammer, and A. Bouhuys, 165–76.

Bouhuys, A., D. F. Proctor, and J. Mead. 1966. Kinetic aspects of singing. *J Appl. Physiol.* 21: 483–96.

Brandl, F. 1985. Bewegungen des Kehlkopfes bei männlichen Berufssängern in Abhängigkeit von der Tonintensität. *Sprache—Stimme—Gehör* 9: 54–58.

Carr, P. B., and D. Trill. 1964. Long-term larynx excitation spectra. *JASA* 36: 575–82.

Childers, D. G., J. J. Yea, and E. L. Boccheri. 1983. Source vocal tract interaction in speech and singing synthesis. In *Proc. of Stockholm Music Acoustics Conference 1983* (SMAC 83) (no. 1), ed. A. Askenfelt, S. Felicetti, E. Jansson, and J. Sundberg, pp. 125–41. Stockholm: Royal Swedish Acad. of Music.

Chowning, J. M. 1980. Computer synthesis of the singing voice. In *Sound generation in winds, strings, computers* (pp. 4–14). Stockholm: Royal Swedish Acad. of Music.

Clarkson, J. and J. A. Deutsch. 1966. Effect on threshold reduction on the vibrato. *J Exp. Psychol.* 71: 706–10.

Cleveland, T. F. 1976. *The acoustic properties of voice timbre types and their importance in the determination of voice classification in male singers.* Ph.D. diss., University of Southern California.

———. 1977. Acoustic properties of voice timbre types and their influence on voice classification. *JASA* 61: 1622–29.

Cleveland, T., and J. Sundberg. 1983. Acoustic analysis of three male voices of different quality. In *Proc. of Stockholm Music Acoustics Conference 1983* (SMAC 83) (no. 1), ed. A. Askenfelt, S. Felicetti, E. Jansson, and J. Sundberg, pp. 143–56. Stockholm: Royal Swedish Acad. of Music.

Clynes, M. 1983. Expressive microstructure in music, linked to living qualities. In *Studies of Music Performance* (pp. 76–181). Stockholm: Royal Swedish Academy of Music.

———. 1969. Precision of essentic form in living communication. In *Information processing in the nervous system,* ed. K. M. Leibovic and J. C. Eccles. New York: Springer Verlag.

———. 1980. Transforming emotionally expressive touch to similarly expressive sound. *Proc. Tenth Int. Acoust. Congr.,* Sydney.

Coleman, R. F., J. H. Mabis, and J. K. Hinson. 1977. Fundamental frequency—sound pressure level profiles of adult male and female voices. *JSHR* 20: 197–204.

Coleman, R. O. 1976. A comparison of the contributions of two voice quality characteristics to the perception of maleness and femaleness in the voice. *JHSR* 19: 168–80.

Crystal, D. 1969. *Prosodic systems and intonation in English.* Cambridge: Cambridge University Press.

Deutsch, J. A., and J. K. Clarkson. 1959. Nature of the vibrato and the control loop in singing. *Nature* 183: 167–68.

Dmitriev, L., and A. Kiselev. 1979. Relationship between the formant structure of different types of singing voices and the dimension of supraglottal cavities. *FP* 31: 238–41.

Draper, M. H., P. Ladefoged, and D. Whitteridge. 1959. Respiratory muscles in speech. *JSHR* 2: 16–27.

Dunker, E., and B. Schlosshauer. 1961. Unregelmässige Stimmlippenschwingungen bei funktionellen Stimmstörungen. *Z. fuer Laryngologie, Rhinologie, Otologie* 40: 919–34.

Erickson, D., T. Baer, and C. Harris. 1983. The role of the strap muscles in pitch lowering. In *Vocal fold physiology: Contemporary research and clinical issues,* ed. D. M. Bless and J. H. Abbs, 279–85. San Diego, Calif.: College-Hill.

Estill, J., T. Baer, K. Honda, and K. S. Harris. 1983. Supralaryngeal activity in a study of six voice qualities. In *Proc. of Stockholm Music Acoustics Conference 1983* (SMAC 83) (no. 1), ed. A. Askenfelt, S. Felicetti, E. Jansson, and J. Sundberg, pp. 157–74. Stockholm: Royal Swedish Acad. of Music.

Fant, G. 1959. Acoustic analysis and synthesis of speech with applications to Swedish. *Ericsson Technics* 1: 1–108. Reprinted in G. Fant: *Speech sounds and features.* Cambridge: MIT Press.

———. 1960. *Acoustic theory of speech production.* The Hague: Mouton.

———. 1968. Analysis and synthesis of speech processes. In *Manual of phonetics,* ed. B. Malmberg, 173–277. Amsterdam: North Holland Publishing Company.

———. 1975. Nonuniform vowel normalization. *Speech Transmission Laboratory Quarterly Progress and Status Report* (KTH, Stockholm) 2–3: 1–19.

———. 1979. Glottal source and excitation analysis. *Speech Transmission Laboratory Quarterly Progress and Status Report* (KTH, Stockholm) 1: 85–107.

Fant, G., L. Qi-guang, and C. Gobl. 1985. Notes on glottal flow interaction. *Speech Transmission Laboratory Quarterly Progress and Status Report* (KTH, Stockholm) 2–3: 21–45.

Flanagan, J. L. 1965. *Speech analysis, synthesis, and perception.* New York: Springer.

Fonagy, I. 1962. Mimik auf glottaler Ebene. *Phonetica* 8: 209–19.

———. 1967. Hörbare Mimik. *Phonetica* 16: 25–35.

———. 1971. Synthèse de l'ironie. *Phonetica* 23: 42–51.

———. 1976. La mimique buccale. *Phonetica* 33: 31–44.

———. 1981. Emotions, voice, and music. In *Research Aspects of Singing* (pp. 51–79). Stockholm: Royal Swedish Acad. of Music.

Fonagy, I., and S. Bérard. 1972. "Il est huit heures." Contribution à l'analyse semantique de la vive voix. *Phonetica* 26: 157–92.

Fonagy, I., and K. Magdics. 1963. Emotional patterns in intonation and music. *Z. fuer Phonetik* 16: 293–326.

Fritzell, B. 1973. Foniatri för medicinare. Stockholm: Almqvist & Wiksell.

Fujisaki, H. 1981. Dynamic characteristics of voice fundamental frequency in speech and singing—Acoustical analysis and physiological interpretations. In *Proceedings of the 4th F.A.S.E. Symposium.*

Gauffin, J., and J. Sundberg. 1980. Data on the glottal voice source behavior in vowel production. *Speech Transmission Laboratory Quarterly Progress and Status Report* (KTH, Stockholm) 2–3 (1980): 61–70.

Gibian, G. L. 1972. Synthesis of sung vowels. *Quarterly Progress Report* (MIT) 104: 243–47.

Goodwin, A. 1980. Acoustic study of individual voices in choral blend. *J of Res. in Singing* 3(2): 15–36.

Gould, W. J. 1977. The effect of voice training on lung volumes in singers and the possible relationship to the damping factor of Pressman. *J of Res. in Singing* 1: 3–15.

Gould, W. J., and H. Okamura. 1974. Interrelationships between voice and laryngeal mucousal reflexes. In *Ventilatory and phonatory control systems,* ed. B. Wyke, 347–60. London: Oxford University Press.

Hagerman, B., and J. Sundberg. 1980. Fundamental frequency adjustment in barbershop singing. *J Research in Singing* 4: 3–17.

Harvey, N. 1985. Vocal control in singing: A cognitive approach. In *Musical structure and cognition,* ed. P. Howell, I. Cross, and R. West, 287–332. London: Academic Press.

Hirano, M., W. Vennard, and J. Ohala. 1970. Regulation of register, pitch, and intensity of voice. *FP* 22: 1–20.

Hixon, T. J. 1976a. Dynamics of the chest wall during speech production: Function of the thorax, rib cage, diaphragm, and the abdomen. *JSHR* 19: 297–356.

———. 1976b. Respiratory function in speech. In *Normal aspects of speech, hearing and language,* ed. F. D. Minifie, T. J. Hixon, and F. Williams, 73–125. Englewood Cliffs, N.J.: Prentice-Hall.

Hixon, T. J., and C. Hoffman. 1978. Chest wall shape in singing. *Transcripts of the 7th Symposium Care of the Professional Voice,* ed. L. van Lawrence, 9–10. New York: Voice Foundation.

Hollien, H. 1974. On vocal registers. *J of Phonetics* 2: 125–43.

————. 1983. The puzzle of the singer's formant. In *Vocal fold physiology: Contemporary research and clinical issues,* ed. D. M. Bless and J. H. Abbs, 368–78. San Diego: College-Hill.

Hollien, H., and G. P. Moore. 1960. Measurements of the vocal folds during changes in pitch. *JSHR* 3: 157–65.

Howell, P. 1985. Auditory feedback of the voice in singing. In *Musical structure and cognition,* ed. P. Howell, I. Cross, and R. West, 259–86. London: Academic Press.

Howell, P., and D. J. Powell. 1984. Hearing your voice through bone and air: Implications for explanations of stuttering behavior from studies of normal speakers. *J of Fluency Disorders* 9: 247–64.

Ishizaka, K., and J. L. Flanagan. 1972. Synthesis of voiced sounds from a two-mass model of the vocal cords. *Bell System Technical Journal* 51: 1233–68.

Isshiki, N. 1964. Regulatory mechanism of voice intensity variation. *JSHR* 7: 17–29.

————. 1965. Vocal intensity and airflow rate. *FP* 17: 92–104.

Iwamiya, S., K. Kosygi, and O. Kitamura. 1983. Perceived pitch of vibrato tones. *J Acoust. Soc. Japan* 4: 73–82.

Johnson, A., J. Sundberg, and H. Willbrand. 1983. "Kölning": A study of phonation and articulation in a type of Swedish herding song. In *Proc. of Stockholm Music Acoustics Conference 1983* (SMAC 83) (no. 1), ed. A. Askenfelt, S. Felicetti, E. Jansson, and J. Sundberg, pp. 187–202. Stockholm: Royal Swedish Acad. of Music.

Johansson, C., J. Sundberg, and H. Willbrand. 1983. X-ray study of articulation and formant frequencies in two female singers. In *Proc. of Stockholm Music Acoustics Conference 1983* (SMAC 83) (no. 1), ed. A. Askenfelt, S. Felicetti, E. Jansson, and J. Sundberg, pp. 203–18. Stockholm: Royal Swedish Acad. of Music.

Karlsson, I. 1976. Vokalers spektrumlutning i tal. In *Avdelningen för fonetik.* Umeå University, Publication no. 10, 68–72.

Kirikae, J., T. Sato, H. Oshima, and K. Nomoto. 1964. Vibration of the body during phonation of vowels. *Revue de laryngologie, Otologie, Rhinologie* 85: 317–45.

Kitzing, P. 1985. Stroboscopy, a pertinent laryngological examination. *J of Otolaryngology* 14: 151–57.

Kotlyar, G. M., and V. P. Morozov. 1976. Acoustical correlates of the emotional content of vocalized speech. *Sov Phys Acoust* 22: 208–11.

Kramer, E. 1963. Judgments of personal characteristics and emotions from nonverbal properties of speech. *Psych Bull* 60: 408–20.

Large, J., and S. Iwata. 1971. Aerodynamic study of vibrato and voluntary "straight tone" pairs in singing. *FP* 23: 50–65.

Leanderson, R., J. Sundberg, and C. von Euler. The role of diaphragmatic activity during singing. *J. Appl. Physiol.* 62(1): 259–70.

Leanderson, R., J. Sundberg, C. von Euler, and H. Lagercrantz. 1983. Diaphragmatic control of the subglottic pressure during singing. *Transcripts of the 12th*

Symposium Care of the Professional Voice, ed. L. van Lawrence, 216–20. New York: Voice Foundation.

———. 1984. Effect of diaphragm activity on phonation during singing. *Speech Transmission Laboratory Quarterly Progress and Status Report* (KTH, Stockholm) 4: 1–10.

Lieberman, P., and S. B. Michaels. 1962. Some aspects of fundamental frequency and envelope amplitude as related to the emotional content of speech. *JASA* 34: 922–27.

Lindblom, B., and J. Sundberg. 1971. Acoustical consequences of lip, tongue, jaw, and larynx movements. *JASA* 50: 1166–79.

Lindgren, H., and A. Sundberg. 1972. Grundfrekvensförlopp och falsksång. Stockholm University, Inst. för musikvetenskap. Stencil.

Löfqvist, A. 1975. A study of subglottal pressure during the production of Swedish stops. *J phonetics* 3: 981–93.

Lottermoser, W., and Fr.-J. Meyer. 1960. Frequenzmessungen an gesungenen Akkorden. *Acustica* 10: 181–86.

McAdams, S. 1984. *Spectral fusion, spectral parsing, and the formation of auditory images.* Ph.D. diss., Stanford University.

McCurtain, F., and G. Welch. 1983. Vocal tract gestures in soprano and bass: A xeroradiographic-electrolaryngographic study. In *Proc. of Stockholm Music Acoustics Conference 1983* (SMAC 83) (no. 1), ed. A. Askenfelt, S. Felicetti, E. Jansson, and J. Sundberg, pp. 219–38. Stockholm: Royal Swedish Acad. of Music.

Makeig, S., and G. Balzano. 1982. Octave tuning—Two modes of perception. Res. symp on psychology and acoustics of music. (Preprint.)

Marshall, A. H., and J. Meyer. 1985. The directivity and auditory impressions of singers. *Acustica* 58: 130–40.

Mason, R. M. 1965. A study of the physiological mechanism of vocal vibrato. Ph.D. diss. Urbana: University of Illinois.

Monoson, P., and W. R. Zemlin. 1984. Quantitative study of whisper. *FP* 36: 53–65.

Morozov, V. P. 1965. Intelligibility in singing as a function of fundamental voice pitch. *Soviet Physics Acoustics* 10: 279–83.

Moses, P. J. 1954. *The voice of the neurosis.* New York: Grune & Stratton.

Navratil, M., and K. Rejsek. Lung function in wind instrument players and glass blowers. *Ann. New York Acad. Sciences* 155, article 1, ed. M. Krauss, M. Hammer, and A. Bouhuys, 276–83.

Nelson, H. D., and W. R. Tiffany. 1968. The intelligibility of song. *National Association of Teachers of Singing Bulletin,* December, 22–33.

Nordström, P.-E. 1977. Female and infant vocal tracts simulated from male area functions. *J Phonetics* 5: 81–92.

Ondrackova, J. 1969. Some remarks on the analysis of sung vowels: X-ray study of Czech material. Phon. Soc. of Japan. *Study of Sounds,* no. 14, 407–18.

Pawlowski, Z., R. Pawluczyk, and Z. Kraska. 1983. Epiphysis vibrations of singers studied by holographic interferometry. In *Proc. of Stockholm Music Acoustics Conference 1983* (SMAC 83) (no. 1), ed. A. Askenfelt, S. Felicetti, E. Jansson, and J. Sundberg, pp. 37–60. Stockholm: Royal Swedish Acad. of Music.

———. 1982. Holographic vibration analysis of the frontal part of the human neck during singing. In *Proc. Int. Conf. Optics in Biomedical Sciences,* ed. G. v Bally, and P. Greguss. Heidelberg: Springer Verlag.

Pawluczyk, R., Z. Kraska, and Z. Pawlowski. 1982. Holographic investigations of skin vibrations. *Appl. Optics* 21: 759–65.

Peslin, R., C. Duvivier, and M. Mortinet Lambert. 1972. Réponse en frequence du système mécanique ventilatoire total de 3 à 70 Hz. *Bull Physio-Path Resp.* 8: 267–79.

Proctor, D. F. 1968. The physiologic basis of voice training. In *Ann. New York Acad. Sciences* 155, article 1, ed. M. Krauss, M. Hammer, and A. Bouhuys, 208–28.

———. 1974. Discussion. In *Ventilatory and phonatory control systems,* ed. B. Wyke, 292–95. London: Oxford University Press.

———. 1980. *Breathing, speech and song.* New York: Springer-Verlag.

Rossing, T. D., J. Sundberg, and S. Ternström. 1986. Acoustic comparison of voice use in solo and choir singing. *JASA* 79: 1975–81.

———. 1985. Acoustic comparison of soprano solo and choir singing. *Speech Transmission Laboratory Quarterly Progress and Status Report* (KTH, Stockholm) 4: 43–58.

Rothenberg, M. 1968. The breath-stream dynamics of simple-released plosive production. *Bibliotheca Phonetica* 6: 1–117.

———. 1973. A new inverse-filtering technique for deriving the glottal airflow waveform during voicing. JASA 53: 1632–45.

———. 1981. The voice source in singing. In *Research aspects of singing,* pp. 15–33. Stockholm: Royal Swedish Acad. of Music.

———. 1985. *Cosi fan tutte* and what it means: Nonlinear source-tract interaction in the soprano voice and some implications for the definition of vocal efficiency. Paper given at Fourth Internat. Vocal Fold Physiol. Conf. New Haven, Conn.: Haskins Laboratories.

Rubin, H. J., M. LeCover, and W. Vennard. 1967. Vocal intensity, subglottic pressure, and airflow relationships in singers. *FP* 19: 393–413.

Ruth, W. 1963. The registers of the singing voice. *Nat Assoc of Teachers of Singing Bull,* May, 2–5.

Rzhevkin, S. N. 1956. Certain results of the analysis of a singer's voice. *Soviet Physics Acoustics* 2: 215–20.

Sacerdote, G. G. 1957. Researches on the singing voice. *Acustica* 7: 61–68.

Sawashima, M., H. Hirose, K. Honda, H. Yoshioka, S. R. Hibi, N. Kawase, and M. Yamada. 1983. Stereoendoscopic measurement of the laryngeal structure. In *Vocal fold physiology. Contemporary research and clinical issues,* ed. D. M. Bless and J. H. Abbs, 264–76. San Diego: College-Hill.

Scherer, K. R. 1979. Non-linguistic vocal indicators of emotion and psychopathology. In *Emotions in personality and psychopathology,* ed. C. E. Izard. New York: Plenum Press.

Schoenhard, C., H. Hollien, and J. W. Hicks. 1983. Spectral characteristics of voice registers in female singers. *Transcripts of the 12th Symposium Care of the Professional Voice,* ed. L. van Lawrence, 7–11. New York: Voice Foundation.

Schönhärl, E. 1960. *Die Stroboskopie in der praktischen Laryngologie.* Stuttgart: Georg Thieme Verlag.

Schultz-Coulon, H.-J. 1978. The neuromuscular control system and vocal function. *Acta oto-lar* 86: 142–53.

Schultz-Coulon, H.-J., and R.-D. Battmer. 1981. Die quantitative Bewertung des Sängervibratos. *FP* 33: 1–14.

Schultz-Coulon, H.-J., R.-D. Battmer, and H. Riechert. 1979. Die 3-kHz-Formant—ein Mass fuer die Tragfähigkeit der Stimme? I. Die untrainierte Normalstimme. II. Die trainierte Singstimme. *FP* 31: 291–313.

Schutte, H. K. 1980. *The efficiency of voice production.* Ph.D. diss., Universität Gronigen.

Schutte, H. K., and D. G. Miller. 1985. The effect of F0/F1 coincidence in soprano high notes on pressure at the glottis. *J Phonetics,* forthcoming.

Scully, C., and E. Allwood. 1983. Simulation of singing with a composite model of speech production. In *Proc. of Stockholm Music Acoustics Conference 1983* (SMAC 83) (no. 1), ed. A. Askenfelt, S. Felicetti, E. Jansson, and J. Sundberg, pp. 247–60. Stockholm: Royal Swedish Acad. of Music.

Sedlacek, K., and A. Sychra. 1963. Die Melodie als Faktor des emotionellen Ausdrucks. *FP* 15: 89–98.

Seidner, W., H. Schutte, J. Wendler, and A. Rauhut. 1983. Dependence of the high singing formant on pitch and vowel in different voice types. In *Proc. of Stockholm Music Acoustics Conference 1983* (SMAC 83) (no. 1), ed. A. Askenfelt, S. Felicetti, E. Jansson, and J. Sundberg, pp. 261–68. Stockholm: Royal Swedish Acad. of Music.

Selkin, S. G. 1982. *Flutes, horns, singers.* Videofilm.

Shearer, W. M. 1979. *Illustrated speech anatomy.* Springfield, Ill.: Charles C Thomas.

Shipp, T., T. Doherty, and P. Morrissey. 1979. Predicting vocal frequency from selected physiologic measures. *JASA* 66: 678–84.

Shipp, T., and K. Izdebski. 1975. Vocal frequency and vertical larynx positioning by singers and nonsingers. *JASA* 58: 1104–6.

Shipp, T., R. Leanderson, and S. Haglund. 1982. Contribution of the cricothyroid muscle to vocal vibrato. *Transcripts of the 11th Symposium Care of the Professional Voice,* ed. L. van Lawrence, 131–33. New York: Voice Foundation.

Shipp, T., R. Leanderson, and J. Sundberg. 1980. Some acoustic characteristics of vocal vibrato. *J Research in Singing* 4: 18–25.

Shipp, T., P. Morrissey, and S. Haglund. 1983. Laryngeal muscle adjustments for sustained phonation at lung volume extremes. In *Proc. of Stockholm Music Acoustics Conference 1983* (SMAC 83) (no. 1), ed. A. Askenfelt, S. Felicetti, E. Jansson, and J. Sundberg, pp. 269–77. Stockholm: Royal Swedish Acad. of Music.

Shipp, T., J. Sundberg, and S. Haglund. 1984. A model of frequency vibrato. *Transcripts of the 13th Symposium Care of the Professional Voice,* ed. L. van Lawrence, 116–17. New York: Voice Foundation.

Shonle, J. I., and K. E. Horan. 1980. The pitch of vibrato tones. *JASA* 67: 246–52.

Smith, L. A., and B. L. Scott. 1980. Increasing the intelligibility of sung vowels. *JASA* 67: 1795–97.

Sonninen, A. 1956. The role of the external laryngeal muscles in length-adjustment of the vocal cords in singing. *Acta Otolaryngologica,* Suppl. 130.

Strohl, K. P., and J. M. Fouke. 1985. Dilating forces on the upper airways of aenesthetized dogs. *J Applied Physiology* 58: 452–58.

Stumpf, C. 1926. *Die Sprachlaute.* Berlin: J. Springer.

Sundberg, J. 1970. Formant structure and articulation of spoken and sung vowels. *FP* 22: 28–48.

———. 1972. Production and function of the singing formant. In *Report of the 11th Congress of the International Musicological Society,* vol. 2., ed. H. Glahn, S. Sorenson, and P. Ryom, 679–88. Copenhagen: Edition Wilhelm Hansen.

———. 1973. The source spectrum in professional singing. *FP* 25: 71–90.

———. 1974. Articulatory intepretation of the "singing formant." *JASA* 55: 838–44.

————. 1975. Formant technique in a professional female singer. *Acustica* 32: 89–96.

————. 1977a. The acoustics of the singing voice. *Scientific American*, March, 82–91.

————. 1977b. Singing and timbre. In *Music, room, acoustics* (pp. 57–81). Stockholm: Royal Swedish Acad. of Music.

————. 1977c. Vibrato and vowel identification. *Archives of Acoustics* 2: 257–66.

————. 1977d. Studies of the soprano voice. *J Research in Singing* 1: 25–35.

————. 1978a. Effects of the vibrato and the singing formant on pitch. *Musicologica Slovaca* 6: 51–69.

————. 1978b. Vibrato and vowel identification. *Archives of Acoustics* 2: 257–66.

————. 1978c. Synthesis of singing. *Swedish Journal of Musicology* 60: 107–12.

————. 1979. Maximum speed of pitch changes in singers and untrained subjects. *J Phonetics* 7: 71–97.

————. 1981. To perceive one's own voice and another person's voice. In *Research Aspects of Singing*, 80–86. Stockholm: Royal Swedish Acad. of Music.

————. 1982a. In tune or not? The fundamental frequency in music practice. In *Tiefenstruktur der Musik, Festschrift Fritz Winckel*. ed. C. Dahlhaus, M. Krause, and P. Freuzel. Berlin: Technische Universität und Akademie der Kunste, 69–98.

————. 1982b. Perception of singing. In *The psychology of music*, ed. D. Deutsch, 59–98. New York: Academic Press.

————. 1983. Chest wall vibrations in singers. *JSHR* 26: 329–40.

————. 1984. Using acoustic research for understanding various aspects of the singing voice. *Transcripts of the 13th Symposium Care of the Professional Voice*, ed. L. van Lawrence, 90–104. New York: Voice Foundation.

Sundberg, J., and A. Askenfelt. 1983. Larynx height and voice source: A relationship? In *Voice physiology*, ed. D. M. Bless and J. H. Abbs, 307–16. San Diego: College-Hill.

Sundberg, J., and J. Gauffin. 1974. Masking effects of one's own voice. *Speech Transmission Laboratory Quarterly Progress and Status Report* (KTH, Stockholm) 1: 35–41.

————. 1979. Waveform and spectrum of the glottal voice source. In *Frontiers of speech communication research, Festschrift for Gunnar Fant,* ed. B. Lindblom and S. Öhman, 301–20. London: Academic Press.

————. 1982. Amplitude of the voice source fundamental and the intelligibility of super pitch vowels. In *The representation of speech in the peripheral auditory system,* ed. R. Carlson and B. Granström, 223–38. New York: Elsevier Biomedical Press.

Sundberg, J., R. Leanderson, C. von Euler, and H. Lagercrants. 1983. Activation of the diaphragm in singing. In *Proc. of Stockholm Music Acoustics Conference 1983* (SMAC 83) (no. 1), ed. A. Askenfelt, S. Felicetti, E. Jansson, and J. Sundberg, pp. 279–90. Stockholm: Royal Swedish Acad. of Music.

Sundberg, J., and P.-E. Nordström. 1983. Raised and lowered larynx: The effect on vowel formant frequencies. *J of Research in Singing* 6: 7–15.

Terhardt, E. 1974. On the perception of periodic sound fluctuations (roughness). *Acustica* 30: 201–13.

Ternström, S., and J. Sundberg. 1984. Acoustical aspects of choir singing. *Transcripts of the 13th Symposium Care of the Professional Voice*, ed. L van Lawrence, pp. 48–52. New York: Voice Foundation.

————. 1986. Acoustics of Choir Singing. In *Acoustics for Choir and Orchestra,* ed. S. Ternström, Stockholm: Royal Swedish Acad. of Music, 12–22.

————. Intonation precision of choir singers. Forthcoming.

Ternström, S., J. Sundberg, and A. Colldén. 1983. Articulatory perturbation of pitch in singers deprived of auditory feedback. In *Proc. of Stockholm Music Acoustics Conference 1983* (SMAC 83) (no. 1), ed. A. Askenfelt, S. Felicetti, E. Jansson, and J. Sundberg, pp. 291–304. Stockholm: Royal Swedish Acad. of Music.

Tiffin, J. 1931. Some aspects of the psychophysics of the vibrato. *Psychol Rev Monogr* 41: 153–200.

Titze, I. 1973 and 1974. The human vocal folds: A mathematical model. Parts 1 and 2. *Phonetica* 28: 129–70; *Phonetica* 29: 1–21.

————. 1983. The importance of vocal tract loading in maintaining vocal fold oscillation. In *Proc. of Stockholm Music Acoustics Conference 1983* (SMAC 83) (no. 1), ed. A. Askenfelt, S. Felicetti, E. Jansson, and J. Sundberg, 61–72. Stockholm: Royal Swedish Acad. of Music.

Titze, I., and D. T. Talkin. 1979. A theoretical study of the effects of various laryngeal configurations on the acoustics of phonation. *JASA* 66: 60–74.

Trojan, F. 1952. Experimentelle Untersuchungen über den Zusammenhang zwischen dem Ausdruck der Sprechstimme und dem vegetativen Nervensystem. *FP* 4. 65–92.

Trojan, F., and F. Winckel. 1957. Elektroakustische Untersuchungen zur Ausdruckstheorie der Sprechstimme. *FP* 9: 168–82.

Vennard, W. 1967. *Singing, the mechanism and the technique.* New York: Carl Fischer.

Vennard, W., M. Hirano, J. Ohala, and B. Fritzell. 1970. A series of four electromyographic studies. *National Assoc Teachers of Singing Bull,* vol. 27, no. 1, 16–21; no. 2, 30–37; no. 3, 26–32; no. 4, 22–30.

Wang, S. 1983. Singing voice: Bright timbre, singer's formant, and larynx positions. In *Proc. of Stockholm Music Acoustics Conference 1983* (SMAC 83) (no. 1), ed. A. Askenfelt, S. Felicetti, E. Jansson, and J. Sundberg, 313–22. Stockholm: Royal Swedish Acad. of Music.

Ward, D., and E. Burns. 1978. Singing without auditory feedback. *J of Research in Singing* 1: 24–44.

Watson, P. J., and T. J. Hixon. 1985. Respiratory kinematics in classical (opera) singing. *JSHR* 28: 104–22.

Williams, C. E., and K. N. Stevens. 1972. Emotions and speech: Some acoustic correlates. *JASA* 52: 1238–50.

————. 1969. On determining the emotional state of pilots during flight: An exploratory study. *Aerospace Med.* 40: 1369–72.

Winckel, F. 1953. Physikalischen Kriterien für objective Stimmbeurteilung. *FP* 5: (Separatum): 232–52.

Wolf, S. K., D. Stanley, and W. J. Sette. Quantitative studies of the singing voice. *JASA* 6: 255–66.

Wyke, B. D. 1974. Laryngeal neuromuscular control systems in singing. *FP* 26: 295–306.

Zemlin, W. R. 1968. *Speech and hearing science.* Englewood Cliffs, N.J.: Prentice-Hall.

Index